Behind Tall Fences

Behind Tall Fences

Stories and Experiences

About Los Alamos

At its Beginning

Los Alamos Historical Society
Los Alamos, New Mexico

Copyright © 1996 by Los Alamos Historical Society
Los Alamos, New Mexico

ISBN 0-941232-91-3

Library of Congress Catalog Card No. 95-78215

1 2 3 4 5 6 7 8 9 0

Los Alamos Historical Society
P.O. Box 43
Los Alamos, New Mexico 87544

co-published with

Exceptional Books, Ltd.
798 47th Street
Los Alamos, NM 87544

CONTENTS

Prelude to Los Alamos

Hugh T. Richards   1
Some 1942 Fast-Neutron Measurements at Rice and Minnesota

Joseph L. McKibben   5
Contribution of the Two Van de Graaff Accelerators Built at the University of Wisconsin to the Los Alamos Project

Alfred O. Hanson   16
Instrumental Developments and Fast-Neutron Fission Studies at Wisconsin During the Pre-Bomb Period, 1940 - 1943

L.D. P. King   32
Early Measurements at Purdue of Some Fusion Reaction Cross Sections

Robert Serber   53
Theoretical Studies at Berkeley

Recollections

L.D. P. King   57
The Development of Nuclear Explosives and Frontier Days at Los Alamos

Nicholas C. Metropolis   69
Random Reminiscences

Arthur Wahl   87
    Los Alamos 1943

Berlyn Brixner   90
    A Scientific Photographer at Project Y

Charles L. Critchfield   101
    The First Implosion at Los Alamos

Edward F. Hammel   103
    Recollections of Plutonium Metallurgy Work in D-Building

Joseph L. McKibben   112
    Timing on the Trinity Bomb Explosion

Hugh T. Richards   116
    The Making of the Bomb: A Personal Perspective

Foster Evans   135
    Early Super Work

John Allred and Louis Rosen   143
    First Fusion Neutrons from a Thermonuclear Weapon Device: Two Researchers' Personal Accounts

J. Carson Mark   155
    A Maverick View

Impressions

Unknown GI   168
    Los Alamos Blues

Charles L. Critchfield   169
    The Robert Oppenheimer I Knew

Karan McKibben   178
    Behind Tall Fences

Serguei Kapitsa   182
    Our Nonlinear World

Richard Rhodes   197
    A Different Country

Glossary   209

To

the Memory of

Charles L. Critchfield

(1910–1994)

Pioneer at Los Alamos

Major Contributor to Physics and Mathematics

A Founder of the J. Robert Oppenheimer Memorial Committee

FOREWORD

The J. Robert Oppenheimer Memorial Committee assembled this volume with the help of Roger Meade, Principal Archivist, Los Alamos National Laboratory, and first published it in August 1994.

The Los Alamos Historical Society found great interest in the book because of its historical importance and the excellence of the material. We were fortunate to have the help of one of the authors, Dr. John C. Allred, who founded his own small press in 1987, in curing the faults of the earlier printing and producing a volume whose appearance is worthy of the contents.

—Marjorie Bell Chambers
President
Los Alamos Historical Society
June 1995

PREFACE

This collection of essays is doubtless the most authentic book ever assembled about the Manhattan Project in Los Alamos, New Mexico, which became Los Alamos Scientific Laboratory, now Los Alamos National Laboratory. It is also arguably one of the best of such books.

The J. Robert Oppenheimer Memorial Committee assembled these materials with the help of Roger Meade, Principal Archivist, Los Alamos National Laboratory and first printed them in August 1994. The demand soon outpaced supply, and I determined to ensure that a suitable document relating these important historical events be published.

As a retired physicist, now a small publisher, I decided the new version would more closely reflect the actual words of the authors represented than did the first version. For that reason, I went back to the original, archived computer files that contained the materials and limited the editing to those changes that facilitate comfortable reading without requiring strict conformance to contemporary editorial style. Transcripts of oral presentations are as nearly literal as possible. Preservation of the style and personality, as well as the knowledge and wisdom, of the original writer has taken precedence over editorial considerations.

The book comprises a collection of 21 papers by 18 authors and a time frame from 1941 to 1951, within which the atomic bomb was produced in 1945 and work on the hydrogen bomb begun. Most of the authors came to Los Alamos during the years 1943–45; these are their stories and recollections. The book is divided into three sections titled respectively, *Prelude to Los Alamos*, *Recollections*, and *Impressions*. These titles reflect the general nature of their sections.

In charge of the scientific effort was J. Robert Oppenheimer, a man remembered with admiration and affection by all of his scientific comrades, surely the man for the time and place. The commanding officer of the Manhattan District in Los Alamos was General Leslie R. Groves, US Army Corps of Engineers. The military and scientists sometimes do not mix well. Somehow Oppenheimer and Groves got along well enough that their joint effort succeeded. Groves's previous assignment was to build the Houston Ship Channel; he was an engineer to be reckoned with, and his contributions in support of the effort at Los Alamos were essential.

There were seven members of the scientific cadre who either were or became Nobel laureates. Niels Bohr and Enrico Fermi had won their crowns; to be awarded this distinction in later years were Luis Alvarez, Hans Bethe, Richard Feynman, Norman Ramsey, and Emilio Segrè.

It was a youthful bunch. The average age of the scientists was 25. They were recruited nationally and came from many parts of the United States.

The concluding chapter is written by the Pulitzer Prize-winning author Richard Rhodes, the author of an important history that includes that of Los Alamos, *The Making of the Atomic Bomb*. His summary of this effort and its consequences over the fifty years since the end of World War II make the book worthwhile—which takes nothing away from the other writings.

Enjoy!

—John C. Allred
Los Alamos, New Mexico
June, 1995

SOME 1942 FAST-NEUTRON MEASUREMENTS AT RICE AND MINNESOTA*
Hugh T. Richards**

Rice University

At that time (late 1941) papers about uranium fission were conspicuous by their absence in physics journals. Hence an obvious implication was that a fission bomb was under consideration. I was therefore not completely surprised when sometime in January 1942 H.A. Wilson sounded me out on the possibility of undertaking (with Bennett) an OSRD [Office of Scientific Research and Development] project to measure energy spectra of fast neutrons.

Apparently Wilson had been at an earlier secret conference with Compton and others (probably at the U. of Chicago or in Washington). I suspect that Bonner [Tom W. Bonner of Rice University] also attended since he was the recognized expert on fast neutron energy measurements. Wilson told me that intelligence reports indicated that the Germans were working on a fission bomb. Perhaps a bomb was not feasible, but if the Germans could even produce large amounts of radioactivities, the military shock possibilities of dropping these on troops or cities might be important. Hence we must carefully explore the possibilities. I conjecture that Bonner believed that his radar work was more important and that Bennett and I could adequately handle the neutron measurements.

We accepted. Since the end of the first semester was near, I would devote full time to the project second semester. I had plenty of research results for my Ph.D. thesis and could use evenings to write up the material. Although I wouldn't formally receive my Ph.D. till June, I became a Research Associate at the then munificent rate of $2700 per annum. The schedule left me almost no free time, but I had already survived several years at Rice with minimal social life.

The new job triggered a security clearance investigation and required a birth certificate. I was born November 7, 1918 on a Colorado ranch without professional help. A Dr. Tucker from Elkart, Kansas, didn't arrive until it was all over, and apparently had neglected to file a birth certificate! However, my mother and Dr. Tucker were still alive and could file a late birth certificate even after a gap of 23 years and two months: hence the certifying doctor's signature is dated <u>January 22, 1942</u>! Dr. Tucker did stretch the truth by certifying that he attended the birth. My mother's handwriting fills in the family details on the certificate although her statement that my father was

---

*Adapted from his book *Through Los Alamos, 1945: Memoirs of a Nuclear Physicist,* Hugh T. Richards, © 1993, Medical Physics Publishing, Madison, WI 53705.

born in Coudey Co., Missouri disagrees with all our other records. It should have been Nodaway Co., Missouri. In fact there is no Coudey Co., Missouri!

Professor Gregory Breit of the University of Wisconsin was then in charge of the fast-neutron studies. Although he was our boss, we only dealt through H.A. Wilson who administered the Rice Project. Many felt Breit was too security conscious. When he resigned in May 1942, Oppenheimer was chosen to replace Breit.

Our first task was to measure the energy spectrum of neutrons from $^{12}C + {}^{2}H$. Only later did we learn that the Minnesota group was using this reaction as a source of fast neutrons to measure important scattering cross sections; if the neutrons were not monoenergic, the measurements would be hard to interpret or useless. Since it was important to detect any low energy group of neutrons, the cloud chamber technique was our method of choice. The geometry correction for recoils leaving the illuminated volume of the chamber is similar to the one I derived for the photographic emulsion case but was considerably more complicated. Bennett and I finally just solved it numerically for five different track lengths and then interpolated between them. We indeed found the neutrons to be monoenergic: our secret report was declassified after the war and published in the *Physical Review*, 71, 565, (1947).

Our next task was to measure the spectra of neutrons from the fission of ^{235}U. To this end Breit had arranged for a small (about 3cm) sphere of ordinary uranium to be manufactured to our design. We used the $^{7}Li + H$ source at a proton energy giving neutrons below that which would fission the ^{238}U isotope. Since the only known measurements were crude and especially inadequate for the low energy part of the fission neutron spectrum, again a cloud chamber with a hydrogen containing gas (e.g. ethane) was our technique.

The uranium sphere came in time to start on these measurements in July 1942. Although the general continuum shape of the spectrum one learns rather quickly, the cloud chamber technique was not practical for the high energy part of the spectrum. This later required my photographic emulsion method. Nor is it easy to deduce the true original ^{235}U spectrum since the fission neutrons can be inelastically scattered in the sphere and/or cloud chamber, and some of the higher energy fission neutrons will fission the ^{238}U isotope. To sort these effects out requires use of smaller and/or enriched spheres. So fission neutron spectra would occupy my time much for the next couple of years.

With Oppenheimer replacing Breit, we learned at the end of summer that various separate OSRD contracts such as ours were to be consolidated into bigger projects with the goal being one central laboratory. To this end we were asked to go in October to the University of Minnesota to help them finish up various measurements of fast neutron scattering cross sections. Fortunately, with my new salary, I had splurged and bought a low mileage second hand 1949 Plymouth two door sedan for $750. I kept this car for 13 years; then sold it to a University of Wisconsin grad student for $20! New cars were of course unavailable because of the war. With the uranium sphere in the glove compartment of the car, I took off for the north. The first leg of the trip was to the Met Lab at the University of Chicago where we were briefed by John Manley and Edward Teller.

University of Minnesota

Manley indicated the need for our helping finish the Minnesota fast neutron cross section measurement so we could all be assembled at the central location for bomb design. He wanted me also to continue on the spectrum measurement of fission neutrons.

The University of Minnesota electrostatic accelerator, completed just prior to WW II, was a huge homemade vertical type (financed largely by the Rockefeller foundation) and housed in an outdoor steel cylinder to contain the pressurized insulating gas. The control room and labs were underground beneath the accelerator and connected to the physics building. Despite the large physical size, the peak terminal voltage (about 3 MeV) did not equal Herb's [Prof. Ray Herb] smaller horizontal machine at Wisconsin; however, the sparks from the terminal to the wall made an impressive sound! The large outdoor container resulted in both pluses and minuses: 1) access for servicing was through the bottom and one need not remove the hoops since one could climb up inside the hoops and insulator support system; 2) the temperature changes of the accelerator system followed the outdoor Minnesota temperatures despite a radiator installed in the bottom of the cylinder. One consequence was that the wax which sealed sections of the vacuum tube became brittle enough when the outdoor temperature dropped to < -20 degrees F that a vacuum leak invariably opened up! Maintenance work inside the tank at these temperatures was impractical so we worked on other projects until the outdoor temperature rose to > -20 degrees F and the leak sealed itself!

Professor John H. Williams who (with Rumbaugh and Tate) had built the accelerator, was a pusher who thought big and worked hard. A Canadian by birth, but with a Ph.D. from Berkeley, he came to Minnesota in 1933 after an NRC fellowship at Chicago. Probably because of the project he became naturalized in 1942. He had a down-to-earth manner and philosophy; hence got along well with colleagues, service personnel and students. I was therefore not surprised that he later headed the electrostatic accelerator group at Los Alamos, was in charge of all services at the Trinity Test, and postwar served a term on the AEC [US Atomic Energy Commission]. He was a sports enthusiast and introduced me to college hockey. After his death from cancer in 1966, the University named their sports arena after him.

**Hugh T. Richards came to Los Alamos in April 1943 from Rice University via the University of Minnesota and continued work begun there on measurements of fast-neutron spectra and cross sections. He was in charge of neutron measurements at the Trinity test, July 1945. He went to the University of Wisconsin after the war and was Professor of Physics until his retirement in 1988. He is presently Professor Emeritus and continues his association with the University.

CONTRIBUTION OF THE TWO VAN de GRAAFF ACCELERATORS BUILT AT THE UNIVERSITY OF WISCONSIN TO THE LOS ALAMOS PROJECT EFFORT
Joseph L. McKibben*

1. Introduction

The Los Alamos research effort in the development of the fission bombs was aided by ion beams from two pressurized electrostatic accelerators that were developed and built at the University of Wisconsin. Research work using them under contract with the OSRD was started February 15, 1942 at Madison. The accelerators were then brought to Los Alamos in April 1943 where for the next two years they played an active role in acquiring needed nuclear physics information. The short version of this paper based on a talk was published[1] by the author in 1991.

2. Development of the Accelerators

A. World's first pressure-insulated electrostatic accelerator. Raymond G. Herb in 1933–34 built the first pressure-insulated electrostatic accelerator. The terminal was charged by the belt system developed by Robert Van de Graaff at Princeton University. It delivered a proton beam and he used it to study the $^7Li(p,\alpha)^4He$ reaction at 400 keV for his Ph.D. thesis. This was the first nuclear physics experiment done at the University of Wisconsin. He was assisted both in the construction of this accelerator and doing the experiment by beginning graduate students David Parkinson and Don Kerst.

B. World's second pressure-insulated electrostatic accelerator. In the fall of 1935 Herb, Parkinson, and Kerst started construction of a pressure-insulated accelerator in a 100-psi vessel 22 ft. in overall length and 5.5 ft. in diameter. The diameter was the largest that could be brought in through a window in Sterling Hall into a laboratory room. In October 1936 they submitted a paper to the *Physical Review*[2] describing the operation of this accelerator. During the next two years it was responsible for several papers in nuclear physics using energies up to 2.6 MeV. The proton-proton scattering experiment was done with it in the energy range of 0.85 MeV to 2.4 MeV and became recognized as a classic paper[3] in nuclear physics.

C. Test Generator, or Short Tank. Herb was interested in building an electrostatic accelerator capable of much higher voltage. He stated to me that not enough information existed—especially concerning the design of the vacuum tube—to proceed with the construction of a large electrostatic accelerator. So in the fall of 1937, at his urging, I abandoned my two-year cloud chamber project and took on the responsibility of building a test generator. The university was lucky enough to obtain a 200-psi pressure vessel that was 17 feet in length by 5.5 feet in diameter as a gift from Chicago Bridge and Iron. It arrived in my Sterling Hall room early in 1938.

With the design help of J.C. Bellamy and construction help of D.B. Parkinson, the basic generator was functioning sufficiently well to do voltage testing by April. Unfortunately, it sparked along the insulating support at only 1.3 MV because these insulators were phenolic-bound paper, an unfortunate selection on my part. In the summer of 1938 R.L. Burling and I bolted 0.75-inch-OD aluminum tubes transversely across the support sheets every 1.25 inches apart. Afterwards, the voltage would go to 1.7 MV using 125 psi air as insulation and to 2.2 MV when several pounds by weight of Freon-12 was added.

Considerable test work went on with the assistance of Burling during the next year on both insulators and single sections of plausible acceleration tubes. We observed, as others had, that it was important to shield the negative corner between the insulator and the metal electrode. We found that a conical shape for the electrodes was optimum provided the voltage polarity was such that electrons were drawn away from the surface of the insulators. And we became aware that metal spinning was a good way of fabricating the steel electrodes since their shape was complicated.

We installed our acceleration tube in September 1939. However, we soon became aware that this tube absorbed a considerable amount of the charging current due to a spontaneous electron current present in it. This current generated a large amount of x-rays even after the surface that the maximum energy electrons struck had been changed to beryllium. Finally, on July 30, 1940, I inserted eleven tilted rings within the electrodes of the tube. The tilts of the rings were alternated in sign. The tilted rings provided a series of inclined electric fields that decreased the length of the electron trajectories. This decreased the magnitude of the electron current loading and the hardness of the x-rays.

D. Herb's Third Electrostatic Generator, or the Long Tank. By 1939 Herb had become convinced that significantly higher energy could be obtained in the same laboratory room and in essentially the same tank by going to a single-ended configuration. One end of this tank was modified so the opening was full size. By supporting the structure from the opposite end, he was able to incorporate two interpotential shells that produced a more uniform gradient of the field. This configuration also significantly increased the length of both the tube and the belt. He took advantage of our tube research and designed a tube using spun steel electrodes of the general shape we used. He decreased the tube diameter and made a change in the design of the spun electrode. He was lucky in that the design change produced a tube that did not current load, at least during the first voltage test. In those days we did not understand what produced current loading.

The accelerator was made operational in 1940 with the help of C. M. Turner, C.M. Hudson and R.E. Warren[4]—the submission date to the *Physical Review* on their paper was August 15. It was stated in it that a top voltage of 4.5 MV had been reached; however, to achieve it 15 pounds by weight of Freon-12 had been added to the 100 psi air. They reported 3.5 MV with air alone and experience over the years is in agreement with that value. However, experience since then showed that the maximum reliable operating value with Freon was only 4.0 MV. The reason for the 4.0-MV limitation was never experimentally determined—I suspect it was due to current loading that developed. Operating experience showed that the use of the large shell did not give appreciable higher operating voltage. Also sparkover of the insulators required to support the outer end of the large shell was a troublesome problem so it was only used a few times.

3. Development of the two Accelerators from mid-1940 until 1942.

A. Herb to Radar Lab. Ray Herb was called upon to work at the Radar Lab and went there early in the fall of 1940. Ernest Lawrence came to Madison to recruit him. His departure left me as the senior man knowledgeable of these accelerators although I was only a postdoctorate fellow—my Ph.D. had been granted in May. Fortunately, the work that got done on both accelerators during this period was ideal for putting them into condition to do the work that was to be requested in 1942.

B. Radioactive Iodine Production. The mission I was given was to convert the short tank into a source of thermal neutrons to make iodine radioactive for John Willard in the Chemistry Department [at Wisconsin]. I brought the deuteron beam into the center of a tank of water which was 4 feet in diameter and depth. There it impinged a thick beryllium target. The largest glass bulb contained the iodine solution and had an inserted glass tube so the liquid in effect surrounded the source. To make the program more viable, I did considerable developmental work on the Zinn ion source in order to obtain more current and reliability. The deuteron energy without Freon was 1.7 MeV and on good days the current may have been 25 μA. In this effort I was assisted by David Frisch, a beginning graduate student.

C. Development Work on the Long Tank. Important developmental work was carried out by A.O. Hanson in this period. He had been a teaching assistant during the construction of the long tank and so had only limited experience before taking on the responsibility alone. Hanson was alone since none of the people involved in the construction were still around.

Before the accelerator could be used to take data, he had a problem to solve. With the interpotential shells in place, the generating voltmeter would no longer indicate the true potential of the terminal. So Hanson[5] built a curved-plate electrostatic analyzer and passed the H_2 beam through it. A signal from the beam position on the pair of detection plates was used to automatically control the voltage on the terminal by varying the charging current of the belt.

Hanson and Benedict[6] for their thesis projects went on to make a determination of four reaction thresholds. To do this they made a flat-plate deflection system and calibrated it by sending an electron beam through it that had accurately known energies in the 8 to 20 keV range. The calibrated analyzer was then installed on the proton beam line. In use, part of the proton beam struck a $^7Li(p,n)$ target located before the analyzer and the remainder of the beam passed on to the detection plates. They obtained the value of 1.883 MeV for this threshold while the generally accepted value was 1.86 MeV. They obtained values for three other reactions that were also ≈1.5% higher than the accepted values. Eventually, their higher values came to be accepted but at the time they were met with skepticism.

4. Neutron Cross-Section Work Performed for the OSRD from February 15, 1942, until April 1943

A. OSRD Contract for Neutron Cross-section Measurements. Early in January 1942, Gregory Breit spoke to me about the possibility of using the two accelerators to make cross-section measurements that were needed to develop the fission bomb. So the author with A.O. Hanson and D.L. Benedict along with graduate students J.M. Blair and D.H. Frisch got the project started. J.M. Hush joined it June 1.

Breit resigned his position at the Metallurgical Laboratory on May 18, 1942. The emotional struggle between him and Robert Oppenheimer has been discussed by Peter Goodchild.[7] Arthur Compton, Director of the Metallurgical Laboratory, turned the responsibility of guiding the research effort under the OSRD at the Universities of Minnesota, Wisconsin and Rice and at the DTM of the Carnegie Institution at Washington, D.C., over to Oppenheimer. However, Oppenheimer wanted an experimentalist to take on the responsibility of visiting these research facilities and obtained the assistance of John Manley of the University of Illinois. For a discussion of his effort see John Manley's[8] paper *A New Laboratory is Born*. Some of our contact with Manley and Oppenheimer was by registered mail with return cards. We did not use the telephone.

B. Neutron Scattering Program. David Frisch and I undertook to determine what elements would be good backscatterers of neutrons. To do this, the deuteron beam from the short tank was passed through the tank of water that had been used in the production of radioactive iodine and struck a target located behind it. It was necessary to remove a wall in order to get space to do the experiment. Unfortunately, our first experimental arrangement was poorly designed and Manley persuaded us to abandon it. We then went to a configuration that had been developed by Aoki *et al.*[9] in Japan which measured differential scattering cross sections. The scattering materials were fabricated in the shape of rings. The neutrons scattered from a ring were detected by a fission detector made with natural uranium oxide. It was shielded from the source of neutrons by a cone. The scattering angle could be varied by changing the positions of the ring relative to the detector. While it was not possible to observe 180° scattering with this arrangement, data were taken at mean angles of 115°, 138°, 148° and in some cases at 156°.

The detector consisted of concentric cylinders covered with natural uranium oxide. The covered surface with an area of 15 sq. in. was inside a cylinder 1.2" in diameter by 1.1" long. This was encased by cadmium 0.05" thick and boron carbide 0.3" thick in order to reduce the troublesome epithermal neutron background present in the room.

Two sources of neutrons were used. One was from deuterons on a thick target of carbon and gave neutron energies up to 1.6 MeV. The other was from deuterons on a thick target of deuterated water that was frozen within the vacuum system by liquid air. This gave neutron energies up to 5.1 MeV. To obtain data using the neutrons from carbon it was important that the highest feasible deuteron beam energy be used. The terminal voltage used throughout this experiment was 1.87 MV. It was necessary to add Freon to the 125-psi air to get this voltage and even so some insulator sparking was present. Without Freon the top voltage was 1.7 MV.

Oppenheimer requested at a meeting about September 1 that we concentrate our scattering measurements on dense elements and tantalum, tungsten, platinum, gold and uranium were suggested. We were not able to get these materials in the form of true rings, but Manley was able to obtain bars of these elements at the Metallurgical Laboratory and from these bars we were able to form approximate rings, i.e. square rings. Now it turned out that lead and bismuth had as large scattering cross-sections as any of the dense elements so pseudo-rings of various shapes were made of the lead to check out the geometrical factors. The geometrical factors were later calculated by A.T. Monk, J.A. Wheeler and G. Young at the Metallurgical Laboratory.

The counting rate was very low and the background was approximately equal to the effect. When the deuteron current on the carbon target got down to 10 μA, the experiment using it was no longer feasible so the ion source had to be repaired. During the last month at Madison, three other people joined the group and we were able to run the accelerator around the clock to get the needed data.

C. Fission Cross-section Measurements using the Long Tank. Hanson, who had received his Ph.D. in November, took on the responsibility of operating and maintaining the electrostatic accelerator as well as carrying out experiments. In this work he was assisted by Benedict, Blair and later Hush.

We had two ways of determining the neutron flux. One way was to use the proton recoils from a paraffin film of known weight that had been evaporated on platinum. This was the simpler method except sensing the number of protons recoils correctly turned out to be difficult. Blair and Hush developed an elegant coincidence proportional counter that was believed to be capable of detecting all the proton recoils and ignoring all other recoils. The other method used measured the total flux from the source in a manganese water bath. The activity created by neutron capture in Mn from exposure to the accelerator neutrons was compared to the activity created from a calibrated radium-beryllium source. It was necessary to measure the angular distribution of the neutrons accurately to get a cross-section value this way and this was difficult. Benedict took on a major responsibility for this experiment.

The nuclear reaction used was the $^7Li(p,n)^7Be$. It gave us neutron energies up to 1.8 MeV at the accelerator's top operating voltage of 3.5 MV without Freon. Breit never discussed with us how this reaction might have a problem. However, at my first meeting with Oppenheimer, which took place at the University of Chicago on about September 1, we had a long discussion about the usefulness of the $^7Li(p,n)^7Be$ reaction. He was concerned that the ^7Be excited state, well known to be present at 0.43 MeV, would make this reaction invalid for neutron measurements above 645 keV or 2.37 MeV proton energy. In my mind this was the only feasible reaction available. On September 4, Oppenheimer wrote me a letter asking that we study the $^7Li(p,\alpha)^4He$ reaction as a function of energy. He stated that he would be concerned if the alpha intensity rose rapidly with proton energy over 1 MeV energy. This measurement was soon made by Blair and Hanson and the alpha intensity rose only monotonically. Upon seeing their report, Oppenheimer wrote me on October 26, stating he was no longer concerned and requested that we now put all our effort on the measurement of the fission cross-sections. (We now know[10] that between 3.0 and 4.0 MeV proton energy, or 1.6 and 2.4 MeV forward neutron energy, $\approx 10\%$ of the neutrons had energies that were reduced by the higher $^7Li(p,n)^7Be^*$ threshold. Nowadays the $^3H(p,n)^3He$ reaction would be used for such work but no tritium was available then.)

In making measurements with a well focused beam of 1 to 2 μA that it was capable of delivering, it was found that the thickness of the evaporated lithium target diminished moderately rapidly. So early in the year Hanson designed and built a rotating lithium target. With it the neutron output was stable over long periods of time; however, this target could not be used for the Mn-bath fission measurements.

The fission cross section for ^{235}U measured by the coincidence proportional counter was essentially constant from 0.5 MeV to 1.8 MeV and had a value of 1.66 barns.[11] The ^{238}U cross section measured with it had a threshold around 1.0 MeV and rose to ≈0.45 barns at 1.8 MeV. On the other hand, the ^{235}U cross section when measured using the Mn bath was 1.34 barns at 0.27 MeV, 1.22 barns at 0.53 MeV and 1.29 barns at 1.1 MeV. Since the ^{235}U cross section was eventually determined to be 1.33 barns at 1.0 MeV, the values encompassed the true cross section. The reason that the cross section given by the coincidence proportional counter was somewhat high may have a simple explanation. There were two wheels carrying absorbers between the two proportional counters. If the detection apparatus was operated so the neutrons associated with the 0.43 MeV excited ^{7}Be level were not counted, then a fission cross section that was too high would have been observed.

The manganese bath gave me an idea. Why not take a moderate sized cylinder of paraffin and put a boron counter along its axis. If then its axis is pointed to a neutron source, it seemed reasonable that its counting rate ought to be rather insensitive to the neutron kinetic energy. I mentioned this idea to Hanson and very soon he made such a counter and put it into operation. It became known as the long counter and was soon recognized as a neutron monitor[12] that had a flat sensitivity[13] but it had dips in sensitivity at neutron energies where the scattering resonances in carbon are located. Still its energy sensitivity is flat enough that it has been used internationally in many neutron counting operations.

5. Work with the Accelerators at Los Alamos from 1943 to the end of 1945

A. Moving the Accelerators and Equipment to Project Y.

On about April 1 operation with the accelerators ceased and getting them ready to travel started. They were shipped by rail in two box cars. The two pressure vessels arrived at site Y during the April 15–16 meeting which in my mind started the Los Alamos operation although a few people had been there over two weeks. Priority was given to putting the long tank into service and it was stated by Hawkins[14] that it was put into service May 15. A very troublesome V-belt drive problem was eliminated in the short tank by repositioning the drive motor so it was directly coupled to the pulley of the charging belt but still a beam was obtained by June 10.

B. Organization of P-2, known as the Electrostatic Generator Group. John Williams from the University of Minnesota was appointed group leader and I was his alternate. The bulk of the members of the group came directly from the University of Wisconsin and included, besides myself, Al Hanson, David Frisch, Morris Blair, Jim Hush, Worth Seagondollar, Rolland Perry and Robert Krohn while Dick Taschek and Clarence Turner came indirectly. Carl Bailey and Dick Nuckolls also came from the University of Minnesota. Hugh Richards came from Rice University via the University of Minnesota. Our SED [Special Engineering Detachment] technician was Po Povi Da, son of Maria and Julian who were already famous as pottery makers at the nearby San Ildefonso pueblo.

C. Long Tank Program. The first experiment done on both the short and long tank was the determination of the number of neutrons per fission of ^{249}Pu. This value was important in determining the critical mass of a plutonium bomb. The sample was an almost invisible speck weighing only 142 μg. It had been made by many days of cyclotron bombardment of a uranium compound at Washington University in St. Louis and by chemical separation at the Metallurgical Laboratory under the direction of Glenn Seaborg. It was measured by comparing to the number of neutrons emitted per fission of it to that produced in the fission of ^{235}U. The neutrons to produce the fissions were obtained from the Li(p,n) reaction at 1.9 MeV and therefore had a maximum energy of about 150 keV; however, the neutrons had been slowed down by passage through some paraffin. The two samples were placed in turn inside a cylindrical paraffin layer and the fission neutrons produced proton recoils from the paraffin layer. The recoils were inside an argon-filled ionization chamber where they were counted. To obtain the ratio of the emitted neutrons, it was necessary to measure the ratio of the two fission cross-sections in this same neutron flux. A comparison chamber was made using a pair of platinum foils—one having ^{239}Pu on it and the other having ^{235}U on it and it was determined that the plutonium cross section was 1.83 times that of uranium. The result of the experiment was that the ^{239}Pu neutrons per fission were greater than the ^{235}U neutrons per fission by the factor 1.20 ± 0.09.

Next the ratio of the fission cross section of ^{239}Pu to ^{235}U was made at many energies and the fission cross section of other elements were also compared this way. Early effort went into comparing the boron reaction cross section to the fission cross section of ^{235}U at a large range of energies. Since the ratio of radiative capture in ^{235}U relative to the boron reaction cross section had been carefully measured at the Metallurgical Laboratory, this gave the ratio of the absorption to fission cross section in ^{235}U. This ratio was extended up in energy to 3 MeV using the D-D source and down to 5 keV using neutrons from the short tank.

Effort was made to determine the variation of ν, the number of neutrons per fission, with the energy of the neutron. More effort was put into the absolute fission cross section. These were both difficult experiments especially at the neutron flux available and the results were still not well verified by the end of the war.

D. Short Tank Program. The short tank, in its state of development when it arrived, was close to being a misfit to the Los Alamos program. The tamper evaluation program, for which it had been used at Wisconsin, was taken over by Barschall (who had considerable experience in making neutron scattering measurements) and Manley. They used the Cockcroft-Walton D(d,n)^{3}He reaction for this program. The short tank, with its 40-μA beam capability, was capable of producing a nice neutron output with the ^{7}Li(p,n) reaction; however, its top usable voltage using considerable Freon was only 2.1 MV and that [only] if the experiment could tolerate occasional sparks within the tank. Now Edward Teller had stirred up interest in a bomb that might be made using uranium hydride instead of pure uranium. If the bomb would function satisfactorily, it would be valuable since the mass of uranium required would be much smaller. Therefore knowledge of the fission cross sections at the low energies that the neutrons would have became important.

I was aware that the voltage needed was very likely obtainable since it was the phenolic-bound support insulators that were limiting the voltage. It appeared that the acceleration tube was capable of somewhat higher voltage. Shellac-bound paper tubing, known as 1824 Textolite, was known to be able to support a much higher voltage gradient and was the insulator in use in the long tank. However, incorporating these insulators, which were only available in the form of tubes rather than sheets, required rebuilding the hoop system and terminal. The design was worked out during that summer with the assistance of Krohn and he supervised its construction. The installation into the pressure vessel was accomplished in only two weeks in December 1943 so the modification did not put the accelerator out of operation very long. Soon afterwards it was operated at terminal potentials up to 2.5 MV using Freon.

It was also important that the accelerator have a precision voltage-control system. So an electrostatic analyzer similar to that built by Hanson at Madison, but upgraded, was built and put on the diatomic beam line. A corona-control system, as conceived by Ashby and Hanson[15] at Madison, was installed. With this equipment in operation, the voltage was known accurately and was stable to ± 1.5 keV.

The neutron energy in the forward direction using 2.5 MeV protons was ≈ 750 keV. At threshold the neutrons all went forward with ≈ 30 keV energy. By working at a back angle and slightly above threshold, data could be taken using neutron energies as low as 5 keV. Los Alamos physicists now had available, by use of the three accelerators, reasonably monoenergetic neutrons from 5 keV to 3 MeV. After the modifications were completed numerous experiments were then done using this accelerator. No attempt is being made to discuss these experiments here. The theoretical physicists found that the cross sections obtained did not support the hydride gadget as being viable as a bomb.

In my mind the most exciting experiment done with this accelerator was the measurement of the number of neutrons per fission of ^{239}Pu. The experiment started June 24, 1943, so was done well before the revision and essentially in parallel with the same experiment on the long tank. The detector of the fissions in this case was thorium since its fission threshold was at 1.2 MeV neutron energy. Hugh Richards[16] took the lead in developing this detector. However, the thorium detector sensed a troublesome background which was traced to photofission. The photons that produced the fission were produced by capture of thermal neutrons by iron, copper, cadmium, etc. so the counter was made of pure aluminum since it was known to have a low cross section for capture of thermal neutrons. Water was eventually used for the moderator. The ratio of the fission cross sections was 1.83 as in the long tank experiment. The ratio of the neutrons from ^{239}Pu to ^{235}U determined by this method was 1.25 ± 0.12. A description of the two versions of the experiment with results are given in a report written by John Williams[17] and dated September 11, 1943. According to Hawkins[18] this was the first experiment completed at Los Alamos.

E. Epilogue. After the war was over, the short tank was purchased by the laboratory and was operated by group P-3 under the direction of Richard Taschek. It was capable of delivering 60 μA beams and was operated at voltages up to 2.7 MV. It eventually was used to accelerate tritium. It was kept in operation until 1964 but then the top voltage was down to 2.2 MV. The long tank was returned to the University of Wisconsin where it was kept quite busy until 1958 training graduate students under the direction of Professors Barschall, Herb and Richards. Its use at Madison was terminated soon after they obtained their EN tandem accelerator from High Voltage Engineering. Professor Herb was able to use the money the university obtained from LASL's purchase of the short tank to build the first electrostatic accelerator that used ceramic insulators with metallic seals to titanium.

JOSEPH L. McKIBBEN

[1] Joseph L. McKibben, *Early history of Los Alamos with emphasis on the two Van de Graaff accelerators from the University of Wisconsin*, Nucl. Instr. and Meth. A303, 1 (1991).

[2] R.G. Herb, D.B. Parkinson and D.W. Kerst, *The Development and Performance of an Electrostatic Generator Operating under High Air Pressure*, Phys. Rev. 51, 75 (1937).

[3] R.G. Herb, D.W. Kerst, D.B Parkinson and G.P. Plain, *The Scattering of Protons by Protons*, Phys. Rev. 55, 998 (1939).

[4] R.G. Herb, C.M. Turner, C.M. Hudson and R.E. Warren, Phys. Rev. 58, 579 (1940).

[5] A.O. Hanson, *Voltage-measuring and control equipment for electrostatic generators*, Rev. Sci. Instr. 15, 57 (1944).

[6] A.O. Hanson and D.L. Benedict, *An Independent Determination of Fixed Points on the High Voltage Scale*, Phys. Rev. 65, 33 (1944).

[7] Peter Goodchild, *SHATTERER OF WORLDS*, Houghton Mufflin Co. in 1981 or paperback by Fromm International Pub. Corp. of New York in 1985. See page 48.

[8] John Manley's chapter in the book entitled *Reminiscences of Los Alamos, 1943-45*, edited by Badash, Hirschfelder and Broida, D. Reidal Pub. Co., Dordrect, Holland (1980).

[9] Aoki, Kikuchi and Wakatuke, Proc. Phys. Soc. Japan 21, 232; 410 & 656 (1939).

[10] R.R. Borchers and C.H. Poppe, *Neutrons from Proton Bombardment of Lithium*, Phys. Rev. 129, 2679 (1963).

[11] Barn was a code name invented at that time for 1×10^{-24} cm^2. The statement was made then that this cross-section for a nucleon was as big as the side of a barn.

[12] A.O. Hanson and J.L. McKibben, Phys. Rev. 72, 673 (1947).

[13] R.A. Nobles, R.B. Day, R.L. Henkel, G.A. Jarvis, R.P. Kutarnia, J.L. McKibben, J.E. Perry, Jr., and R.K. Smith, *Response of the Long Counter*, Rev. Sci. Instr. 25 334 (1953).

[14] *Project Y: The Los Alamos Story*, PART I Toward Trinity by David Hawkins, Tomash Publishers 1983.

[15] R.M. Ashby and A.O. Hanson, *Grid-controlled corona*, Rev. Sci. Instr. 13, 128 (1942).

[16] Hugh Richards, Los Alamos Report No. 19.

[17] John Williams, Los Alamos Report No. 25.

[18] See page 93 of reference 14.

---

*Joseph L. McKibben came to Los Alamos in April 1943 from the University of Wisconsin and continued work on accelerator development and fast-neutron measurements begun there. After the war he remained at the Laboratory, where he continued his career in nuclear physics. He retired in 1980 and continues to pursue his scientific interests.

INSTRUMENTAL DEVELOPMENTS AND FAST-NEUTRON FISSION STUDIES AT WISCONSIN DURING THE PRE-BOMB PERIOD OF 1940 TO 1943
Alfred O. Hanson*

During my master's year at the University of North Dakota a physics professor and a few students got together to report on physics articles. I reported on an article by R.G. Herb, D.B. Parkinson and D.W. Kerst on their 2.4 MeV electrostatic generator operating under high air pressure. I was pleased to get a teaching assistantship at Wisconsin in the fall of 1938 following two previous graduate assistants from North Dakota, Gil Plain and Francis Davis.

After two years teaching as a teaching assistant, I joined Herb's research group in the summer of 1940 just after they had completed rebuilding the electrostatic generator with three concentric electrodes. This generator is shown in Fig. 1. The new arrangement gave the charging belt almost twice the length of that in the previous generator and a longer and improved accelerating tube. It was very successful in that it reached 4.5 MeV with a well focussed beam. With the concentric electrodes in place the generating voltmeter at the tank wall would sense only the potential of the outer electrode and a different method of measuring the energy of the beam had to be devised. The energy of 4.5 MeV was determined by the range of the proton beam in air. I was given the project of making an electrostatic analyzer to be placed in the diatomic hydrogen beam. It was my first experience with making any experimental equipment and I was left mostly to my own resources when Professor Herb left for war work at MIT in the fall of 1940. I eventually put together the analyzer shown in Fig. 2. It does not depend only on a collimator for determining the path of the incident beam. Although the position of the beam could be located visually, it was not convenient to do so. A detector was devised which consisted of two small metal plates placed opposite one another. The beam was centered when the beam fell equally on both plates. The undeflected beam passed through a channel in the lower plate to the lower detector. The detector plates were kept at a negative potential to repel the secondary electrons released from the glass covers and from the detectors themselves. The latter secondaries resulted in an amplification of the current to the detectors by a factor of two or three. Signals from the detectors were amplified and displayed on a double electric eye tube at the control panel so the operator could tell at a glance whether the beam was on one or the other detector plate or if it were centered between them.

The same signal went to an electronic regulator controlling the current sprayed on the accelerator belt which kept the beam average energy constant to about 0.1 percent. The regulation could have been improved by controlling a corona load from the tank wall where the charge would reach the electrode in a shorter time than on the belt. Bob Ashby and I investigated a corona triode arrangement shown in Fig. 3 for this purpose. It was not installed immediately but it was found to be useful at Los Alamos. Although this work was published in *Review of Scientific Instruments* in 1942, a New York lawyer looked me up in 1974 to get a copy of my notes on this device since some competitor was trying to patent a corona triode device for use to spray electrons in a photocopier.

Since the beam energy measurement and control system was working very well, Don Benedict and I carried out some absolute voltage measurements of some nuclear reactions which could be useful reference points in our energy region. We made a special analyzer shown in Fig. 4. It was calibrated by measuring the voltage required to deflect electron beams of precisely known energies of 8 to 20 keV between fixed detectors. It turned out that the threshold yield of neutrons from the Li(p,n) reaction was very sharp as can be seen in the graph. We found a value of 1.883 MeV for this threshold which was higher than the value of 1.86 MeV which was used until the higher value was confirmed by Professor Herb's group after the war. This work was the major contribution to our thesis projects which were completed during the summer of 1942.

As Joe McKibben mentioned, Gregory Breit, who was on the National Office of Scientific Research and Development Committee supervising work, needed to develop the fission bomb, arranged a contract to use the Wisconsin accelerators for fast neutron fission measurements starting on February 15, 1942. After suggesting that we make some preliminary measurements of the intensity and angular distribution of neutrons from the Li(p,n) reaction, Breit arranged for me to come to Washington, D.C., to present the data at a meeting which included Eugene Wigner. The yield in the forward direction is shown in Fig. 5. The extremely sharp rise at threshold and the maximum at 2.3 MeV was interesting but puzzling. The graphs in Fig. 5 are from the work of Taschek and Hemmendinger in 1948. I have no copies of those in the original report. I did not understand all their concerns but it was clear that they would like to know more about ^{7}Be which was expected to have an excited state around 450 keV and the effect it would have on the usefulness of the Li(p,n) as a neutron source. I remember the date well, it was May 15, 1942, and I went directly from Washington to Columbia, Missouri, where Betty and I were married on the following day.

Robert Oppenheimer took over the supervision of the fission bomb work shortly after that date. John Manley assisted with the experimental work at several universities. Joe McKibben was the official investigator for our group. The people involved and the list of the experimental reports are summarized in Joe's letter to Professor Compton at the end of the contract. This letter is shown as Fig. 6. Copies of these reports were sent to me by Joe and were my main source of information about the fission cross section measurements.

Oppenheimer had a lengthy talk with Joe McKibben about the Li(p,n) source shortly after he took over. He asked us to look for any resonances in the Li(p,alpha) reaction below the Li(p,n) threshold. This experiment was carried out very quickly by Morris Blair and myself. The arrangement for measuring the yield at 0 and 90 degrees and the results are shown in Fig. 7. The yield in both directions rose smoothly by a factor of three from 1.0 to 1.9 MeV where the protons began to be as penetrating as the 8 MeV alpha particles. A report was sent to Oppenheimer. He thanked us for the report and was apparently satisfied that the Li(p,n) neutrons were monoenergic up to about 0.450 MeV and asked us to go ahead with neutron cross section measurements below that energy. We found no evidence for the second group of neutrons either at Wisconsin or at Los Alamos but it was clearly seen in nuclear emulsions by Johnson, Laubenstein and Richards at Wisconsin in 1950. Their results showed a second group of about 10% associated with a 0.431 MeV level in Be^7 for neutron energies above 1.5 MeV.

Oppenheimer then wanted us to check the fission cross section for ^{235}U (which we referred to as 25) for 0.300 MeV neutrons and arranged for us to be supplied with well separated foils produced at Berkeley. It was useful to measure a pair of foils back to back to check the separation factors. The fissions were easy to count; one used a simple air chamber and one didn't need much of an amplifier. The determination of the neutron flux through the samples was a challenge for our inexperienced group.

We tried two ways of measuring the flux. One way was to compare the total neutron yield from the Li(p,n) by placing the target tube at the center of a water tank two feet in diameter containing solution of $MnSO_4$ and comparing the radioactivity it produced with that produced by a calibrated neutron source supplied by John Manley of the Metallurgical Laboratory. The difficult part, for which Donald Benedict took the major responsibility, was to measure the angular distribution and to determine accurately the fraction of the total flux which passed through the samples at each energy. This was done measuring the total ionization in a cylinder filled with seven atmospheres of hydrogen as measured with a Victoreen electroscope at a number of angles. Considerable work was required to correct the measurements for backgrounds and to calculate the response for the known neutron proton cross sections at each energy. The ^{235}U cross sections for neutron energies of 0.27 MeV, 0.53 MeV and 1.1 MeV were found to be 1.34 barns, 1.22 barns and 1.29 barns respectively. These values were close to a value eventually determined to be 1.33 barns at 1.0 MeV.

A second method of determining the neutron flux was to measure the number of proton recoils in the forward direction from a thin paraffin film of the same size and location as the ^{235}U samples. This method was being experimented with by Bacher's group at Cornell. Bacher suggested to Morris Blair that although there would be a lot of spurious pulses due to recoils from carbon and the argon gas these could be reduced by using a coincidence arrangement. After many difficulties Morris Blair and Jim Hush developed an elegant proportional counter coincidence system that they believed could detect proton recoils having energies above 0.1 MeV. A sketch of their counter is shown in Fig. 8. It has a target disk holding three thin paraffin films on platinum backings, one clean platinum disk and a polonium source. Two absorber wheels each containing nine absorbers are mounted between the two counters to analyze the energy of the recoil protons. With some help they also made the amplifiers, the pulse height discriminators, a coincidence circuit and a scaler. Blair also designed and built an improved current integrator which was published in R.S.I in 1943. With this system we found fission cross sections for ^{235}U which remained essentially constant at 1.66 barns from 0.5 to 1.8 MeV. This value was somewhat high and may be due in part to the fact that the counters discriminated against the lower energy group of neutrons. The fission cross section for ^{238}U was found to have a threshold of about 1 MeV and rose to 0.45 barns at 1.8 MeV.

One instrument which was very useful during the long runs required to measure the angular distributions was the rotating lithium target shown in Fig. 9. With it a lithium film could be evaporated directly onto the target in the vacuum over an area increased by a factor of 50. This provided neutron beams which were stable over periods of 100 hours or more.

Another instrument associated with these experiments was the long counter. Joe McKibben saw it as a section of the manganese bath where a long neutron counter pointed to the neutron source would be rather insensitive to neutron energy. A counter which was found to be very useful was called the Long Boron Monitor. It was simply a long boron lined ionization chamber about 2.5 cm in diameter and 20 cm long. It was surrounded by 10 cm of paraffin. In use the tube was pointed towards the neutron source and seemed to have a sensitivity quite independent of neutron energy. A shielded version which was used at Los Alamos is shown in Fig. 10 together with a response curve found by a Los Alamos group including Joe McKibben in 1954. The response to energies up to 5 MeV was flat but was down about 10% at 25 keV. They also found some sharp fluctuations of about 5% at neutron scattering resonances in carbon around 2 MeV and around 3 MeV. A pair of these long counters were used extensively at Los Alamos for measuring neutrons from small radioactive neutron sources with and without being surrounded by spheres of fissionable materials to determine the absorption when surrounded by spheres of heavy metals considered as possible tamper materials.

The research contract for preliminary fission bomb research was terminated after a little more than a year. A decision was made to concentrate the work of all groups working on the bomb project to the new laboratory being built at Los Alamos. By April 1, 1943, we had stopped operating the accelerators, written reports on what was done and started packing up the accelerators and all research equipment for shipment to Santa Fe by train.

By April 15 we had arrived in Santa Fe and followed a truck carrying the long tank dangling precariously over the shorter truck bed towards Los Alamos. The road up the hill was rough and narrow with several hairpin turns which took considerable maneuvering to complete. Once on the hill the long tank was quickly reassembled. The main difficulty was that the accelerating tube had developed a pressure-sensitive leak on the trip over. Some of us took turns staying in the tank while it was pumped up sufficiently for the leak to show up on the vacuum gauge and to locate and stop the leak by spraying shellac around the seals between the tube sections.

By June 1, the long tank was operating again with only a pair of army diesel generators in the back yard supplying power to the laboratory and the town site. We were soon comparing the fission cross sections of ^{239}Pu and ^{235}U and eventually the number of neutrons per fission in each case. The long tank was in use almost continually until the war ended in 1945. It was then returned to Wisconsin where it was kept busy by graduate students and others under the direction of Professors Herb, Richards, and Barschall until 1958.

Figure Titles and References

1. Electrostatic generator with concentric electrodes. R.G. Herb, C.M. Turner, C.M. Hudson, and R.E. Warren. Phys. Rev. 58, 579 (1940).

2. Second Analyzer. A.O. Hanson. Voltage measuring and control equipment for electrostatic generators. Rev. Sci. Inst. 15, 57 (1944).

3. Corona triode characteristics. R.M. Ashby and A.O. Hanson, Grid controlled corona. Rev. Sci. Inst. 13, 128 (1942).

4. Li(p,n) Threshold Measurement. A.O. Hanson and D.L. Benedict. An independent determination of fixed points on the high voltage scale. Phys. Rev. 65, 33 (1948).

5. The neutron yield from the Li(p,n) reaction. R. Taschek and A. Hemmendinger. Reaction constants for Li^7(p,n)Be^7. Phys. Rev. 74, 373 (1948).

6. J.L. McKibben. Letter of April 9, 1943, to Compton at the Metallurgical Laboratory in Chicago transmitting reports of the work at Wisconsin.

7. Li^7(p,2 alpha)Be^7 experiment. J.M. Blair and A.O. Hanson. Report on alpha particles from lithium bombarded by protons. CF 624 to Chicago.

8. Coincidence proportional counter. J.M. Blair and J.M. Hush. Coincidence proportional counter. CF 617 to Chicago. Related reports: A.O. Hanson, J.M. Blair, and J.M. Hush. A measurement of fission cross sections by use of a coincidence proportional counter. CF 618 D.L. Benedict and A.O. Hanson. A measurement of the uranium 235 cross section by the manganese solution method. CF 638.

9. Rotating Lithium Target. (patented at Los Alamos, July 3, 1951).

10. The shield long counter as used at Los Alamos and a measurement of its efficiency. A.O. Hanson and J.L. McKibben. A neutron counter having uniform sensitivity from 10 keV to 3 MeV. Phys. Rev. 72, 673 (1947). R.A. Nobles, et al., Rev. Sci. Inst. 25, 334 (1954).

*Alfred O. Hanson came to Los Alamos in April 1943 from the University of Wisconsin, where he had been working with Herb's group on electrostatic generators, to continue work with the "long tank" measurements of the fission cross sections of plutonium 239 and uranium 235. After the war, he left for a position at the University of Illinois, Urbana, where he continues his interests in accelerator development and nuclear physics and has been Professor of Physics since 1951.

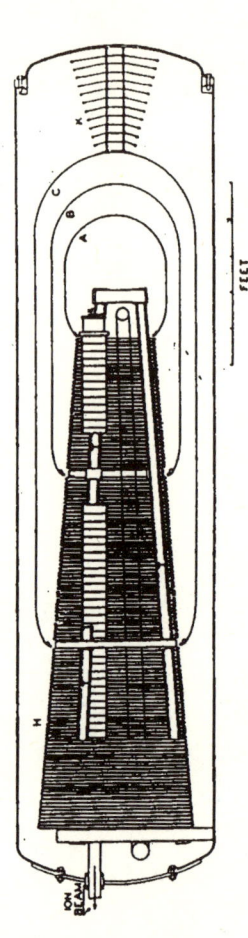

ELECTROSTATIC GENERATOR WITH CONCENTRIC ELECTRODES
BUILT AT
THE UNIVERSITY OF WISCONSIN DURING 1939-40
BY
R. G. HERB, C. M. TURNER, C. M. HUDSON AND R. E. WARREN

THE 100 PSI VESSEL WAS 5.5 FT. IN DIAMETER BY 22 FT. IN LENGTH. THE TANK DIAMETER WAS LIMITED BY THE WINDOWS IN STERLING HALL.

THE THREE INSULATING SUPPORT TUBES WERE OF TEXTOLITE. THESE TUBES WERE MADE USING PAPER BOUND WITH SHELLAC.

CHARGE WAS CARRIED TO THE TERMINAL USING A COTTON BELT. THIS FAMOUS METHOD WAS INVENTED BY ROBERT VAN DE GRAAFF.

THE ACCELERATION TUBE CAN BE SEEN LOCATED ABOVE THE CHARGING BELT.

Fig. 1.

Fig. 2. Second electrostatic analyzer.

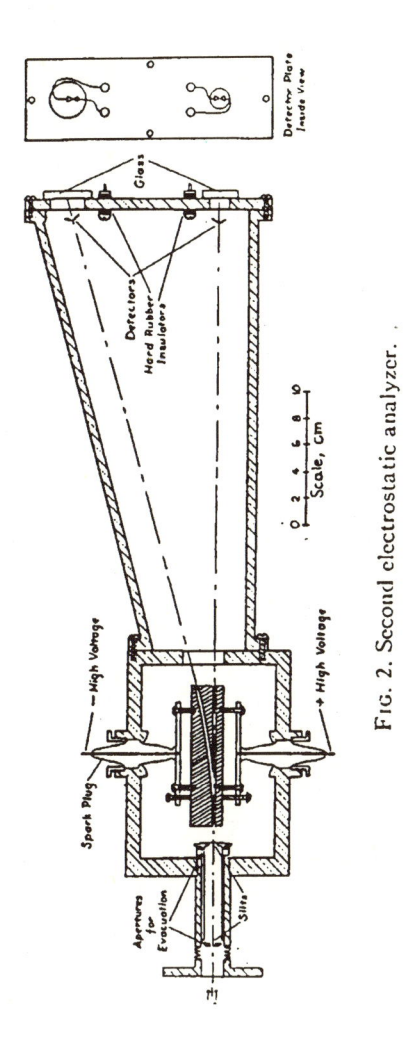

Fig.2.

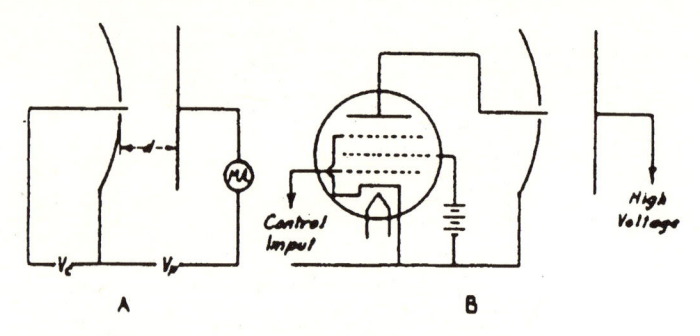

A. Schematic diagram of experimental triode. B. Vacuum-tube control of corona triode.

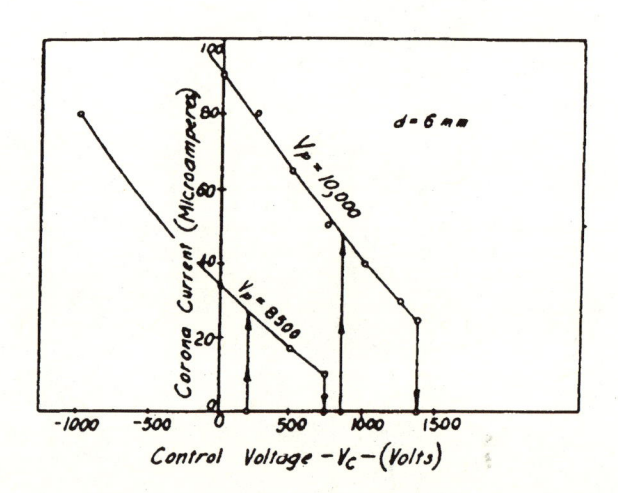

FIG. 3. Corona triode characteristics.

Fig.3.

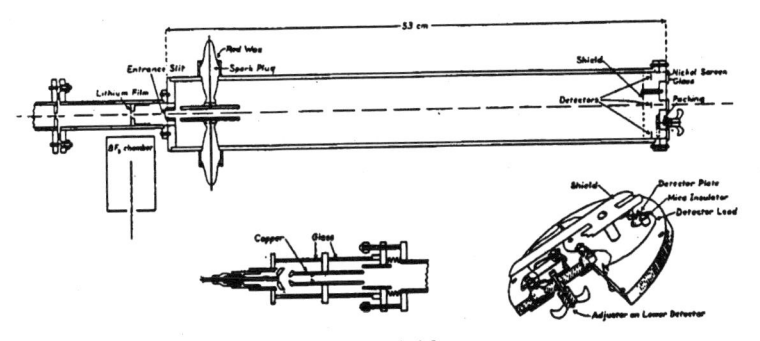

Electrostatic deflector.

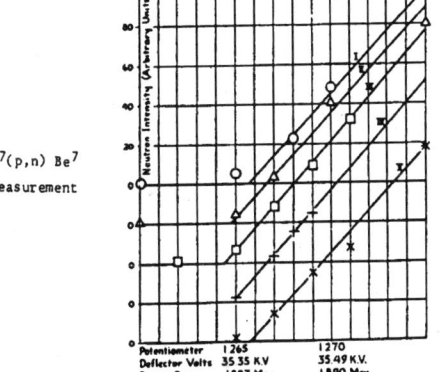

Fig. 4. Li^7(p,n) Be^7 Threshold Measurement

Neutrons from the Li(p, n) reaction. Runs I, II, and III taken with the beam on the upper detector. Runs IV and V taken with the beam on the lower detector.

Fig. 4.

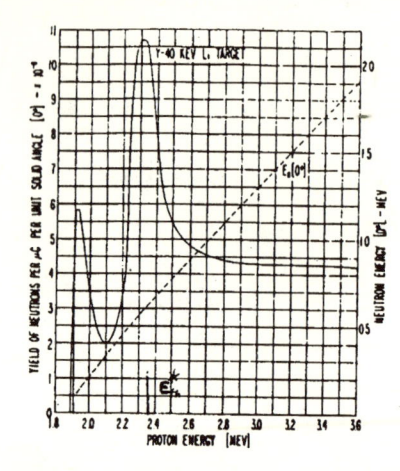

The yield of neutrons in the forward direction from a 40 kev thick lithium target and the energies of the neutrons in the forward direction as a function of the incident proton energy.

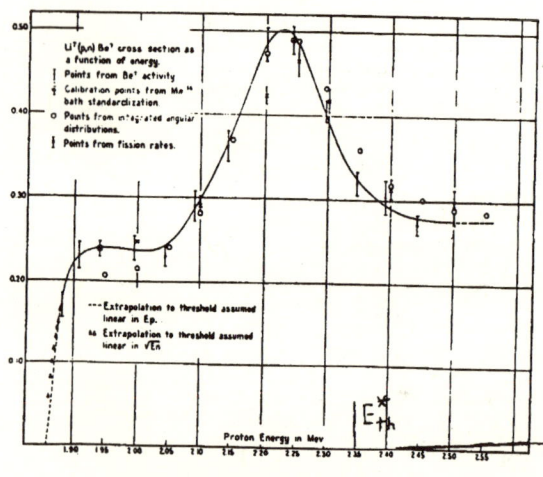

The $Li^7(p,n)Be^7$ total reaction cross section as a function of proton energy.

Fig. 5. The neutron yield from the Li(p,n) reaction as reported by Taschek and Hemmendinger at Los Alamos. Note the thresholds for the neutrons associated with the 0.43 MeV excited state of Be^7 at about 2.35 MeV.

Fig. 5

This letter was written on the stationery of the Physics Department of the University of Wisconsin. This is a copy made from a yellow copy I have.

April 9, 1943

Professor A. H. Compton
Metallurgical Laboratory
University of Chicago
Chicago, Illinois

Dear Professor Compton:

This is the final report on OEM sr-402, Department of Physics, University of Wisconsin, Madison, Wisconsin. The information given in this letter is general. The contract started on February 15, 1942, and ended April 15, 1943, personnel dropped from payroll March 31, 1943.

Personnel:
- J. L. McKibben, Official Investigator
- A. O. Hanson, Ph. D. Nov. 1942
- D. L. Benedict, Ph. D. Dec 1942. Left Feb. 15, 1943 to work with Sylvania Tube Corporation, Emporium, Pa.
- J. M. Blair, Graduate student.
- D. H. Frisch, Graduate student.
- J. M. Hush, Graduate student. Joined project June 1, 1942.
- R. D. Krohn, Graduate student. Joined project Mar. 15, 1943. Has been on payroll since February as an assistant to Professor Wahlin doing consulting work.
- L. W. Seagondollar, Graduate Student. Joined project Mar. 13, 1943.
- R. Perry, Graduate student. Joined Project Mar. 1, 1943 (On Los Alamos payroll).

The important results obtained on this project are being reported in five parts by the authors named.
1. Differential scattering cross-sections of dense elements.
   D. H. Frisch and J. L. McKibben......This designated CF-625 by the by the Metallurgical Laboratory.
2. Coincidence proportional counter. J. M. Blair and J. M. Hush.........This was designated CF-617.
3. A measurement of fission cross-sections by the use of a J.M. Blair & J.M. Hush coincidence proportional counter. A. O. Hanson. & .....This was designated CF-618.
4. A measurement of the 25 cross-section for 0.53 MeV neutrons by the manganese solution method. & A. O. Hanson........This was designated CF-6 8.   D. L. Benedict

Fig. 6.

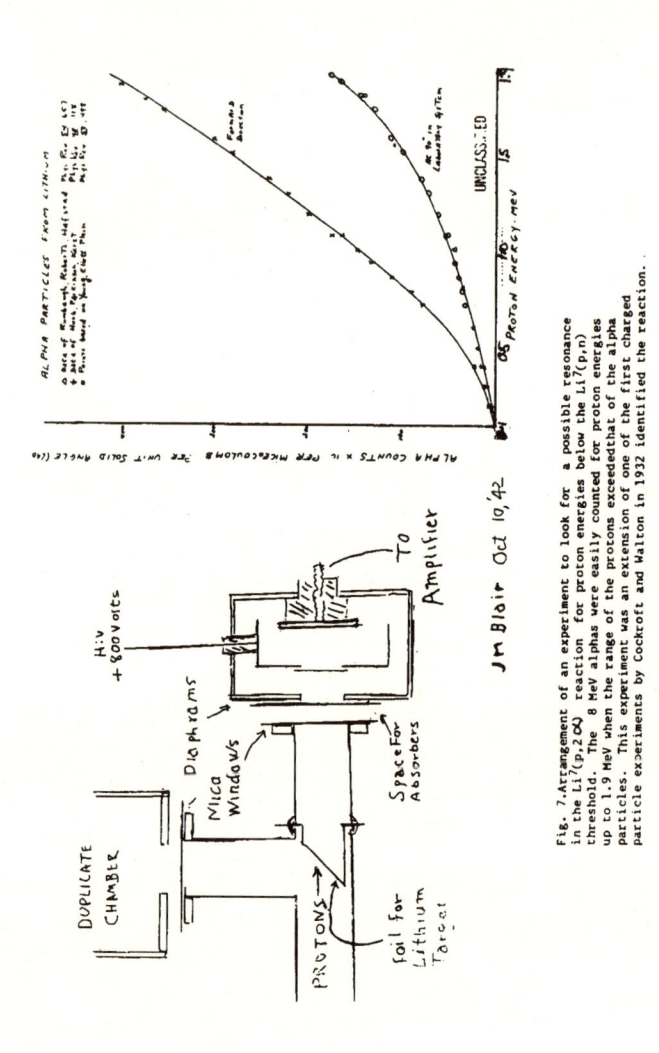

Fig. 7. Arrangement of an experiment to look for a possible resonance in the Li7(p,2α) reaction for proton energies below the Li7(p,n) threshold. The 8 MeV alphas were easily counted for proton energies up to 1.9 MeV when the range of the protons exceeded that of the alpha particles. This experiment was an extension of one of the first charged particle experiments by Cockroft and Walton in 1932 identified the reaction.

Fig. 7.

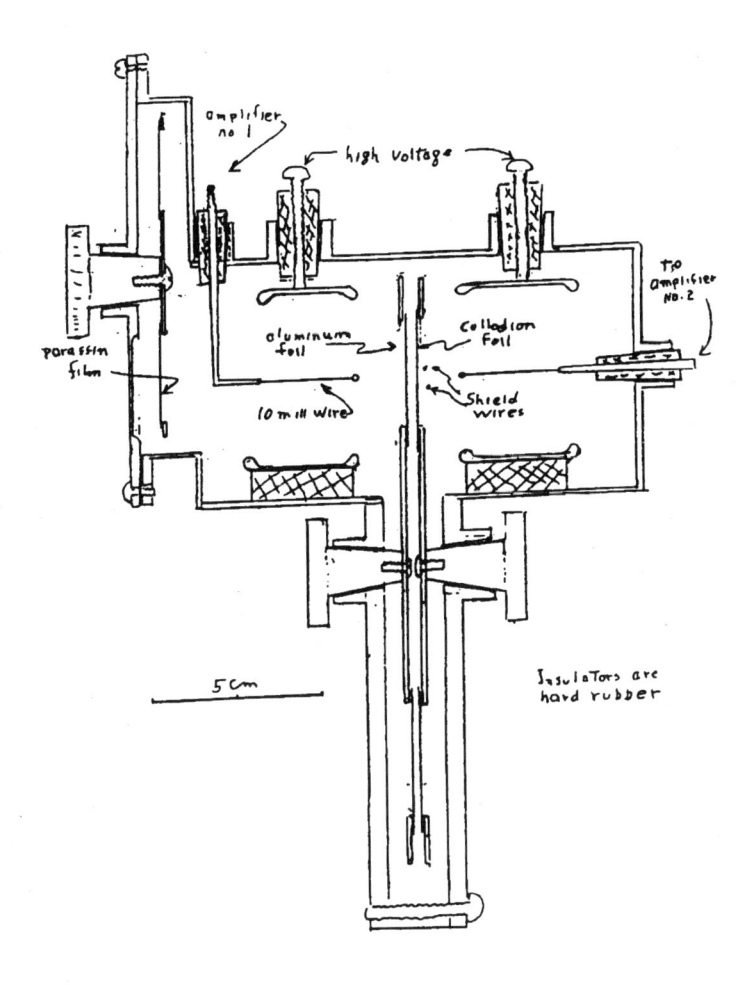

Fig. 8. Blair - Hush coincidence proportional counter for determining fast neutron flux by measuring the number of proton recoils from paraffin films. The target wheel contained 3 paraffin films, a clean platinum disk and a polonium alpha source. The two absorber wheels each contained an open aperture and 9 aluminum or collodion foils for energy identification and selection.

Fig. 8.

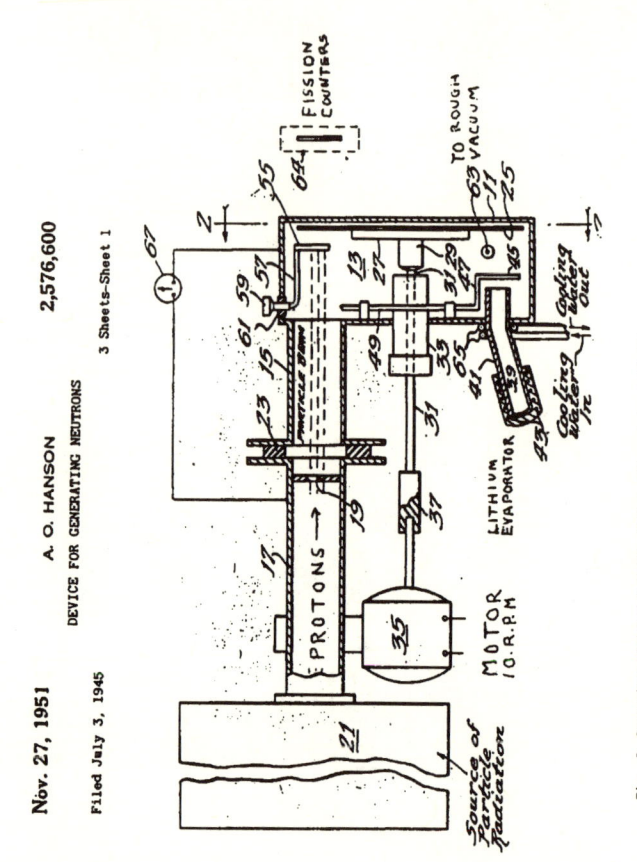

Fig. 9. Rotating lithium target with self contained lithium evaporator as shown in a patent obtained at Los Alamos.

Fig. 9.

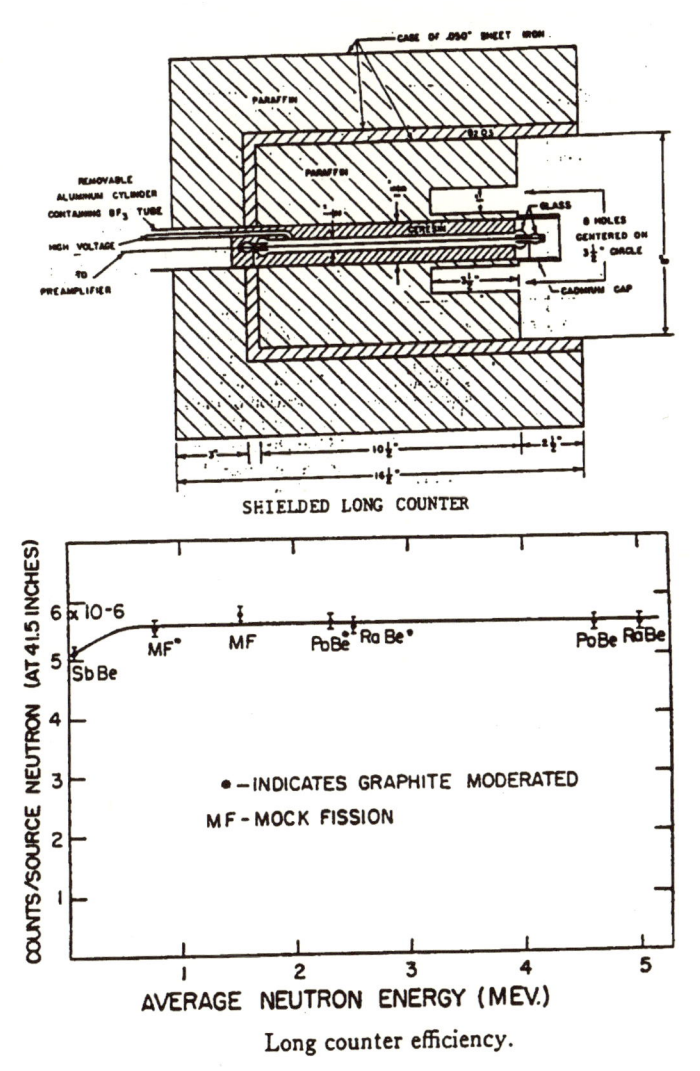

Fig. 10. The shielded long counter as used in Los Alamos and a measurement of its efficiency for a number of bare and carbon moderated radioactive sources.

Fig. 10.

EARLY MEASUREMENTS AT PURDUE OF SOME FUSION REACTION CROSS SECTIONS*
L.D.P. King**

I was a little hesitant at first to agree to give this paper on work I participated in over 50 years ago. However, I decided it was a great idea to have this historical session about work closely related to Los Alamos that was done at numerous universities and predates Los Alamos Laboratory. It also comes close to the 50th anniversary of the Laboratory.

Much of this work with its personnel and advanced accelerator equipment made it possible to perform the astounding feat of creating a modern laboratory on a remote mesa in New Mexico in less than one year. Both equipment and personnel were bodily moved to New Mexico when the time came to create this new laboratory.

I was pleased to note that all the speakers on this program were at some time closely associated with the University of Wisconsin. When I went back to Wisconsin for a reunion a couple of years ago, I learned that Don Kerst, Ed Creutz, and I were the first to earn Ph.D.'s in nuclear physics there, when we graduated in 1937.

This paper is presented on almost the 50th anniversary of the last paper I presented to the American Physical Society. My 30 years of work at Los Alamos was mostly concerned with specialized nuclear reactions. When some of this work was declassified, it seemed to me more appropriate to talk about it at the meetings of the newly created American Nuclear Society. Hence my long absence from American Physical Society meetings.

I became involved in Los Alamos rather unexpectedly when, in June 1942, J. Robert Oppenheimer appeared at Purdue University to find out whether the Purdue cyclotron could be used to carry out some classified experiments he was interested in. Because I was then in charge of moving the cyclotron from its rather cramped quarters to a space specially planned for it in a nice new Physics Building; of course, I became involved.

First, let me give you a little history—as I remember it—concerning the Purdue cyclotron. It was not as well known as some, perhaps because in late 1939 the head of the Physics Department, Dr. Lark Horowitz, insisted that the paper describing the cyclotron be sent to the Journal of the Franklin Institute,[1] rather than where we wanted it sent—to the American Physical Society. He must have had some kind of feud with the American Physical Society!

---

*Paper prepared for Division of Nuclear Physics of the American Physical Society October 16, 1992—*Some Preludes to Los Alamos*.

In 1937 jobs were not too easy to get, so I had been pleased to accept an invitation to become an instructor in the Physics Department at Purdue. When I arrived I found there were three other new appointments besides mine—and that a beautiful unused 37-1/2" cyclotron magnet sat in the basement of the old Physics building. It had been put in working order the previous year by Dr. Yearian and Mr. Howe.

Three of us—Bill Henderson (who I believe came from Canada), Jacob Risser (from Rice) and I—were given the job of creating a running cyclotron with this beautiful magnet.

Because none of us had any cyclotron experience—or contact with Berkeley where the cyclotron was, of course, invented—we had to do considerable research in the literature to get things going. This gave us an opportunity to incorporate many new features, which perhaps influenced Dr. Oppenheimer in his choice of the Purdue cyclotron.

(1) The pole pieces had already been tapered from 40" to 37-1/2" according to a formula derived by Hans Bethe for giving minimum fringing flux.

(2 The dees or inner electrodes were shaped according to calculations by Rose,[2] which showed that the focusing of the ion beam produced by the combination of the electric and magnetic fields was such that the ion current realized depends on the height of the dees halfway out from the center. For a given electrostatic capacity it is possible to obtain higher ion currents by shaping the dees to accommodate the shape of the ion beam. Figure 1 shows the shape we adopted.

(3) Experiments I had carried out at Wisconsin on high-voltage accelerator tubes for a Cockcroft-Walton accelerator had shown that tapered internal corona shields prevented sparkover and bombardment of the glass section of an accelerator tube. This design was incorporated in the dee support and deflector plate mountings as shown in Figures 2 and 3.

(4) Rose[4] had done some recent calculations on the use of an internal shim to improve the uniformity of the magnetic field at the edge of the magnet. We incorporated such a shim—and Figure 4 shows the improvement achieved.

(5) Livingston[5] had in 1939 described some early experiments at Cornell using a low-voltage arc instead of the usual filament for the ion source; our design is shown in Figure 5. This provided an ion current five or six times greater than did the conventional cyclotron filament source.

When the cyclotron was put into operation, all our initial experiments were for the purpose of studying various nuclear reactions, using high-energy alpha particles. The cyclotron equation with the chosen values of the magnetic field and radius of the exit slit yielded 16.5 million volt alpha particles for these experiments.

After construction of the new Physics building in late 1941, the cyclotron was moved into the new facility shown in Figure 6. The move had been completed, and the cyclotron was operating again, when in June 1942, as I mentioned earlier, Dr. Oppenheimer arrived.

The experiments he wanted done on the cyclotron were to determine cross sections for two nuclear reactions in the energy range of 0.3 MeV to 1.0 MeV.

(1) Bombarding deuterium with He^3 ions and observing the number of disintegration alpha particles.

(2) Bombarding deuterium with tritium ions and observing the number of disintegration alpha particles.

These experiments were secret, so this was going to be my first experience in working with a guard at the entrance to the room. In fact, even the head of the Physics Department was not allowed in!

Because it appeared that our cyclotron would be suitable for doing these experiments, an arrangement had been worked out between the Purdue Research Foundation and the Office of Scientific Research and Development (OSRD). This office had been established in June 1941 to coordinate all United States work on the production of fissionable materials and the production of a nuclear weapon.

The team that Dr. Oppenheimer chose to carry out these classified experiments consisted of four physicists. Two were from Cornell, and were experienced in cross section measurements on the small Cornell cyclotron. They were Marshall Holloway and Charles Baker. The other pair were from Purdue: R. E. Schreiber, who had recently received his Ph.D. at Purdue, and myself. The Cornell group brought some of their measuring equipment with them.

The first job was to change the cyclotron from the high energy adjustments used to obtain the 16.5 MeV alpha particles we had been using. The magnetic field had to be reduced from 14,500 gauss to 5,000 gauss, and the oscillator frequency from 10.9 megacycles to 5.5 megacycles.

This large decrease in magnetic field required the removal of the internal Rose shim, because instead of providing a more uniform field to the edge of the magnet, it produced a hump. Further shimming adjustments were required to obtain a satisfactory beam.

The frequency adjustment in the oscillator proved to be easy because the oscillator was a tuned grid and plate circuit using quarter wave lines in both the grid and plate circuits, the latter being the dee circuit. The large closed end of the original elements had been made from a copper eave downspout 3" in diameter, which we had to replace with a coil of 3/4" copper tubing. The range of frequencies required by the experiment was obtained by a slight change in spacing the turns in the coil.

Adjustments in the arc source were found to be very important. Changing the relative positions of the dummy and arc cones had a marked effect on the beam intensity. We found the final arrangement giving the best beam intensity was obtained by putting a cap on the arc cone of such shape that a dummy cone was unnecessary, and the ions leaving the arc could see only one dee (Figure 7).

I will try to give you a rough outline of how these experiments were carried out. The first experiment was done with He^3 ions. Air reduction gas of 99.9% purity was used. The final beam through a 1/8" x 1/2" exit opening gave approximately 2×10^5 particles/sec, representing about 30% of the total beam.

A schematic layout of the irradiation chamber and cyclotron connections is shown in Figure 8.

(1) Deuterium gas was used for the target material.

(2) Disintegrations were observed in two directions from the incident beam because there was a possibility that anisotropy existed in the center of the mass system. The ionization chamber was therefore designed to observe disintegration alphas emitted in a cone about the forward direction and in a zone about the 90° direction.

Screens A and B were used to decrease the intensity of the beam without changing the running conditions of the cyclotron.

An alpha particle source could be inserted for calibration measurements of the energy distribution of the bombarding particles.

The target chamber was the region between the exit foil and the defining foil.

The "hairpin" electrode in the target chamber was used to collect the ionization produced by the incident particles.

The 0° and 90° collectors were used to collect the ionization produced by the disintegration alpha particles emitted in their respective directions.

The gate valve could be used to completely stop the beam for background measurements.

Figure 9 shows the detail of the ionization chamber. The exit foil was an aluminum foil having an air equivalent of 1.5 cm for the He^3 having the energies used in the experiments.

The defining foil is an aluminum foil of thickness 1.01 air cm. The air equivalent of the foil added to the air equivalent of the deuterium gas between the exit foil and the end of the cone nearest the zero degree collimator was calculated to be just sufficient to stop all scattered deuterium ions and still allow all disintegration particles to have at least 0.5 cm air range in the collecting region between the end of the cone and the 0° collector.

The physical depth of the target chamber was 1.06 cm including correction for the curvature of the exit foil.

The linear pulse amplifier used was of a conventional design.

The beam current of about 2×10^5 particles/sec was measured indirectly by measuring the irradiation current produced by the incident beam in the target chamber. The ratio of the number of He^3 particles producing the ionization current was determined in a separate experiment. The ionization current was measured with a direct current amplifier, or pliotron.

The target material, deuterium, was highly purified in order to remove all non-hydrogenous material by passing it through palladium. The concentration of deuterium gas was then determined by Dr. Nier in a mass spectrograph to be 96% to 98% pure.

The number of target atoms was determined from the temperature and pressure at the time of the deuterium gas filling. The depth of the chamber was a constant determined by the planes of the exit foil and defining foil, so the number of target atoms could be expressed as the number of atoms/cm^2.

The energy distribution of the bombarding particles was measured immediately before or after each disintegration run by a comparison of the distribution in pulse height of the He^3 particles with the distribution in pulse height of polonium alphas, which had lost a known amount of energy in the chamber. For these measurements the ionization chamber was filled with nitrogen to such pressure that all He^3 ions in the beam were completely stopped in the target chamber and the polonium alphas gave pulses of comparable size.

The energy loss of the alphas in the chamber was computed from their range, the thickness of the exit foil, and the air equivalent of the chamber. From this it was possible to translate the measured height distribution of the He^3 to energy distribution.

The calculation of the solid angle in which particles are detected had to take into account a number of things, and was quite complicated.

(1) The solid angle in the center of mass system varies appreciably with energy.

(2) The target chamber is too large to be considered a point source.

(3) The target is thick in terms of energy loss.

For these reasons, the solid angle was computed as a function of energy, and the target subdivided into cells sufficiently small so that each cell could be considered a point source. The upper corner of Figure 10 shows how the region between the exit foil and the defining foil was subdivided into four equal levels by planes perpendicular to the direction of the beam, and each of these levels divided into four equal cells. Calculations were made for each cell, except where symmetry made this unnecessary.

Calculations for the 90° collector were even more complicated because there was no symmetry in the cells with respect to the openings in the 90° collimator, and also because the hairpin subtends an appreciable angle in the various cells.

To make a long story short, Figure 11 shows an approximation to the true cross section from the initial analysis of data. A distinct peak in the cross section is apparent in the energy range of 0.7 - 0.8 MeV.

The ratio of the yields in the 90° collector to those in the 0° collector at various energies is designated by circles in Figure 12.

It was concluded that the anisotropy does exist in the center of mass system. It further appeared that the size of the anisotropy changes with energy, there being a larger yield at 90° than at 0° at low energies and the reverse at higher energies.

The second experiment was to accelerate tritium particles in the cyclotron with energies between 0.3 MeV and 1.0 MeV, and again bombard a deuterium target and determine the number of disintegration alphas.

The source of tritium was 60 cm^3 (at NTP) of gas containing 0.025% T's. This sample was supplied by Emilio Segrè and Milton Kahn. Rough calculations indicated that this could be diluted by almost a thousand to one with ordinary tank hydrogen and still give a beam of suitable magnitude (2 x 10^5 particles/sec).

The same capped arc was used as in the He^3 experiments and a beam of 5 x 10^5 T's/sec was obtained after some shimming of the magnet.

The deuterium gas for the target chamber was again purified by passing it through palladium.

At first it was thought that the same ionization chamber could be used as in the He^3 experiment, but a number of difficulties were encountered requiring several changes.

(1) There was a great variation in the energy of the disintegration alphas with the incident energy of the tritium particles. This necessitated taking data for the 0° collector to be done in two stages. For incident energies between 0.2 MeV and 0.65 MeV, a 1.0 cm air equivalent defining foil was used, and for mean energies between 0.5 MeV and 1.0 MeV, a 2.0 air equivalent defining foil was used.

(2) The direct measure of the incident tritium particles was done in the same manner and in the He^3 experiment—comparing the pulse height produced by the tritium with that of polonium alphas passing into the nitrogen-filled target chamber. For this method to be valid required that the tritium particles lose all their energy in the target chamber. This was not possible for the complete energy range of the tritium particles used. A mica foil mounted vertically to the beam, equipped with a protractor disk and an index so that it could be set at any angle to the direction of the beam, was installed. This had the dual purpose of stopping singly charged H and D molecules, and of varying the energy of the tritium particles. This foil is shown in Figure 13.

(3) It was found that tritium particles are scattered by aluminum. This necessitated the incorporation of a shield to hide the exit foil from the 90° collector. This shield is shown in Figure 14.

Calculations for the solid angle were similar, but somewhat more complicated than in the He^3 experiment. The shield for the scattered tritiums from the exit foil complicated the 90° calculations. The use of two thicknesses of the defining foil complicated calculations for the 0°.

Again, making a long story short, Figure 15 shows the average cross section for the 90° collector. The 0° collector gave a similar shape but consistently lower values.

In view of the uncertainty of the solid angle and number of target atoms in the 90° direction, it was not determined at the time of the report whether any anisotropy existed until completion of solid angle calculations.

Before completion of this second experiment, we were visited by Dr. Oppenheimer's right-hand man, John Manley. He informed us that these experiments were being made for a secret Laboratory recently created in New Mexico. He persuaded all of us to go there—which we did in late October 1943. I don't think I knew that our measurements were to create a super nuclear explosive until after some lectures by our next speaker, Robert Serber.

With some parts of the world still in the Stone Age, the Atomic Age was being born. Absorbed in the fascination of unraveling the mysteries of nature, we scientists did not concern ourselves with the use to which our discoveries would be put. We became unwitting tools in the hands of a government vying with another government to forge the most terrible weapon in human history. At the same time, we were learning things with incredible potentialities for good.

REFERENCES

[1] W.J. Henderson, L.D.P. King, J.R. Risser, H.J. Yearian, and J.D. Howe, "The Purdue Cyclotron," Reprint from the *Journal of the Franklin Institute*, Vol. 228, No. 5 (November 1939).
[2] Rose, Phys. Rev. 53, 392 (1938)
[3] Haworth, King, Zahn, and Heydenburg, *Rev. Sci. Inst.* 8, 486 (1937).
[4] Rose, Phys. Rev. 53, 715 (1938).
[5] Livingston, *Rev. Sci. Inst.* 10, 63 (1939)
[6] Baker, Holloway, King, and Schreiber, AECD-2189, LADC-541, LAMS-2.
[7]. Baker, Holloway, King, and Schreiber, AECD-2226, LADC-540.

**L. D. P. King came to Los Alamos in October 1944 from Purdue University where he had begun experimental studies on fusion reaction cross sections of deuterium and tritium at the request of Oppenheimer. He remained at the Laboratory in various scientific and administrative capacities until his retirement in 1973. He has been a member of the J. Robert Oppenheimer Memorial Committee since 1969.

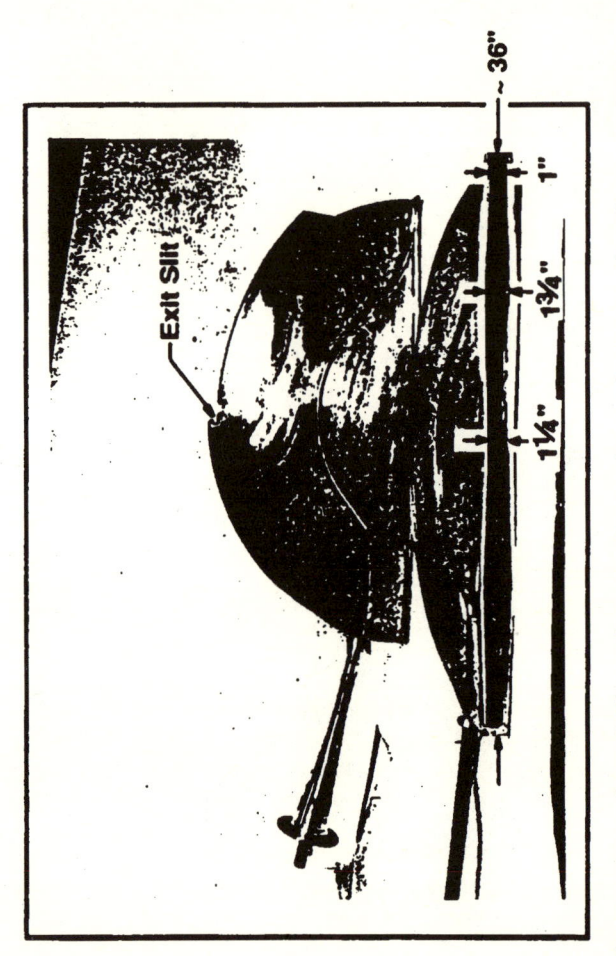

Photograph of the dees showing the conical support and inner gasket seal.

Figure 1

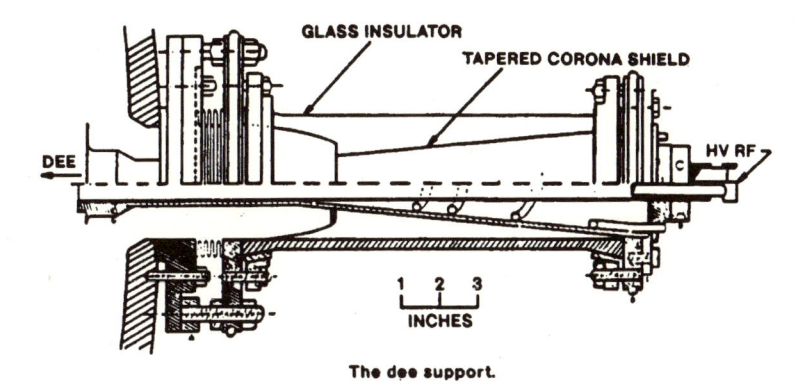

Figure 2

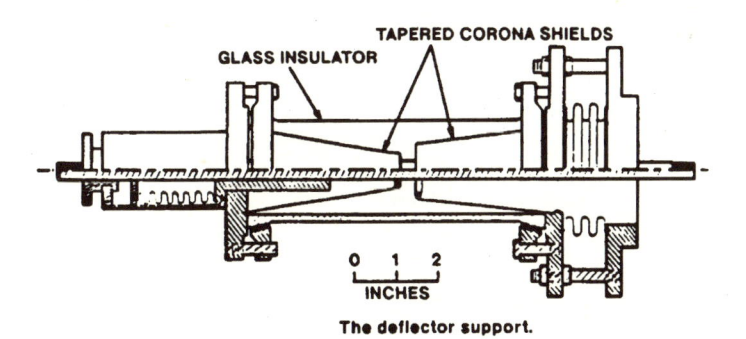

The dee support.

Figure 3

The deflector support.

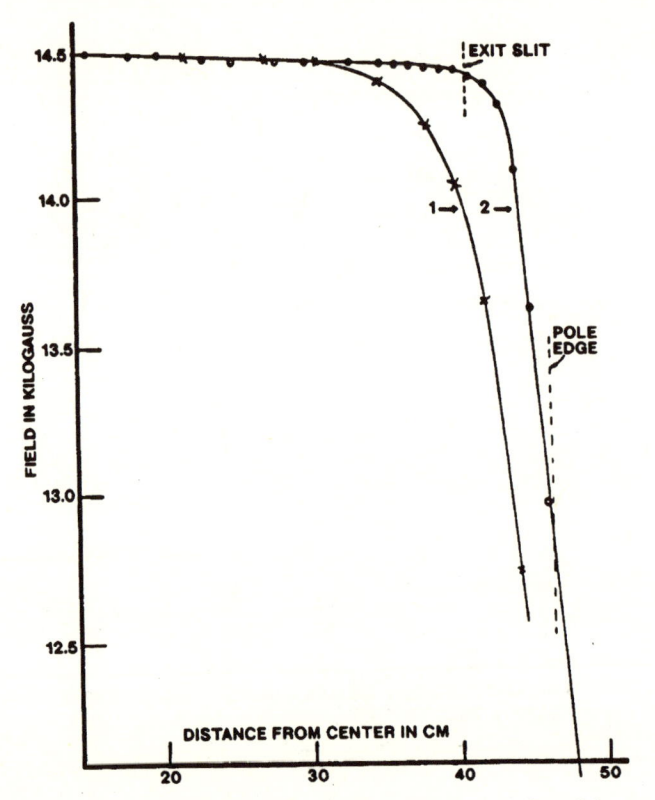

The magnetic field near the exit slit. Curve 1 is the uncorrected field. Curve 2 the magnetic field after the insertion of the ROSE shims $\frac{3}{8} \times \frac{5}{16}$ inches.

Figure 4

The arc source.

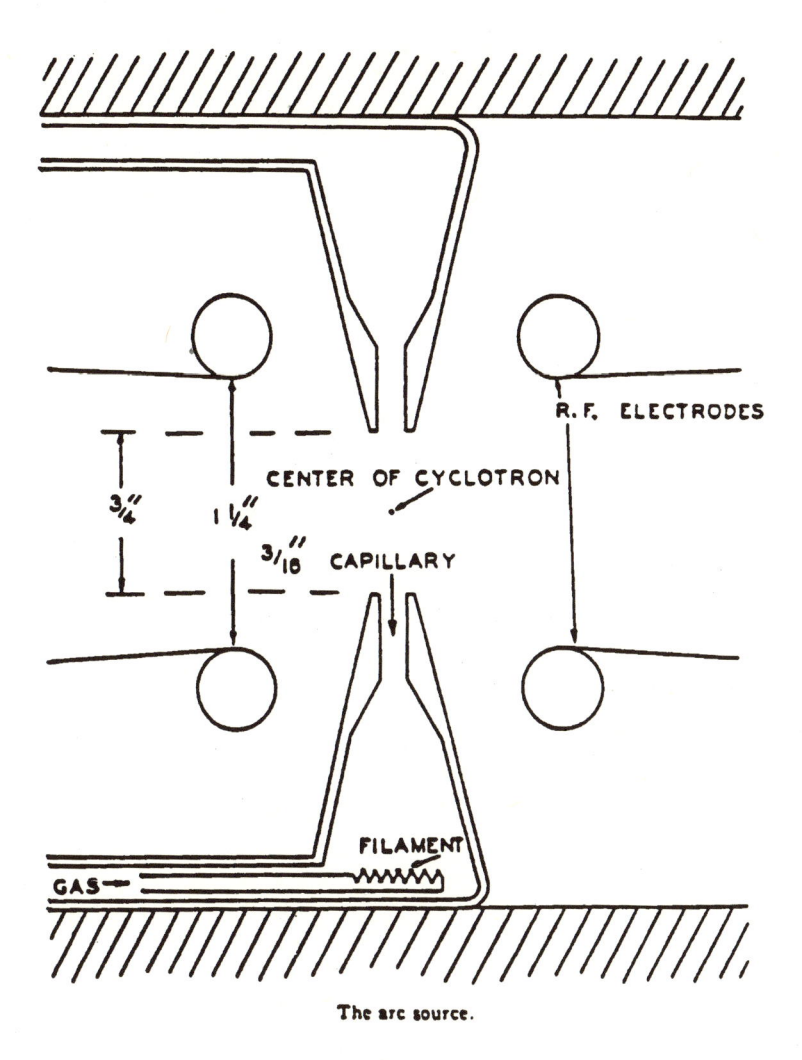

Figure 5

16.5 MeV ^{4}He Cyclotron Facility
$D(^3He, \alpha) p$ E_{3He} (0.3 → 1.0 MeV)
$D(T, \alpha) n$ E_T

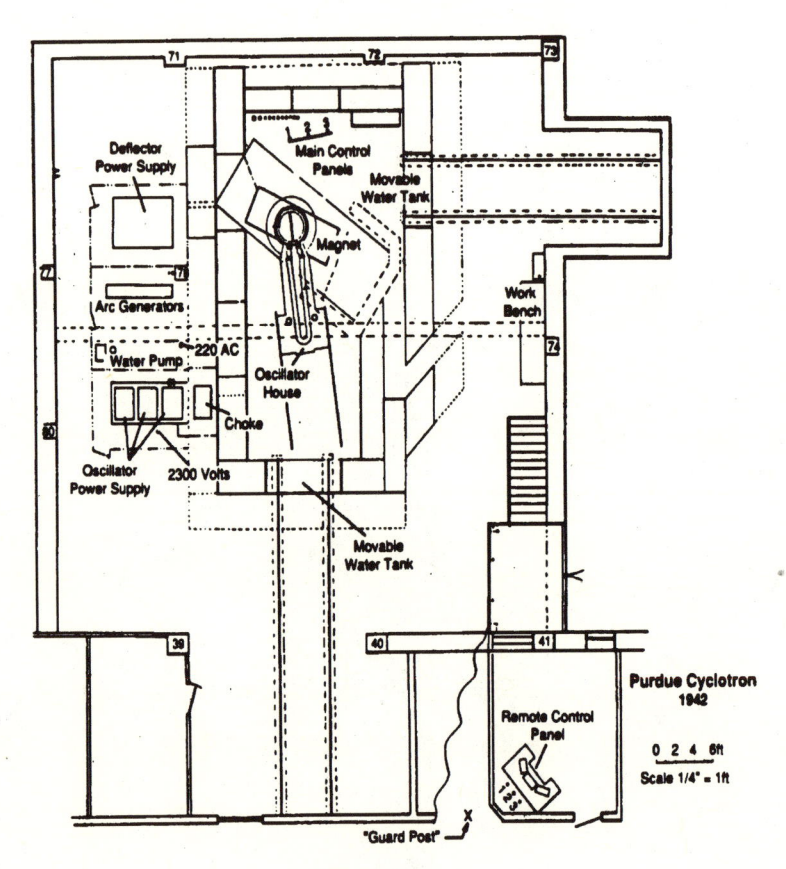

Figure 6

Capped Arc Ion Source

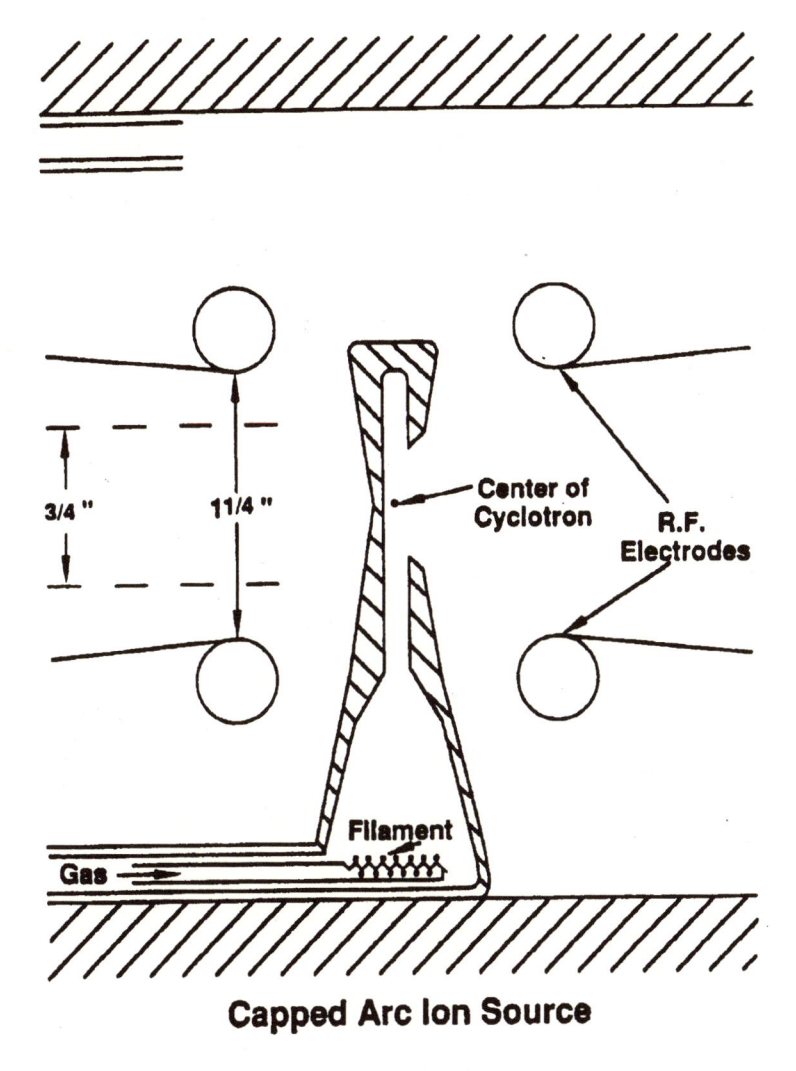

Figure 7

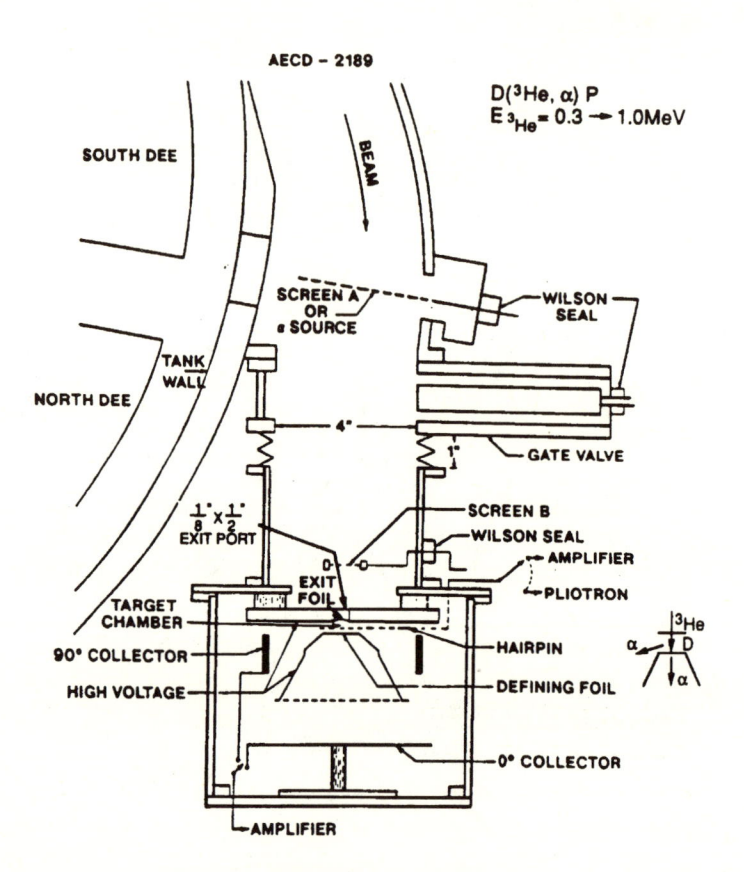

Figure 8

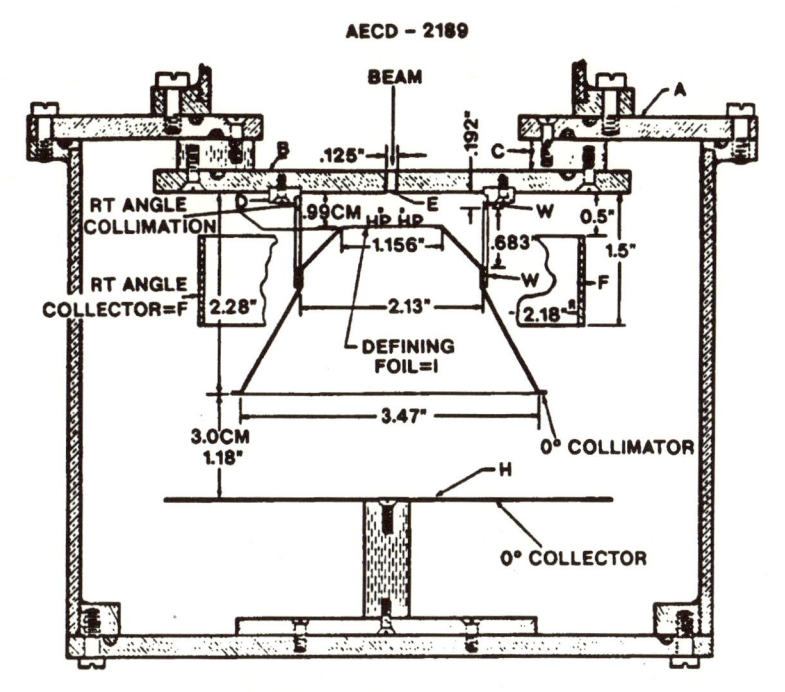

Disintegration chamber, section viewed from side. E = exit foil. H.P. = .011 in. wire. ▨=Lucite. ◉ = round rubber gasket. ▬ = soft solder. W-W .005 in. Ni wires spot-welded on cylinder with 3/16 in. spacing. 0° collimation cone and collector are Cu, other parts are brass. Entrance slit = .125 in. by .50 in. Foil pulled in averaged .07 cm by vacuum.

Figure 9

Figure 10

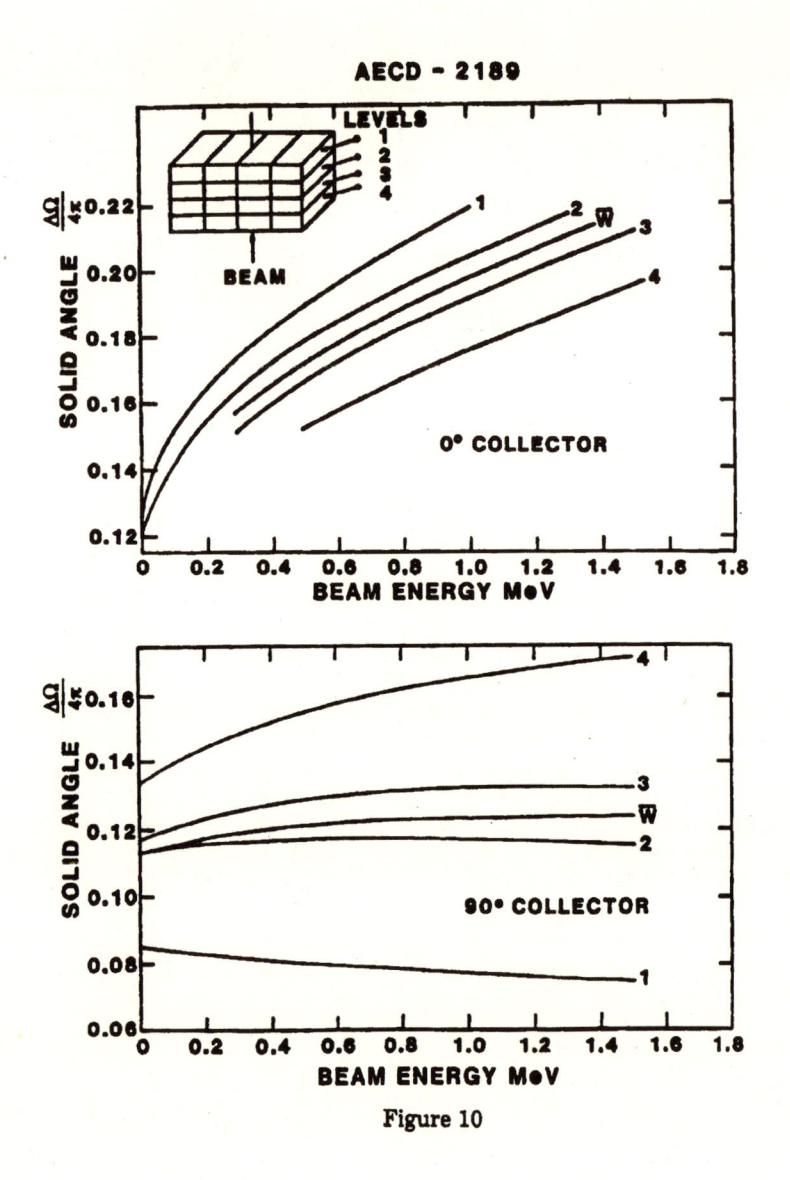

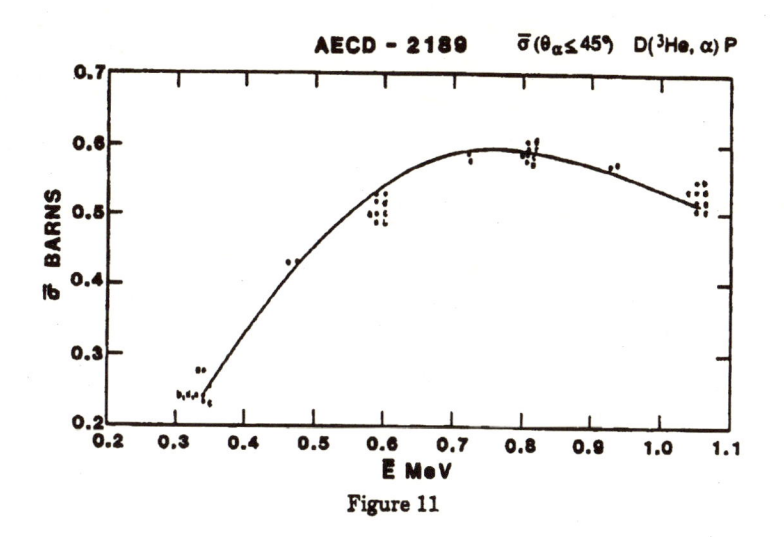

AECD - 2189 $\bar{\sigma}(\theta_\alpha \leq 45°)$ $D(^3He, \alpha)P$

Figure 11

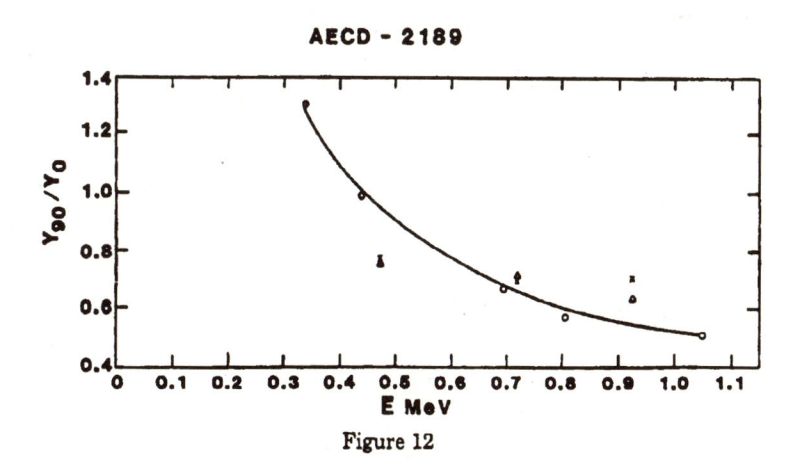

AECD - 2189

Figure 12

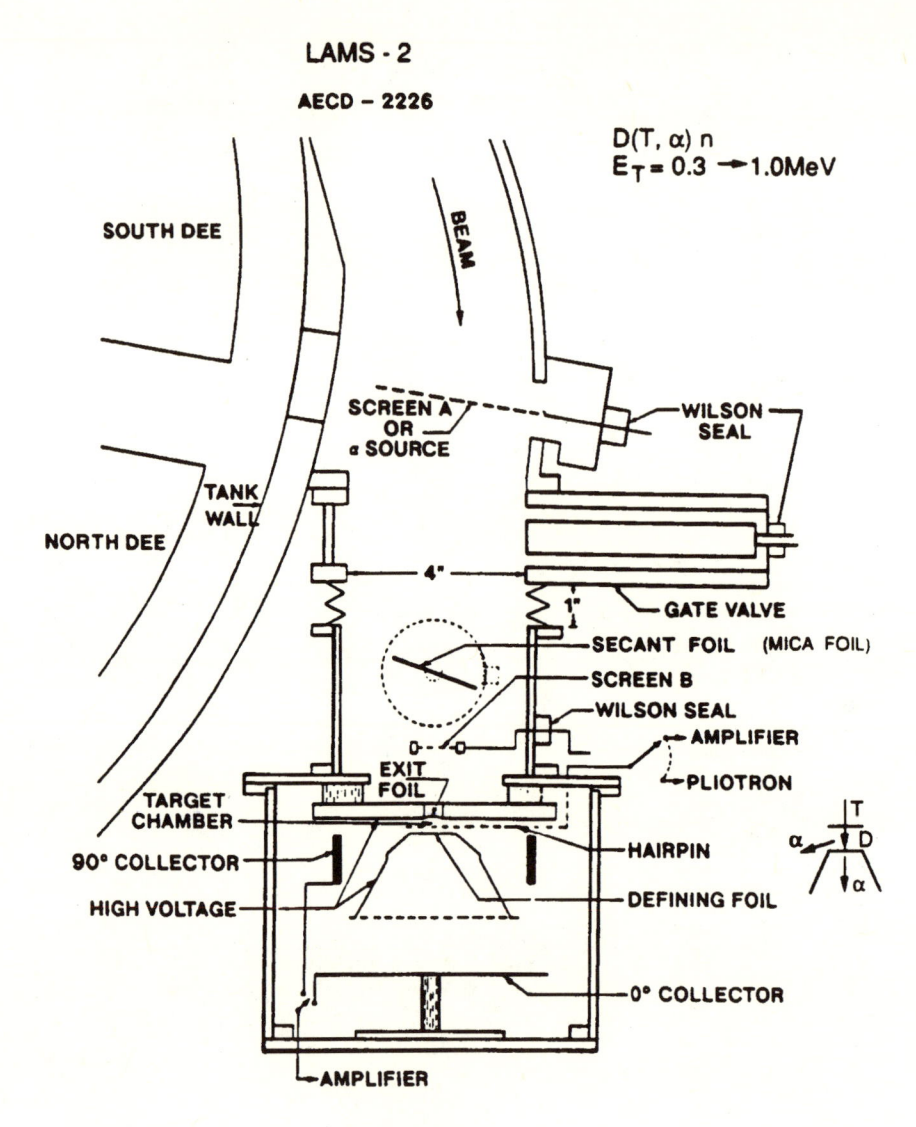

Figure 13

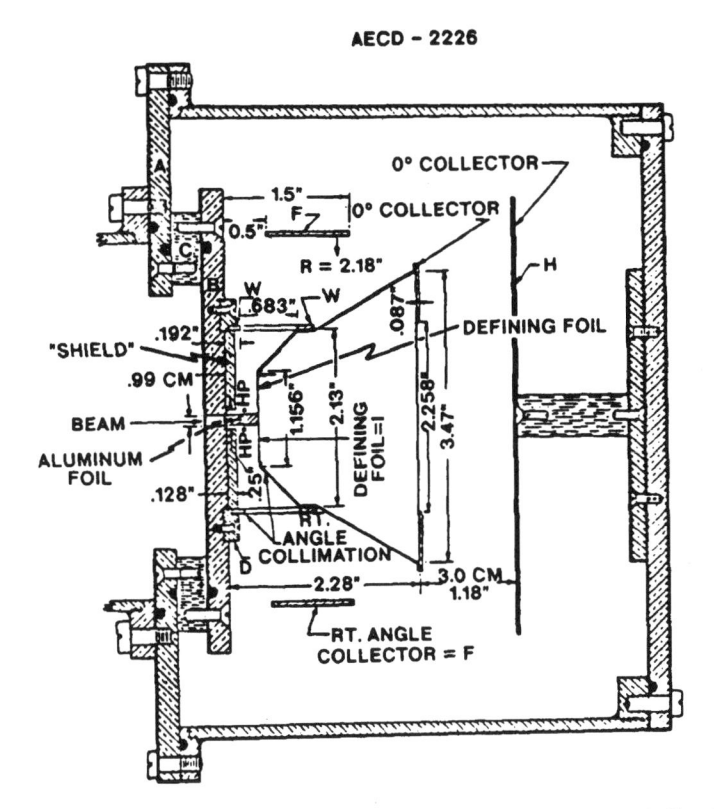

Disintegration chamber, section viewed from side. E = exit foil. H.P. = .011in. wire. ▭=Lucite. ⊗ = round rubber gasket. ⌐ = soft solder. W-W .005 in. Ni wires spot-welded on cylinder with 3/16 in. spacing. 0° collimation cone and collector are Cu, other parts are brass. Entrance slit = .125 in. by .50 in. Foil pulled in averaged .07 cm by vacuum.

Figure 14

$\bar{\sigma}$ D(T,α)n 90° COLLECTOR

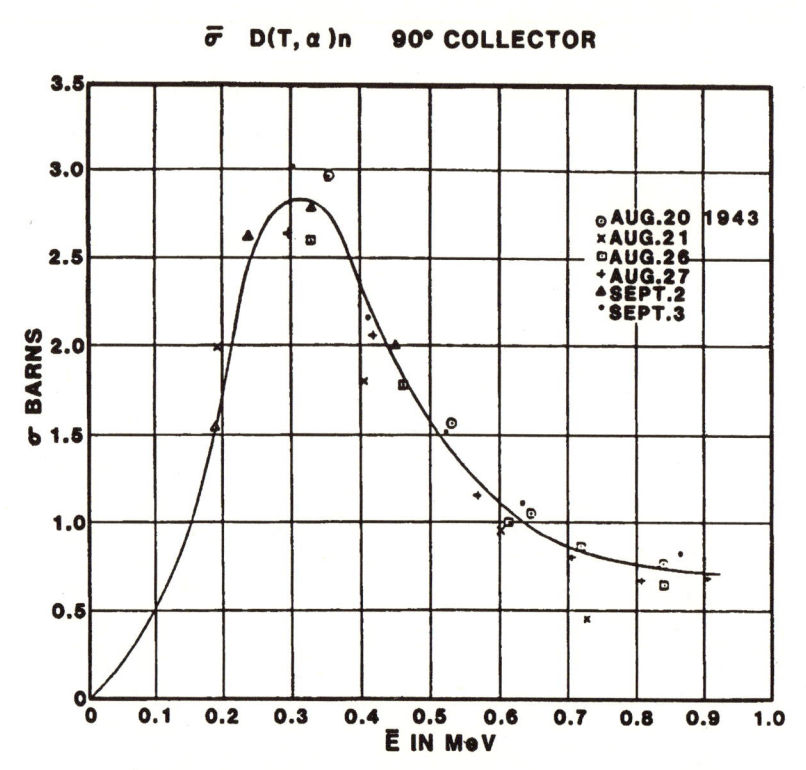

Average cross section as a function of average energy at center of chamber

Figure 15

THEORETICAL STUDIES AT BERKELEY
Robert Serber[*]

My story begins with a phone call from Robert Oppenheimer just before Christmas 1941. I don't remember the actual date. Let me mention a little history first. In March 1940, Frisch and Peierls wrote a memorandum to the British Government in which they described what a nuclear bomb would be like—a fast neutron reaction in ^{235}U, a rare element. They also said it would be feasible to separate the elements. This was the main part of their report. Their optimism on this score was greatly aided by an enormous underestimate of the critical mass—they gave it as 600 grams of ^{235}U. This got the British government interested and they appointed the MAUD Committee in 1941.

The MAUD committee reported that a bomb could be built in two years at a cost of 50 million pounds. The MAUD report plus a lot of prodding by the British finally persuaded the American authorities to take the fission program seriously. This took until 6 December 1941, the day before Pearl Harbor, when the project was taken out of the hands of Lyman Briggs and turned over to Compton, Lawrence, and Urey. A phone call came from Oppy, who was in Chicago, shortly after this meeting. Oppy wanted to come to Urbana, where I was teaching at the University of Illinois, to talk to me about something. He came, we took a walk, and he told me he was going to be appointed to replace Gregory Breit as the "Coordinator of Rapid Rupture" in charge of the weapons end of the project and the various university contracts. He wanted me to come out to Berkeley to be his assistant.

It was difficult to get away from Urbana immediately because so many people had already left for war work. No one was left to teach. It was agreed that I would come after classes were over. So, at the end of April my wife, Charlotte, and I left and drove out to Berkeley and moved into a little apartment over the garage at Oppy's Eagle Hill House. We were supposed to stay only a day or two while Charlotte went looking for an apartment. But she found that wasn't so easy. Berkeley was so crowded with shipyard workers—the Richmond Shipyard was there—we actually stayed for ten months. Charlotte gave up and took a job in the shipyard herself. She was called a statistician because she knew how to add and subtract!

I went to Oppy's old office in Le Conte Hall. He had some English (British) papers there about bomb problems—critical masses and efficiency. These were on a very elementary level but quite helpful because they pointed to a number of problems and outlined ways of attacking them. It was quite striking in that there wasn't a sign of an American paper on this subject. I don't know how much this was due to Gregory Breit's paranoia about secrecy. In any event, there was no sign that any thought at all had been given in this country to what a bomb would be like before the MAUD report arrived.

Oppy had a group of students and post docs who were calculating orbits for Ernest Lawrence's electromagnetic separator. Some of the people there were Frankel, Nelson, Richman, Lominintz, Weinberg, and perhaps Bohm. I could use their services as long as Ernest's work got done. I asked Frankel and Nelson to look at improvements in the simple diffusion theory that had been used previously for critical mass calculations. I had in mind a perturbative approach, but they did a lot better. They wrote down the exact integral equation for the diffusion and found properties of the solution. They also looked at the literature and found the exact solution for one-directional diffusion. With this background, we were able to make a fairly accurate critical mass calculation provided, of course, that our experimental friends told us what the cross sections were and what the number of neutrons per fission was.

I, meanwhile, was working on the efficiency problem and had the hydrodynamics for the untamped bomb in pretty good shape, but not yet for the untamped case. Oppy oversaw this whole work, but he was away a lot of the time. He and John Manley were busy with the various contracts. Oppy did get some information on blast damage by high explosives and on guns that the Army and Navy had. We also worked on predetonation and initiators.

In July 1942, Oppy called a conference of theorists at Berkeley to look over the situation. Attending were Bethe, Teller, Tolman, Van Vleck, Bloch, Konopinski, Frankel, Nelson, Oppy, and myself. I reported on the present status of things and Frankel and Nelson told what they had done. Everybody agreed that things looked pretty good. The main problem was plutonium—getting light element impurities low enough to keep the neutron background down and getting a high enough velocity gun to assemble the pieces. Then we talked about different shapes so you could assemble larger masses. Edward brought up various autocatalytic schemes such as using absorbers that would be squashed by the explosion. This didn't look very good because the masses were too big and the efficiencies were too low.

And then a really remarkable thing happened. Edward brought up the super—a detonation wave in liquid deuterium heated by an atomic bomb. Everybody turned eagerly to discuss the super forgetting all about the atomic bomb as if that was an accomplished fact already! Old hat. Here was something new and interesting. At first, Edward claimed it was a cinch until somebody brought up cooling by radiation. Edward then said "Well, equilibrium wouldn't be established because radiation processes are too slow." The next morning, Hans [Bethe] came in with a nice fast radiation process—namely the Inverse Compton effect. It looked as if the super were quite dead. Konopinski suggested adding some tritium. The super still had a little bit of life left. You can see we were having a nice, lively, and exciting time. Everybody was really enjoying themselves.

While all of this was going on, Tolman, who was a relativist, not a nuclear physicist, came to me wanting to talk about implosion—assembly of pieces by high explosives. We discussed this quite a bit and wrote a memorandum on the subject of implosion. By the way, this particular memorandum is not available now. When we all left for Los Alamos, the files of the Summer Conference were moved to the Radiation Laboratory and nobody knows what became of them.

The conference ran full blast for about a week and then piddled out over the summer. Some of us continued in a fashion into the fall. Oppy and I traveled to Chicago two or three times to talk to Edward [Teller], Konopinski, and Hans about various parts of the project—such as equations of state and opacities. It happened that Oppy and I were there when General Groves first met the Met Lab scientists. I remember, just before the meeting Compton rushing around looking for Szilard, wanting to make sure he didn't get anywhere near Groves. We were all sitting around a big table when Groves came in. Everybody around the table was introduced and Groves began to give a rather tough speech along the lines that we worked for him now and had better toe the line. Just then he was called from the room for a telephone call, and he never came back. A couple of days later back at Berkeley, Oppy and I were in Oppy's office when Groves came in followed by Colonel Nichols. Groves unbuttoned his uniform jacket, took it off and handed it to the Colonel, saying, "Find a dry cleaner and get it pressed." The colonel took the jacket and walked out of the room. We had been thinking about enlisting in the Army. So you can see what kind of lesson that was!

After that, during the fall and winter, I worked mostly on efficiencies. I did the theory of exponential shock waves, shock waves with pressure increasing exponentially with time, which was needed for the hydrodynamics of a tamped sphere. This involved some numerical calculations which were undertaken by Frankel and Nelson. They were greatly surprised that they needed much more accuracy than they originally thought. This got them interested in computing. Later, in Los Alamos, they played an important role in the transition from the desk calculators we were using—Monroes and Marchants—to the IBM punch card machines, which were state-of-the-art in those days.

We also did a lot of work on two- or three-group-velocity critical mass calculations. During this time, Oppy was busy setting up the Los Alamos Laboratory with the help of Ed McMillan. We went out to Los Alamos in early March 1943, ten months after I first arrived in Berkeley. The results of the Berkeley year were summarized in the Los Alamos Primer [LA–1, the first Los Alamos report, written by Serber].

POSTSCRIPT

We talked about blast damage [during the summer conference in Berkeley], which we scaled up from known data. This work proved to be quite accurate. We talked about neutrons, which didn't seem all that important since we didn't think the effects would extend past the blast damage. We talked about radioactive fission products, but couldn't say much because it depended on the circumstances of how you set off the bomb. We missed two things at Berkeley: the fireball and consequent flashburns, but that was studied at Los Alamos during the first Summer in 1943. The only surprise at Hiroshima and Nagasaki was the x-rays from the fission fragments in the fireball. That I don't think anybody thought of.

It's rather amazing how accurate the predictions in the Primer were. A lot of it was just luck, I think, because the cross section numbers and the neutrons per fission were both inaccurate. One changed up and the other changed down and it didn't make any difference.

*Robert Serber came to Los Alamos in March 1943 from the University of California at Berkeley, where he had been involved with theoretical bomb design studies with Oppenheimer, Bethe, Teller, and others. He returned to the University of California, Berkeley, after the war from 1945-51, and then was at Columbia University from 1951–77. He is now Emeritus Professor of Physics at Columbia.

THE DEVELOPMENT OF NUCLEAR EXPLOSIVES AND FRONTIER DAYS AT LOS ALAMOS
L.D.P. King[1]

I. Introduction

The title of this talk is "The Development of Nuclear Explosives and Frontier Days at Los Alamos." I understand this is the first of a series of events this group plans, so I thought I would try and trace for you the various steps that were involved in the creation of an atomic bomb and then show you how Los Alamos fits into the picture. Then I will tell you of a few personal recollections and reminiscences I have of the early townsite and laboratory. Following that, I will be glad to try and answer any questions you may have. I have incorporated the word "frontier days" since I think these are very appropriate for they not only indicate how we lived in the early days but we were also working on a new frontier of physics.

It is a pleasure to be able to talk to the Los Alamos Historical Society here in Fuller Lodge. This building was not only intimately connected with the Los Alamos Ranch School, but played an important part for Project Y, as Los Alamos was called during the war. I can remember many pleasant meals, parties and meetings in this fine building which is constructed of logs cut on the old school property. Some of the skits were extremely good and made fun of, usually, living conditions, the army, etc. There was the old timers square dance group which met here; the first ski club meeting was held in front of that fireplace there. I recall the pleasant appearance of this room with its rustic tables and chairs, the stuffed owl and deer and antelope heads; the numerous beautiful Indian rugs hanging from the walls. I hope some of this early atmosphere can be returned if this building could be used as some sort of museum. I understand some of these things are still in the possession of the AEC. But I mustn't forget the marvelous party put on here by the British Mission before they left. The wives did the cooking and waiting on table, and we all drank a toast to the Queen.

So this original building area retains for some of us the old Los Alamos charm. The original beautiful view east to the mountains from the portal is gone. Originally, there were long fields in the middle with a row of poplar trees. The big house was on the left about where Hall's Shoe Store is, and the Ranch School Store only a short distance on the right, much closer than the post office. We had victory vegetable gardens one year about where the Firestone store is. Then followed the housing shortage and some of the area became covered with some of the worst Los Alamos slums—the army hutments. And then came the Community Center.

---

*Talk presented to the Los Alamos Historical Society at Fuller Lodge January 18, 1968.

II. Stepping Stones to Los Alamos

Let us now look at how Los Alamos, or rather Project Y, got started. To appreciate the sense of excitement, urgency and great importance of this original community one has to have a fairly complete background on what led to Los Alamos. Many of the people who formed the scientific nucleus of this project were actually involved elsewhere in the program for one or even two years prior to coming here.

The discovery of the fission process by Hahn and Strassman in Germany in 1938 is probably the first link of a chain of events in which this Laboratory forged the final brilliant link. The correct theoretical interpretation of this physical phenomenon of fission was quickly forthcoming when Hahn wrote his former colleague, Lise Meitner, at Copenhagen, of their results. She and her nephew, Otto Frisch, interpreted the apparent disappearance of mass, i.e., that the sum of the fragments did not add up to the uranium mass but there was a conversion mass to energy according to Einstein's theory of 1905, $E = mc^2$. The energy released was of the order of 200 million electron volts/fission. This meant that the complete fissioning of one pound of uranium was equivalent to the burning of 1,400 tons of coal, or an energy gain of 2,800,000 for the same material weight. One gram of uranium explosive force equals 17 tons of TNT.

Such a discovery in physics, of course, immediately stimulated work to confirm these results in many laboratories all over the world. If it hadn't been for the ominous political situation in Europe, this would have resulted—at a somewhat slower pace, no doubt—in the numerous exciting peaceful applications of atomic energy we have today. Military applications would have been slow in following in times of peace. Hitler changed this, however. A few wise men in England and the United States immediately worried about the military potential if the tremendous energy release of fission could be harnessed into explosive power. The outbreak of the war and the stopping of all uranium exportation from Germany greatly enhanced the sense of urgency to find out more about the fission process and keep ahead of the enemy.

It was this sense of urgency, moving slowly at first, but building up pressure with each new experimental measurement, which led these few wise men to do some fantastic gambling. They gambled on the success of an all-out effort to make a military explosive out of the energy released in the fission process with little actual evidence that it could be done. Huge sums of money and many valuable people were involved. Los Alamos played a major role in this fantastic gamble.

Experiments under Fermi at Columbia in early 1939 first indicated a chain reaction might indeed be possible since more than one neutron was emitted in each fission. This led to an unheard of step in the United States. Fermi, Szilard, Wigner and Einstein composed a letter to President Roosevelt advising him of the power of a potential nuclear explosive and advised that some money be made available to step up the experimental program as well as to make sure the United States could procure an adequate supply of uranium, if necessary. The Columbia group at this point imposed a secrecy requirement on themselves and published no further data on fission.

Roosevelt appointed an advisory committee November 1, 1939, and, for the first time, government money, indeed in small amounts at first, became available under the administration of the Office of Scientific Research and Development, known as the OSRD, to support certain work like that at Columbia for obtaining more information on the fission process. In another one of these projects at the University of California, a new element, plutonium, was discovered in March 1940 under Ernest Lawrence. The urgency of the situation was greatly increased when it was discovered that this new element would also undergo fission. This discovery was followed at Columbia in July 1941 by a number of experiments which indicated that a chain reaction could very probably be produced in a uranium-graphite system.

These two discoveries led to the establishment of a loose central organization in late 1941 under Arthur Compton, and the establishment of the Metallurgical Laboratory at Chicago, under the OSRD to coordinate further work on the production methods for fissionable material and to take charge of the construction of a chain reacting system. Fermi's group at Columbia moved to Chicago and formed the nucleus of a nuclear physics group. This group was to develop the first chain reaction. A chemistry group was formed under Professor Spedding of Iowa State to determine the properties of plutonium, even though only micrograms were available, and to develop methods of producing pure uranium. A theoretical physics group under Professor Wigner of Princeton was to worry about the production of plutonium in large nuclear reactors, assuming, of course, Fermi would succeed in making a chain reaction operate in a pile. Several additional OSRD subcontracts under the Met Lab were started at various universities on special projects.

Up to this time, actual work directed towards a weapon design had been almost completely neglected. In June 1942 Oppenheimer was appointed by the Met Lab to coordinate this work which, after all, was the ultimate aim of all the entire project.

After erecting 300 piles (graphite structures to determine the critical mass of uranium), the Fermi team accumulated sufficient experimental data by July 1942 to work on the design and construction of a pile of purified graphite and uranium metal. The uranium for this experiment was being produced, by now, at Iowa State University, Westinghouse, and the Metal Hydrides Company.

Almost all the effort so far had gone into making this first chain reacting pile and learning how to make pure fissionable material and none towards obtaining an explosive release of the energy from fission. It became evident that if large amounts of fissionable material were to be actually produced for some sort of weapon, better coordination and more engineering capability would be required. Dr. Vannevar Bush, who headed the OSRD, recommended to President Roosevelt therefore that a special Army engineering organization be established. This was done in September 1942, when General Leslie Groves was appointed to head the Manhattan District of Engineers which was to incorporate all organizations working on an atomic bomb.

On December 2, 1942, Fermi's team passed the important milestone of demonstrating the first real chain reaction in the old West Stands Building of the University of Chicago. The 25th anniversary of this world-shaking event occurred last December ... .

By the spring of 1943, the various groups of the former OSRD projects had developed three methods for producing fissionable material suitable for a weapon. At Berkeley, the California group had demonstrated the electromagnetic method for producing the rare ^{235}U isotope needed for the bomb rather than the more common ^{238}U isotope. At Columbia, Professor Urey's group had developed a diffusion method for accomplishing the same thing. Fermi's first chain reacting pile demonstrated that if very large scale reactors were made, the element plutonium could be manufactured atom by atom by the excess neutrons existing in the piles.

The gambling really had to get under way on a grand scale now if ever enough fissionable material was to be made available to build fission weapons. Hundreds of millions of dollars were committed by the Manhattan District for the great Hanford Engineering Works for advance planning and construction of the large reactors to produce plutonium. This was done even before Fermi proved that the chain reaction was possible. Similarly, huge amounts of money were committed to Oak Ridge, which was known as Project X, to construct giant uranium separation complexes. Both the electromagnetic and diffusion plants were constructed. The latter turned out to be more efficient so that the electromagnetic work was discontinued later.

Initial work by Oppenheimer on the design and planning for a weapon, following his appointment under the Met Lab in June 1942 as already mentioned, uncovered many difficulties and really brought this almost neglected angle into perspective. The huge amount of money and effort going into the production of fissionable material brought an enormous pressure to bear on this group which had to come up with something that could make use of this costly material in time to influence the outcome of the war. It became evident to Oppenheimer that a special project for weapon design and development was a necessity. This led to the creation of a new Project Y in Los Alamos in November 1942, only two months after the creation of the Manhattan District of Engineers. Project Y, or Los Alamos, was created to forge the final and most important link in an incredibly complicated and costly chain of events which led to the development of the first atomic bomb. Initially, it was thought that some 100 top scientists would be able to come up with the basic design in a small project based on early OSRD-type contracts with universities. Later, for the actual construction and testing, the army would move in and the scientists continuing would receive commissions. Fortunately, this latter arrangement never became necessary. The Laboratory, however, grew in leaps and bounds to keep ahead of their complex task.

III. Project Y, or Los Alamos

The Los Alamos site was chosen over several other possibilities because of Oppenheimer's familiarity with the Los Alamos School site. Due to its isolated location, security measures promised to be easier to enforce in order to assure the extreme secrecy thought necessary for this project.

This site, together with the surrounding area, was established as a military reservation. The community was fenced and guarded like an army post. The Laboratory was built within an inner fenced region. Both military and technical direction were, in principle, under General Groves as director of the Manhattan District.

The commanding officer, who reported directly to Groves, was responsible for the conduct of the military personnel, the maintenance of adequate living conditions, and the prevention of trespass and special guarding. Oppenheimer, as scientific director, was also responsible to Groves, who had as his scientific advisor Harvard president J. B. Conant. Oppenheimer was also made responsible for the policy and administration of the Laboratory security. This was done so that there would be a guarantee of no military control over the exchange of information among the scientific staff members. Oppenheimer was given the assistance of a military intelligence officer to help in security problems.

Let us go over the steps again of the history for the design of a nuclear weapon. Prior to the creation of the special Project Y, work directly concerned with the design and development of an atomic bomb was scattered through the Met Lab and its OSRD subcontractors at several universities. When Oppenheimer was picked to begin coordination efforts he set up a series of conferences at Berkeley and Chicago. These meetings brought out the difficulties, as well as the magnitude, of the job. This led to the creation of Project Y.

Oppenheimer's first step following the creation of Project Y was to hold a series of conferences at Los Alamos on April 15-24, 1943. These meetings were to brief the initial staff on the present state of knowledge and chart a course for theoretical and experimental work at Los Alamos. A series of indoctrination lectures by Robert Serber prior to these conferences is the first Los Alamos document, LA-1.

Where did Oppenheimer get his staff for a new project when most scientists were already busy on various other war efforts? As already mentioned, a number of OSRD projects were already under way at various universities in some way related to Manhattan District work. As many as possible of these projects were used as sources of equipment and men. Scientists came from projects at Washington, University of Wisconsin, Purdue University, Stanford, Cornell, Princeton, University of Minnesota, and the Met Lab. Research equipment was brought by many of these groups. Two Van de Graaffs [accelerators] came from Wisconsin, a cyclotron from Harvard, and a Cockcroft-Walton accelerator from the University of Illinois. Chemical and cryogenic equipment was brought from Berkeley. In addition, all groups brought specialized electronic and other small pieces of equipment. This technique made it possible to create a new, well-equipped, going research lab in an amazingly short time.

The initial plan for buildings at the lab was drafted by Oppenheimer, Manley and McMillan. An office building, T, contained administration, the theoretical physics group, the library and classified documents, conference rooms, a photo lab, and drafting room. Building U was a general laboratory building, V a shop building, and buildings X, Y and Z were specialized laboratory buildings to house the Van de Graaffs, cyclotron, cryogenics lab, and the Cockcroft-Walton accelerator.

Oppenheimer and a few staff members first arrived on March 15, 1943. Buildings were not ready so the first project office was set up in Santa Fe. Early staff members were put up in surrounding guest ranches rather than hotels for security reasons.

The late John Williams lived at the site at this time as acting site technical director. Conditions were difficult and primitive during these early days. Only one forest service telephone connected the site to Santa Fe until mid-April. Problems arose frequently between the technical personnel and the army due to different feelings of urgency, speed, and their widely divergent backgrounds.

The group at Purdue University was engaged in June 1942 to make some cross-section measurements related to early concepts of a hydrogen-type bomb. In order to finish their job, this group did not arrive in Los Alamos until October of 1943. I was a member of this group.

The initial plan for a small group of 100 scientists did not last long. The more measurements were made, the more new problems were uncovered. The entire group was working on a brand new area of technology. Almost nothing was known about the problems of most importance to the design of an atomic bomb. Yet at this very time those costly neutrons at Hanford were making plutonium, and the magnetrons and diffusion plant at Oak Ridge began to produce enriched uranium.

A tremendous pressure was placed on Los Alamos. It had to come through with scientific developments which would enable the intelligent use of materials being produced by several very fantastic and costly gambles. It had to come through quickly with the correct answers if the outcome of the war was to be influenced.

The job of trying to assemble as-yet-unavailable fissionable material in such a manner as to release at least a portion of the nuclear fission energy was indeed a formidable task. One first had to make countless measurements to determine the unknown nuclear properties of almost all the elements in the periodic tables plus a new one, plutonium. Then one had to decide on how best to assemble material to optimize the energy release. The amount of purified ^{235}U and ^{239}Pu required to make a self-sustaining chain reaction could only be estimated since sufficient material was not available until 1944 for ^{235}U and not until April 1945 for ^{239}Pu.

Two basic assembly approaches were initially considered—a gun assembly in which two subcritical masses were fired at or into each other at sufficient speed so that many fissions would occur before the material had a chance to disassemble; or the so-called implosion method might be used whereby fissionable material would be blown together by some technique from an initially subcritical spherical geometry. The gun technique looked easier, so was initially chosen and followed through to completion. The high spontaneous fission rate of the reactor-produced plutonium could not be determined until material in some quantity was available; and then it turned out to be unsuitable at this late date for the gun method. This necessitated a crash program to come up with some means for using plutonium, now in full production. By a tremendous effort, the implosion technique was developed and successfully tested at Trinity on July 16, 1945. This was indeed a scientific triumph over many obstacles. I was fortunate to be on hand at the nearest point of observation at 10,000 yards. I was lying next to Fermi and had another opportunity to witness his genius in obtaining physics data with the simplest of equipment. He stood up after the initial flash and before the sound reached us, and started dropping some small pieces of paper he had torn up, and then came up with an excellent answer on the energy yield of the test. When the shock wave hit the falling pieces of paper, he was able to determine the yield (about 20,000 tons of TNT equivalent) from the amount the still-falling paper was displaced by the shock wave.

IV. Reminiscences of Early Los Alamos

Let me now tell you about a few reminiscences of the early townsite that come to my mind.

1. First, there is, of course, the excitement of going to a secret new place. We were told confidentially before coming that the site was about 35 miles from Santa Fe near a former school. We had two clues to work on based on this bit of information—first, the New Mexico PWA book, which we procured in Indiana, listed only one school about 35 miles from Santa Fe—the Los Alamos Ranch School, and second, one of the Physics professors at Purdue was brought up in Frijoles Canyon and he was quite sure we must be going there. The PWA book gives some very nice descriptions of this area including one of the old road up to the school. Some of you who haven't read this book might be interested in getting it out of the library.

2. I remember, after staying overnight at Eagle Nest on our way here and coming in through Ranchos de Taos, my first look at an architecture which was quite new to me: the flat-roofed adobe houses. And then we wondered, driving down from Taos to Santa Fe to check in, where in those mountains or valleys we were going to end up. We had to retrace our steps to Pojoaque after getting instruction from Mrs. McKibben at the Project office at 109 E. Palace Avenue.

3. The first ride to the hill was memorable. Wandering through the several little Spanish villages past San Ildefonso Pueblo and then climbing an incredible series of switchbacks to get to the top of Los Alamos Mesa, all on a rough gravel road, is not easily forgotten. You can still see the last switchback of this early road when you make the last turn coming up the hill. The guard gate used to be at the narrowest region of the mesa just before the last rise to the hill.

4. We had received a floor plan of the house we were going to have before starting out from our Indiana home. It gave room and window sizes, etc., so one could plan on curtains and rugs, etc. It was a brand new Sundt quadruple unit. We had none of our furniture for about three weeks, but we were helped out by friends and neighbors to supplement the sparse GI furniture consist-

ing of beds and dressers. One of our tables was a box, I remember. There were no bathtubs for economy reasons. The old school buildings near the Lodge were therefore known as Bathtub Row, since they were the only houses with tubs. The kitchen had a double sink, one side deep enough to give the kids a bath. We had what was known as a Black Beauty stove which looked like a wood stove but burned kerosene. Everybody that could get an electric oven and hot plate did, so that before long the electric power was inadequate for the Laboratory and home use. No cooking could start until after 5:00 p.m. The house was heated by a central furnace which was stoked by janitors that made the rounds several times a day. These furnaces were stoked with New Mexico soft coal, and the bin was right by the back door so the air wasn't always as clean as it is today. Our janitors had no experience stoking soft coal and just piled it on so it would last as many hours as possible. Quite frequently there were loud booms as the coal gas ignited anywhere from five minutes to half an hour after the stoking was done. Occasionally the blast was serious enough to break something or blow soot into the house through the air vents. One day when the grounds started thawing, my neighbor's car next to our bedroom window settled with all four wheels up to the hubcaps. We had mail censorship and all guns were collected for safekeeping including my .22 rifle. There were no phone books and no street addresses except a GI number. Our house number was T-131.

5. There were a few advantages to living on an army post, however. We were given enough gas ration stamps to go to Santa Fe once a week to shop—by doubling up, we always had enough gas to go on trips into the mountains and surrounding areas. GI cars were even made available to the staff for a while for recreation on weekends. There was better meat at the commissary than was available at most meat markets during the war. We got lots of cheap, edible food at the army messes when we wanted to eat out. To be sure, the atmosphere and noise were not like at a fancy restaurant. We even had free bus service to Santa Fe and Indian maid service delivered to the hill by the army.

6. Everyone wasn't as lucky as we were in finding our way up here. I remember the excitement when Bill Ogle's wife disappeared. She had checked in at 109 Palace Avenue and then gotten a ride with a new machinist who was also checking in and then coming on the hill. Bill was already there. It was the winter of 1943 and the machinist didn't follow instructions closely enough and had taken the Puye road and, of course, got stuck in the snow. We had people driving all over looking for them for hours.

7. As a special treat some of us had wonderful meals at Edith Warner's Tea House about once a month. Part of her house still stands just this side of the river on the left. The part where we ate has been torn down long ago. The wonderful old San Ildefonso Indian, Tilano, used to wait on tables.

8. Trips in the mountains in those days were quite hazardous. All the roads were rather bumpy gravel and dusty, with no guard rails, and very frequently dead trees would fall across the road which you either had to remove or drive around. There was no Highway Department maintenance. We soon learned to travel with a saw, axe and shovel.

9. Once, just to see if we could fool the guard system, we drove out the main gate and drove up an old road up the walls of Bayo Canyon and got up on the hill without showing a pass. It was fun once but we well might have gotten stuck on the narrow canyon shelf road made for wagons.

10. We eventually had two movie theaters. Number one was down in the army barracks area which was near the ZIA buildings and opposite the big empty parking area. Number two was put up later and sat about where the photo shop is now. This building was also used for the staff meetings when we outgrew the original room in the tech area proper. Number one is now the large building of the Baptist Church and theater number two is the gym you can see from the highway when you drive by Ojo Caliente.

11. New batches of prefab houses of all types and description kept appearing in order to keep up with the lab growth. First were the Sundts, then the Fort Leonard Woods, Hanford, Wingfoots, and of course, those terrible army hutments. The population growth, especially in children, was such that the schools became a real problem. General Groves supposedly was ahead of the times. He had an early look at the consequences of a population explosion and tried to influence the administration in promulgating birth control information.

12. Many of us became ardent outdoorsmen and took up hiking and skiing at every opportunity. One of the most ardent enthusiasts was Enrico Fermi who always went on weekend expeditions as the best form of relaxation from the pressures of the Laboratory. I was along on most of these.

13. Then there was the big scandal of the freezing of the brand new pipe line from Guaje Canyon which was to solve the water shortage. The winter was cold and someone turned the wrong valve. It didn't take long for water to freeze when not moving fairly rapidly. I don't think it ever was completely thawed out again until spring. Tank trucks brought up water, from holes made near the Rio Grande River, to the angry housewives. Our family was fortunately below those on Bathtub Row, so we were low enough to always have water.

14. One can't forget how well poor Dr. Oppenheimer tried to take care of not only the lab problems, but he also had to soothe some of the irate scientists' wives for all sorts of domestic problems and failings in the townsite.

V. Reminiscences of the Laboratory

1. My first contact with J. R. Oppenheimer, later always affectionately known as Oppie by all the staff, was at Purdue in 1942 when he picked our cyclotron to do a supersecret job related to the hydrogen bomb which the head of the department was never even cleared for.

2. There was a pleasant, informal university atmosphere during the early days at the site in spite of the great political pressure. Oppie's insistence on the complete exchange of all information between all staff members paid off. This was in complete contrast to normal army security procedures where great compartmentalization is the approved method.

3. I was initially surprised to hear so much German spoken in the tech area until it was banned so everyone could understand what was spoken. We had, of course, numerous prominent scientists of German, Swiss, and Austrian extraction.

4. I will never forget how comical the Swiss pair of scientists, Hans Staub and Egon Bretscher, were when together. Staub was always swearing loudly about army incompetence.

5. The never forgettable early loudspeaker system initially installed in the tech area to help find technical staff members when needed was always a source of amusement and, finally, irritation. The most important "scientist" turned out to be J. J. Gutierrez if one went by his frequent paging. He turned out to be the head janitor. The speaker system was soon discontinued.

6. I worked at Omega site from its initial ground breaking in 1943 for a period of about 10 years. In the early days this was a very important site. There were two towers with manned machine guns there for a while. We had all of the first batches of enriched uranium to come out of Oak Ridge in order to find out how much it took to go critical. There were five of us who formed the nucleus of that group and during the period when this uranium was first received at least one of us had to be in the building 24 hours a day to guard it. The drive down there was rough in the winter since the running stream crossed the road a half dozen times and there were no bridges; as a result, high banks of ice built up on either side. I remember how one of our prominent theoretical physicists started edging to the door to be ready to run when Fermi took the first enriched chain reaction critical and let the sensitive counter system buzz loud and fast as the assembly went up to a few watts of power. I remember how, after tying a piece of tubing up one of the pine trees to carry the radioactive gases out of the reactor, we discovered an inversion layer was trapping the gas in the canyon. There was literally a cloud of gas sitting over the building. Fermi and I drove up and down the canyon to find out how far

the gas was spreading. Then there was the now-incredible problem we had of getting a thin one-foot-diameter stainless steel sphere welded up to contain the uranyl sulfate solution of the reactor. With the highest national priority, two spun halves were sent out to be welded. They finally came back useless since portions were silver-soldered. The welding of this material, like almost everything else we needed, had to be developed here. The security restrictions were very successful, yet our first badge consisted of only a white plastic button with a number on it which I succeeded in losing while skiing. The lab was given a very high priority for almost anything it needed. Things were routed and rerouted, addressed and readdressed, in a fantastic manner to assure secrecy. The final address was always "Box 1663, Santa Fe, New Mexico." Our local procurement office was quite good in obtaining almost anything. When Bob Wilson, now heading the new Midwest accelerator program, found out one had to wait long times frequently for a hair cut, he ordered a barber chair and got it through procurement so one could now have tech area haircuts.

VI. Conclusions

I would like to say that to have been able to work at this Laboratory during those early, vital and important years was indeed a memorable experience. The excitement of a small frontier community plus the excitement of working on a new frontier of science and technology cannot often be combined. Where else could one have had so many technical developments in so short a time; where else could one culminate the efforts and singleness of purpose of so many famous men but here in those momentous years of 1943, '44, and '45. This place deserves a place in history and you people of this Historical Society should be able to help.

---

[1] L.D.P. King came to Los Alamos in October 1943 from Purdue University where he already had begun experimental studies on fusion reaction cross sections of deuterium and tritium at the request of Oppenheimer. He remained at the Laboratory in various scientific and administrative capacities until his retirement in 1973. He has been a member of the J. Robert Oppenheimer Memorial Committee since 1969.

RANDOM REMINISCENCES
Nicholas Metropolis*

I am honored beyond all bounds for the opportunity to address you this evening. I am also grateful to the Oppenheimer Memorial Committee for that privilege. There is, however, a moral that derives from it: namely, don't ever miss a meeting when that Committee is selecting its annual speaker.

Before launching into the talk proper, I should perhaps mention that next year is the 50th anniversary of the founding of the Laboratory. To help recognize that numerical occasion, the committee-in-charge at the Laboratory plans to invite Edward Teller as a principal speaker. He was a member of the original staff in 1943. A consistent remark for the raison d'etre of that action is the following:

Both protagonists, namely Robert Oppenheimer and Edward Teller, were seriously hurt by an event of 1954 and what followed it. Great as was their suffering in that period, and the suffering was great, it was science itself that was the biggest loser. In 1962, Oppie was awarded the prestigious Fermi Prize and it was to be presented by the President of the United States, John F. Kennedy. But fate intervened and it was Lyndon Johnson who actually was present on that occasion. Edward, a prior recipient, was in the audience and was the first to congratulate Oppie. The evening news recorded the event.... What better gesture could the committee-in-charge make to demonstrate that science had suffered enough!

The talk this evening will attempt a short history of computing inspired by the vertiginous set of events of wartime Los Alamos. To begin at the beginning: Not since classical times has there been such a collection of talent gathered in one place. The concentration of scientists on a first name basis was impressive indeed. By scientists I mean more specifically physicists, chemists and engineers. Among the native-born Americans, there were both Oppenheimers, Robert and Frank, Feynman, Neddermeyer, Konopinski, Serber and Wilson as examples; then there was the European exodus—Bethe, Bohr, Fermi, Teller, Kistiakowsky, von Neumann and Rabi (these last two were consultants, seemingly ubiquitous). Early on, there was the British Mission made up of magical names, primarily Penney and G.I. Taylor. The younger scientists were delighted to be in the daily company of all of the above.

It was quite clear that the theoretical physicists were dealing with unheard of pressures, densities and temperatures of materials, all high! The subject was fluid dynamics and the associated equations were nonlinear, because of the equations of state; these equations of state relate pressure, volume, temperature for each particular volume element being considered. Traditionally, theoretical physicists learned to stay away from nonlinearities, focussing on linear forms, which were difficult enough. Nonlinearities always had one recourse—specific examples could always be solved numerically; that is to say, one could always compute a particular example. Such solved examples were important albeit highly specific, for our understanding of the questions facing us and perforce taken seriously. After all, this was war!

So scientists learned to deal with nonlinearities. Rather than trying to explain the difference between linearities and nonlinearities, perhaps a striking analogy can be made, something more familiar: those of you old enough at the time may remember the difference between before and after Marlon Brando made his debut on the stage and screen in vehicles such as Streetcar and Viva Zapata! Drama was qualitatively changed—so was science, even a bit earlier.

So, many a theorist at Los Alamos would be seen clanking away on his electromechanical desk computer, the popular kinds were Marchants, Fridens and Monroes. Whenever they got jammed, and this happened frequently, they were quickly boxed and sent off to San Diego, California, to be repaired. When the situation became desperate, the shipping time seemed exorbitant—a not unfamiliar phenomenon today.

Feynman, in his characteristic fashion, took matters into his own hands. He started the study of computer reliability by converting his office, complete with a shingle hanging on the outside to announce that heretofore desk calculators would be repaired on the spot—no charge. His *modus operandi* was to uncover a good one and compare detailed operating procedures with the sick one. This was how he learned to cure them; I know because I became his assistant. Then one day Hans Bethe, the division leader, happened by and wondered whether it was appropriate for Feynman to be taking time off to repair computers. Feynman's immediate reaction was to close down the shop. It was not long after that when Bethe conceded defeat (the number of effective electromechanical computers had dwindled) and urged Feynman to reopen his repair business. Later, much later, the Challenger Committee of Space was formed; on television we see Feynman again making direct and simple, but very important observations.

The British Mission, mentioned earlier, was most welcome for it brought Britain's best in our midst. That group had as its leader James Chadwick, the discoverer of the neutron slightly more than a decade earlier; his experiments earned him a Nobel Prize. Then there was G.I. Taylor, perhaps England's best known scientist, also a member; he was rushed back to

England when the Nazis started dropping their V-bombs in the Battle of Britain; there was William Penney, a great scientist. He headed the postwar atomic bomb project in England and successfully tested the A-bomb in Australia for which he was knighted. Later he headed the team to develop the fusion bomb, tested successfully also in Australia, for which he was made a lord.

Also a part of the British Mission were Rudolph Peierls, later knighted, ending up at Oxford University, and Otto Frisch, who in collaboration with Lise Meitner, his auntie, explained fission. He and Peierls worked on the critical mass for ^{235}U and pointed out the importance of the fast fission. Then there was Klaus Fuchs, brilliant, hardworking, turned idealist; after the war he was head of the theoretical group at England's Harwell Laboratory and served on the Declassification Committee, U.S.-England postwar. Also, James L. Tuck, who returned to Los Alamos after the war and led the Sherwood Project, so named by Lewis Strauss, Chairman of the A.E.C. for obvious reasons. There were at least a dozen other distinguished scientists from the British Mission.

Most distinguished of the visitors was Professor Niels Bohr, who was traveling with his son Aage, also a physicist and later, like his father, a Nobel laureate and head of the world famous Danish Institute of Physics in Copenhagen that his father founded.

To return from the digression, it was Dana Mitchell who first proposed that business machines be rented for the routine calculations of fluid dynamics so necessary for weapons design, our central mission, especially since it was not realistic to use fissionable material as part of an experimental program. Mitchell had observed these business machines back at Columbia University on some relatively simple problems in astronomy. Once again, Feynman was on the scene when the crates arrived that contained the various units; this time Stanley Frankel and Eldred Nelson were to join him. All this without the usual engineer who was to show up several days later to find that the team had temporarily managed without him! Later that week, Feynman had organized a group of five women calculators, mostly wives of scientists, to "race" against the machines. The competition was keen.

The idea was obvious—to provide a computer program and to check that the business system wasn't making numerical errors. At first, the women took the lead, but as the day wore on, the system caught up, especially since the machines were on a 3-shift basis, around the clock. But Feynman had established the basis of reliability testing. The machines went on to do yeoman service from their inception, even though the so-called "shock fitting" had, because of its complexity, to be done by human computers for each time-step, based on the previous time-interval of automated data.

BEHIND TALL FENCES

One repeats the obvious to say that Feynman was a genius, but he was also respected as a human being. Whenever he made a point, especially in science, it was always expressed in simple terms and it always covered the principal aspects and principles.

I learned much from all the learned people around: most I learned from him and it was always a lot of fun—more physics and mathematics; computers and nonlinearities.

An aside on the lighter side that I am reminded of was the incident of the ducks. One fine day, early on, in wartime Los Alamos, ducks appeared out of nowhere. They were a joy to everyone, parents and children in particular. So successful, in fact, that soon one wanted to acknowledge the originator of the idea of the ducks. Especially because of Ashley Pond Pond (to give it its proper name). Matters became very serious when members of the firehouse, by the northeast edge of the pond, made no claims of being the responsible ones, just part of the interested audience and duck feeders. The quest of ownership continued (and nontrivially)—perhaps the ducks had microtransmitters under their wings!

On one occasion I was late for lunch at Fuller Lodge and sat with a bunch of silent strangers. To cause a thaw, I raised the question of the origin of the ducks. To my amazement a second lieutenant claimed responsibility. When I regained consciousness, I asked the obvious question. This was his story: His previous assignment involved the construction of a rest-and-recreation project in Texas for the shell-shocked military. Naturally it was a deluxe affair complete with a stunning rivulet and stocked with fowl; swans, geese and ducks graced the scene. To the satisfaction of the designers, the inhabitants spent long periods of time completely fascinated, on the shore of the artificial rivulet. In due course, the second lieutenant was reassigned to the Santa Fe area. For the first time ever, none of his fellow officers was aware of any military activity in the Santa Fe area. He inferred that the Army was planning a truly rest-and-recreation center for the seriously shell-shocked and was keeping it classified. Recalling that the inhabitants stationed in Texas found the fowl a great source of interest and relaxation, he straightaway ordered some six ducks to be shipped to him in Santa Fe. This was the source of the ducks that made their appearance early one spring day in 1943. I hurriedly excused myself in order to report to my friends—Feynman, Ashkin, and Ehrlich—the event of the lunch table. Anyone familiar with the topography between Fuller Lodge and the wartime Laboratory knew that Ashley Pond Pond had to be circled. There was Feynman hard by the shore. "Come here," he cried, "and watch these ducks. They're absolutely fascinating!" "Now hear this," I replied, and proceeded to tell him what I heard at lunch.... Much relief at knowing that the ducks were not a part of an espionage scheme!

Among the youngsters (a fresh Ph.D. from Columbia) was aforementioned Julius Ashkin. I won't say "bright" because all of the staff was at least bright who came to Los Alamos early in its memorable history. Early on, he grew a most beautiful beard. As the New Year began in 1944, he decided to visit his parents in Brooklyn. Not by airplane, but four days on the crowded train, one way. When his mother saw him, she shook her finger at the sight of the Talmudic beard, really among the loveliest of beards. He had to shave it off. So he returned, after another four days on the train, to the southwest. At the time, a military bus ran from Santa Fe to Los Alamos, and conversely. When the bus arrived at the guard station in Los Alamos for pass inspection, he, since the photograph on his badge differed from the clean-shaven Ashkin, was taken to the guard house and told that if he belonged within the gates, then he must know people within the gates. This was Sunday night and it was around 11:00 when the phone rang in the dormitory and someone knocked on my door after a slight delay. "Could you go to the guard station and identify Ashkin." I could awaken Feynman to join me in that trek of a least a couple of miles at best in two feet of snow! So I knocked on Feynman's door. "Let him sleep in the cooler and we'll go down in the morning to fetch him!" I successfully pleaded with Feynman and off we went. Then Feynman opened the guard house door after a trek through deep snow and exclaimed, "Where's this guy who claims he's Ashkin?," cocking his ear with a free hand, as he approached the forlorn Ashkin, who tried to reassure Feynman. "No, that's not Ashkin. Let's go, Nick, we're wasting our time!" Ashkin cried out, "Don't fool around, I'm dead tired, honestly." "Hey, that is Ashkin," replied Feynman, cocking an ear a second time in the direction of the desperate voice. Obviously, the guard was confused by these shenanigans. But they were straightened out eventually. Needless to say, we weren't offered a jeep ride back to the dormitory—it was annoying since there was plenty of luggage!

I should like to interrupt whatever thread is left of my story to tell a story of Enrico Fermi. Segre, his first student back in Roman times, was an excellent fisherman. He would work hard, if only he could persuade Fermi to accompany him on one of his expeditions. "It's nontrivial knowing which flies to use as bait, knowing the habits of the various fish, when and where to go, what the weather should be, and so on" Segre would argue. "I'm beginning to understand," Fermi would slowly reply, "it's a case of matching wits with the fish."

A somewhat later story involving Fermi was in the summer of the postwar period when von Neumann was also here. When Fermi returned to Chicago, he called Herb Anderson into his office to relate his experience with von Neumann. Finally Fermi said, "You know how much faster I am, compared to you. Well, that is how much faster von Neumann is, compared to me," Enrico confided to Herb, who was last seen with his chin falling past his ankles.

There is a slightly more serious story that involved John von Neumann of the Institute for Advanced Study in Princeton and his experience with parallel processing involving one of the rented business machines, called a tabulator. Johnny, as he was affectionately called, learned much of his experimental experience in computing on the business machines that the Laboratory had to do the routine computations on. Anticipating the present day development in computer design, he tried to understand the principal issues involved with parallel processing, that is, having concurrent processing of several different paths of the computation at hand, rather than the serial operation where the computer followed a single sequence of computation. But despite the fact that the tabulator was an electromechanical device and relatively slow compared to electronic speeds, nonetheless Johnny had his difficulties with his sophisticated notion of parallel processing and had to abandon his pursuit. He vowed that thereafter he would confine himself to the much simpler serial computation in designing any set of controls for a computer. End of that story.

Among the consultants that visited Los Alamos during the war was a Navy pilot, one officer Chick Hayward, friend of von Neumann, obviously a nontrivial visitor. One day he "buzzed" Death Valley (he was stationed at the time in Channel Lake, California) and was observed by a tourist, who made a note of the wing number and reported it to the commandant, who called Hayward "on the carpet" to explain his foolish antics. He pleaded that he had been a member of the submarine corps before he became a Navy pilot and he wanted to be able to tell his future grandchildren that he had dived DEEPER in an airplane than the maximum depth allowed in a submarine of 180 feet. The commandant relented. End of short story.

Among other things, von Neumann was a consultant to the Los Alamos Scientific Laboratory, and was also a consultant to Aberdeen Proving Ground in Maryland; it was the Proving Ground that had issued a contract to the Moore School of Electrical Engineering of the University of Pennsylvania in Philadelphia, for the construction of the first electronic computer, the ENIAC, with John Mauchly and Presper Eckert as the designers and builders. It was physicist Mauchly who had realized that the electronic counting apparatus used to study experimentally cosmic rays in physics laboratories could be used as a fundamental building block for the design of electronic computers. For if one could count, then one could do arithmetic; and if one could do arithmetic, one could solve differential (difference) equations, among other mathematical forms, whether linear or nonlinear. And thus von Neumann had argued that, as the time came for the testing of the ENIAC, since the problems of Los Alamos were superior, they could test at least 95% of the electronic computer compared to the ≈ 25% that Aberdeen Proving Ground could come up with in a typical problem, involved with firing tables, a relatively simple problem. So with the proper security installed, Stan Frankel and I undertook the task of learning the details of the ENIAC to prepare the program and run the problems. Later Anthony Turkevich joined us. Thus we learned about electronic computing as well as nuclear devices in wartime Los Alamos. The rest of the world history of the war is well-known, especially among the older generation.

Edward Teller had insisted that a proper documentation of those calculations be recorded and, moreover, that a conference be held in the spring of 1946, since it was not clear what the subsequent history of the world would be; certainly this applied to Los Alamos.

By this time, Stan Ulam, who had left for the University of Southern California early in September of the previous year, had returned and it occurred to him that with such calculational speeds then possible using the ENIAC one could resuscitate the sampling process and mathematically expand the method where it would be useful for our purposes. Thus was the statistical sampling scheme reborn and later came to be known as the Monte Carlo Method.

In due course, the ENIAC was actually moved from Philadelphia to its permanent home in Aberdeen, Maryland, where the Proving Ground was located. This was no small task considering its size; many of the new-born cognescenti predicted that the ENIAC had seen better days. Nonetheless, the ENIAC did survive its journey, thanks in large part to the meticulous care that Richard Merwin and Josh Gray exercised in that move.

Thus ended the wartime period of Los Alamos, a most glorious history of scientific endeavor, vividly remembered by the participants. But it was only the beginning. Norris Bradbury was made the Director of the Laboratory and saw it through its most critical phase. To impart a flavor of the immediate surroundings of the first days of peace on this mesa top, permit me to describe that first weekend.

The inhabitants had been advised that photography was permitted for the first time, provided it did not include portions of the Laboratory. So Turkevich and I walked around familiar places on that Sunday morning as if it were the last time. On bathtub row, suddenly appeared Oppie and Kitty, he wheeling a stroller that contained their first child, a girl called Toni, for short. This was a very unusual role for the Director; so I thought it should be documented. I asked Kitty for permission and Oppie urged expediency by saying "If it didn't take too long." I replied that it would take only one-fiftieth of a second. He could hardly object to that!

BEHIND TALL FENCES

A chance visit by Klari von Neumann (Mrs. John von Neumann) and me to Aberdeen resulted in a new mode of preparing computational problems for the ENIAC. It was a theoretical idea of Richard Clippinger of Aberdeen and implemented by us who used the new programming method on some Monte Carlo problems. This new mode of operation enabled a more efficient programming technique as well as a more efficient way of operating the computer. This method of operation endured for the lifetime of the ENIAC.

When it was dismantled (late '60s, early '70s) one of the twenty so-called accumulators was given to this Laboratory as a museum piece of the early days of computing.

It should be noted that all of ENIAC was built with vacuum tubes, resistors and other electronic parts that were Army-Navy rejected parts, the so-called JAN-specifications. A corollary of this fact was that the ENIAC could have been built before the start of World War II. Imagine the consequences if that had been a fact! Perhaps even the development time of the bomb could have been in time to have made a qualitative difference in the story of the European theater.

What is particularly sad about that conjecture is the fact that it takes wartime conditions to solicit financial support of government for such a project. Of course, it would have been better if industry, in the course of human events, could have seen the handwriting on the wall of progress. Perhaps it is an instance of the perfection of hindsight. Nonetheless the brilliance of Mauchly and Eckert is even more impressive under the actual conditions.

Not long after these Monte Carlo problems were run on the ENIAC, I returned to Los Alamos to start a group here on building a second generation electronic computer. We were to follow in the footsteps of the Institute of Advanced Study; the idea being that a subgroup of electronic engineers could be trained as computer engineers. The difference between electronic and computer engineers was the basis for Fermi to miscalculate the time between errors that the ENIAC would operate successfully. From the very beginning, Fermi took a great interest in modern computing, and especially the ENIAC. After an early visit to Philadelphia, I was asked by Fermi, "How many double triode tubes did you say were in the ENIAC?" "18,000," I answered. Based on a comparison with his laboratory equipment used for counting nuclear events, he pronounced the ENIAC an ill-fated construction by uttering that the ENIAC would operate about a few seconds as a "mean free time between errors" because of vacuum-tube failure. His pessimism was based on just the difference between electronic and computer engineers! For his apparatus in the laboratory, there was no point in achieving unnecessary high-reliability whereas a self-respecting computer engineer would design circuitry much more conservatively in order to achieve the desired reliability! As anyone knows, much higher reliability is usually demanded for computer operation than for a mere physics experimental setup. And thus it was that Fermi underestimated the mean free time between errors for the ENIAC. This was the only time in my memory that Fermi was found wanting—in itself a miracle!

I must counterbalance the above remark with another story of Fermi. This is due to Emilio Segrè, his first graduate student in Rome and later, after the war, a professor of physics at Berkeley. It was the period when Fermi was then an experimental neutron physicist, having shifted from being a theoretical physicist! The year was approximately 1935. Fermi was an insomniac then, and utilized his waking hours playing games of chance on his electromechanical computer to predict the results of the following day's experiments. When his colleagues were sufficiently impressed by the accuracy of his predictions, he came forth with his statistical analyses that were the basis of his predictions. Thus he was ahead of Stan Ulam in his resuscitation of sampling techniques based on statistical analysis.

Talking about electronics reminds me of the Army Engineer in charge of the generating station where electricity for the Lab was produced. One day, several experimentalists were complaining that the timing of their experimental setup was off; it was based, as usual, on the good old reliable 60 cycles. So they decided to check everything, beginning with the generator itself. When they accosted the chap in charge of the powerhouse, he replied that he wanted to make sure the Lab people engaged in some mysterious war work got their share of cycles, so he simply added a few more in case a few cycles were dropped on the way over to the Lab (an in-joke for the experimentalists!).

Returning to the story before the Fermi interruption, we were discussing the training of computer engineers on our project in Los Alamos and, of course, reliability was a part. Progress was a song, since it was much easier to make a copy of circuits rather than to develop them; we started with the so-called arithmetic unit. But the Princeton group ran into a snag developing a memory system. Actually, the research team at RCA-Princeton Junction was having a difficult time developing the Selectron. It doesn't matter what the details of the Selectron are; what matters is that at the University of Manchester, England, Williams and his colleagues came up with the tube that was named after him. It was essentially a cathode-ray tube with the necessary hardware on the outside of the tube. The Princeton group was saved, after some delays. In the meantime, back home, good things were also happening. Mr. James Richardson came to work for us from the University of Toronto, where some experience was had on the so-called Williams tube mentioned above. So while the Princeton group was developing a memory system based on a 5-inch cathode-ray tube, we decided to utilize the time gaining experience on a smaller 2-inch cathode-ray tube.

It turned out that there was an awkwardness in the above delay and it was decided to proceed with our own memory system. The associated control system was developed, then the input-output apparatus, including a magnetic drum and the first line printer ever. In early March of 1952 we were ready, having completed various test runs, for the first serious nuclear weapons calculational problems.

The computer was called the MANIAC. It was a conscious effort to end the naming of computers, but somehow it had just the opposite effect. The interpretation, of course, came after the name was noted. George Gamow, the astrophysicist, came up with an alternative facetious interpretation; he called it Metropolis and Neumann Invent Awful Contraption.

Several names of prominent members of the group should be remembered: Richardson has already been mentioned, then Richard Merwin, Howie Parsons, Walter Orvedahl, Howard Demuth, and Al Klein of the engineers; then John Jackson, Marge Devaney, Mary Tsingou, Elaine Alei, Bob Bivens, Lois Cook, and Verna Gardiner on the programming side. Mark Wells and Paul Stein also made their presence felt. Some obvious names must have been omitted innocently, as is always the case.

These were the early days of electronic computing. We subjected the MANIAC to a variety of computing problems so that it would be clear whether or not the computer, as designed, would indeed be fairly universal in handling a wide variety of different problems. We had a strong feeling it could handle the fluid dynamics problems; after all, it was designed with that capability, given a lot of spatial symmetry. But what of a wider variety of problems? Fermi and his group at the University of Chicago had been experimentally determining the properties of scattering of nuclear particles called pions on hydrogen nuclei. The computational problem in this case was to determine the so-called phase shift angles. It was an ideal problem for the computer, but then Fermi had a keen sense of knowing just what the capabilities of a computer were; he had earlier demonstrated this when he suggested a problem for the electromechanical system that the Laboratory used during the wartime, his first step in learning modern computing. (Nuclear masses as a complicated function of two integers, A the atomic number and Z the nuclear charge.) Returning to the problem at hand, Fermi was interested in all the details of computing and had the desire of doing every step himself, beginning with the actual program, to the "running" of the problem on the computer. In short order he was to become an "expert" of the new electronic computer, quite a step from the earlier days of his 6-inch slide rule.

In collaboration with Drs. Pasta and Ulam, Fermi was also to study the so-called relaxation time of a chain of anharmonic oscillators, what came to be known as the F-P-U problem. It was an accident that led to a proper understanding of the so-called relaxation time. One day, when all three were present, they were arguing some point of the theory and completely oblivious of the MANIAC "running" the computation. Finally they settled the point being discussed and wondered about the MANIAC and whether it had finished the calculation. To their amazement, the MANIAC went way beyond the point of "normal" completion and actually returned to its so-called initial conditions to within a 2% deviation and was about to begin its "second round," when it returned to approximately a 4% deviation, etc. Thus, the "theorists" revised their notion of the relaxation time to a much larger value. All this is a bit technical; the main point is the element of surprise even in mathematics, perhaps computational mathematics! Or even experimental mathematics is a better expression. Later, J.L. Tuck and M. Tsingou followed up on these "supercycles" and published their results.

Also later, H. Bethe and F. de Hoffman had their version of the scattering problem of pions by hydrogen nuclei and confirmed a resonance phenomenon. H.L. Anderson participated in the pion scattering taking into account all of the experiments performed at the various laboratories.

Then there was the problem of what happens inside a complex nucleus when each of the kinds of pions suddenly finds itself in such a nucleus. This problem was suggested by A. Turkevich, a nuclear chemist of the University of Chicago who was a consultant to the Laboratory. We knew that nuclear chemistry was a relatively new field and we felt compelled to learn how the MANIAC would react to problems in this area, especially with such experts around.

The versatile Edward Teller was also in the neighborhood and was interested in collisions of hard spheres, actually disks, since the problem was two-dimensional. Much good came from that research, and Edward made quite an impression on the surrounding personnel.

A quite different type of problem was the game of chess and the associated strategies. In those days of vacuum tubes, before the days of transistors and integrated circuits with their associated storage, the chess board was restricted to a 6 x 6 arrangement, instead of the usual 8 x 8 board. We called it anti-clerical chess, since the two bishops on each side were removed. It took about 20 minutes for the computer to calculate its next move. The strategy was programmed by Mark Wells and looked two and one-half moves ahead. Stan Ulam and Paul Stein contributed. Mary Tsingou, later to become Mrs. Menzel, and one of our best programmers, who had not learned the traditional chess, was selected to challenge the MANIAC. Later that summer when the program was debugged, Martin Kruskal, who was professor of mathematics at Princeton University, and who had a chess rating in New York City, happened to be visiting and was asked to play the MANIAC. He agreed, but with our stipulation that his "queen would be forfeited." He, however, was told the strategy MANIAC would use. Two interesting events took place: (1) After some moves, the MANIAC made what seemed to the onlookers a stupid move. We surmised that the computer had made an error, but let it pass. Two moves later, we realized that the MANIAC had earlier made a brilliant move. (2) Several moves later, Kruskal was perspiring and said, "I wonder why HE did that!", using an anthropomorphic reference to the MANIAC. Cornered, Kruskal relied on knowledge of the MANIAC's strategy and feinted the MANIAC and he won after being nearly scooped by the computer. (He had, in all fairness, forfeited his queen.)

George Gamow, who had solved the enigma (riddle) of the DNA code structure, made some preliminary computational experiments. This brought to a close the preliminary investigation of the vocabulary system of the MANIAC.

One underlying motive was to get the scientist introduced to electronic computing if he had numerics or symbolic computing to be done. The alternative of having a computer assistant works if the problem originator knows computing; otherwise the assistant solves the problem he <u>thinks</u> his boss wants. Often the boss benefits and gets suggestions by watching the development unfold, as the computing proceeds. Soon, industry was involved in the construction of so-called main frames. A salutary commentary of experienced problem solvers was that they knew what new features in a computer would be desirable for their kind of computational problems. This feature was not always appreciated.

Clearly in this young field of computer development and computing, the completion of the MANIAC was only a <u>first</u> step, so it was not a big surprise that MANIAC II was started. It coincided with the construction of the new Administration Building in 1955 in the new area and MANIAC II was indeed housed there in 1956. At first ruggedized vacuum tubes were used, but were soon replaced by transistors, without the user being for the most part any the wiser, since all improvements were made on the weekends. These were the so-called hardware improvements. The integrated circuits were still a thing of the future.

But progress was also being made in the matter of problem preparation. This was the <u>software</u> aspect of computing. One of the real steps forward was <u>visualization</u> that permitted the unfolding of the computing process on some screen while the process was in flight. This capability enabled the human brain to be brought into the loop in an effective manner. The human brain is a subtle instrument and eliminated the element of surprise in a calculation, not to mention a more complete understanding of the calculation at hand, enabling one to interpolate, or even extrapolate, between any two solutions.

I remember an incident in the postwar days, halcyon days they were. Edwin McMillan from Berkeley was visiting the Laboratory. He had been here during the war period. In the meantime, he had won a Nobel Prize in Physics, constructed the synchrotron, became director of the Radiation Laboratory at Berkeley, and [was] a wonderful guy, interested in number theory as a serious amateur. So he wanted to see MANIAC I. When we entered the room, a couple of programmers, lovely females and bright, were running a problem and using clip leads to change the state of a flip-flop, a double triode vacuum tube. So it was a very busy atmosphere, with input tapes, both paper and magnetic, as well as output line printer. "Do you think they actually know what they are doing?" asked Ed. His jaw dropped past his ankles when he was reassured that they did. It made my day to see that they had so impressed someone not easily impressed.

Computer development, both hardware and software, kept pace with nuclear developments. It was the heyday of scientific progress! What a time to be alive! Imagine following the era of the automobile, the telephone, the radio and the television. It was possible, however, to be too optimistic; while all sorts of applications, like airline reservations, were being made in the marketplace, the costs were underestimated. But in the scientific horizon, it was all too easily imagined that because of the natural electronic speeds, the problem of language translation was grossly underestimated. The subtleties of the human brain, even in the matter of simple languages, used in the course of simple exchanges, were not fully appreciated.

After some two generations of computing, the central problem of arithmetical computation has been scarcely investigated, if not forgotten! What do I regard as the central problem? Except for the study of integer arithmetic, all arithmetical inputs have an approximate nature, that is to say, have a numerical error associated with them. The question is what are the errors associated with the answers, or output numbers. Most computational problems associated with or related to natural phenomena have errors in the input numbers. Are such problems merely random number generators? The basic nature of error propagation is essentially interaction of errors. Were there no interactions, this problem would have been solved a long time ago. But interactions exist, and as a consequence, so does the central problem of arithmetical computing. This lack of progress gives the wrong impression of computer development and should not be used to end a talk on the subject of computer progress. Permit me some further digressions.

BEHIND TALL FENCES

When Lord Penney received the invitation to join Britain's most prestigious group, called the Order of Merit, he was both delighted and slightly disappointed. The reason for his delight was obvious; it is the most exclusive club in the world, there are 24 members, unlike the various classes of the French Legion d'Honneur. Any member invariably puts after his name, first the O.M., and the others, like F.R.S., etc.; it is the Queen's organization and upon the death of a member of the Order, someone is nominated to take his place.

The cause of his slight despair was his thought that Sir Geoffrey Taylor, his teacher at Cambridge, should have been nominated instead of him. After all, Sir Geoffrey was older and did deserve that honor. There would be time for Lord Penney.

History took kindly to Lord Penney's thought. There was an interval between the notice of his nomination and the actual ceremony. During the interval, Lord Russell, blessed with an O.M. (the Order of Merit), did pass away. The next nominee was Sir Geoffrey. So at the ceremony Lord Penney and Sir Geoffrey both became members of the Queen's group. One can only imagine Penney's pleasure of that moment.

As all of you know, computer design has concentrated on building computers that operate more rapidly; a figure of merit is sometimes used, namely how many operations is a particular computer capable of doing [in a given time]. One may have noticed that modern computers are being built that are (relatively) smaller and smaller in size. This is not a coincidence. Actually the operational speed is subject to the laws of special relativity! The speed of a signal cannot exceed the speed of light. Thus the shorter distance is an advantage. The pocket calculator or the hand-held computer reflects a given direction of design. It was enabled by what is sometimes called the "miracle of the chip". The chip itself is the laying down of electronic components on a substrate that is essentially a photographic process. The development of the chip is a new direction that increases the reliability of computers as well as the storage size, not to mention the decrease in cost of the ubiquitous expense of operation. It is just the miracle of the chip, whose translation is the very large scale of integration, that has led to a new logical design, that in turn has led to a speedup of solving computational problems. It is, in essence, the increased reliability by having no moving "macro-parts" in the electronic circuitry.

We interrupt once more to discuss an interesting problem, first suggested by Steinhaus, who visited here in the immediate postwar period and was an old timer friend of Stan Ulam, when they were in prewar Poland. We all know that if two persons are to divide something so as one has himself only to blame for being "short changed," one person does the "dividing" and the other does the "choosing." Question: what is the solution if there are no persons? It is not easy, but elegant. It is part of the game theory. First it was Borel in 1921, then the famous book of von Neumann and Morgenstern that gave birth to game theory.

Shortly after Dr. Donald Kerr became the fourth Director of the Laboratory, I sent him a memo pointing out that in 1983, the Lab could celebrate the fortieth anniversary of its founding. One possibility was to have some of the pioneers give talks on some of their researches in the post world war to be called "New Directions in Science." In fact, there could be a session of Nobel Laureates of scientists who had received their recognition after 1943, e.g., people like Feynman, Bloch, McMillan, Alvarez, Segre, Chamberlain, Bethe and Rabi. In any case, the invitations of all these famous people would have to be started in plenty of time, at least a year in advance.

When I didn't hear from the Director in early 1982, I did nothing. When he did phone me in October I thought it much too late, at least for the 40th Anniversary. He remarked that it was worth a try. When several people rearranged their schedules, it was encouraging. The rest is history. The anniversary took place, primarily because those pioneers had a very warm spot for the memories of Los Alamos as a wartime experience.

Earlier in 1976, an international meeting on the history of electronic computing was held in Los Alamos during the week of June 10-15; the National Science Foundation broke with tradition and sponsored this meeting being held at a national laboratory. It was an attempt to record historical perspectives of computing pioneers during their lifetimes. Already we had lost two of the most famous such pioneers, namely Enrico Fermi and John von Neumann. Both were victimized by cancer. In late 1954 Fermi had died and in slightly more than two years later, von Neumann followed him, before he had a chance to give the Silliman Lecture at Yale on the human brain and the analogy to the modern computer.

The British and Europeans were represented by Brian Randell of Newcastle-upon-Tyne, and his colleagues A.W.M. Coombs, J.H. Wilkinson, I.J. Good; then from Europe, F.L. Bauer, M.V. Wilkes, E.W. Dijkstra, A. Svoboda and K. Zuse among others. Japan was represented by R. Suekane, while Russia had A.P. Ershov and M. Shura-Bura. Therein hangs a tale of American frustration. The organizers of the conference wanted the Russian representation badly, despite the relatively late excuses for which the Russians had developed a distinguished reputation. So we had Shura-Bura as a backup to Ershov. We had not counted on Mrs. Ershov breaking a leg on the day her husband was to board an airplane in Moscow, too late for Shura-Bura to take his place.

BEHIND TALL FENCES

The Americans were adequately represented by D.E. Knuth, D.H. Lehmer, A.S. Householder, J.W. Mauchly, P. Eckert, J. Bigelow, G. Birkhoff, S. Ulam, and J. Backus, again among others. Atanasoff elected not to come. The set of reports has been published as <u>A History of Computing in the Twentieth Century</u> and is dedicated to John Pasta.

It was Randell who created quite a stir with his talk about the Colossus, a "symbolic processor" that was used to break German codes in World War II. Randell prevailed upon the British government to release classified information after some 32 years of classification. His main argument was that here was an international conference and the British had something to say. The impression he created was a good one, so much so that an evening session was held at which Randell and Coombs, an engineer, presided. The British Post Office gathered in long overdue praise for its part in computer development, not to mention the war effort! The whole affair couldn't have been better programmed.

Sometime later, a stage play called <u>Breaking the Code</u> with Derek Jacobi, the great English actor who played I Claudius, in the lead role of Alan Turing, complete with the occasional stutter. It played in this country in New York City. There is a curious agreement on an imported play and its cast, owing to Equity: Subject to negotiations, an imported play may be staged for six months with its original cast. After that, it is a requirement that an American cast takes over. In this instance, the British company closed the play—a tribute to its lead. I saw the play late in its six-month period and it played to a full house.

I must apologize for the episodic nature of the talk. It is a compromise between the scientists and all others.

In order to provide some background on von Neumann, he had two younger brothers. The older of the two was Michael von Neumann and the younger was Nicolas von Neumann. Michael was an engineer in Chicago, actually at the University of Chicago in the Physics Department. I did not know that Michael even existed at the time of my decision to return to the University in the fifties, but my friendship of an earlier decade with his older brother helped a great deal and Michael became a good friend. In fact, he became a member of our staff. He was a self-effacing and very shy person, hardly aware of the many talents he possessed. In those days spark chambers were in fashion and occupied part of his time. He was a tremendous colleague. When I returned to Los Alamos in the middle sixties, he joined the staff of my longtime colleague Herb Anderson.

Up to the relatively recent present, the focus of logical design of computers has concentrated on having <u>one</u> arithmetical process only, along with the memory and input/output, and trying to increase the speed of the various operations. But such increases as were achieved became more and more difficult, for there was a natural limit, given by the special theory of relativity, as mentioned earlier.

But it became very natural, given the increased reliability of the miracle of the chip, to have more than just one arithmetic processor, i.e., in fact to have many such arithmetic units. This implies restructuring the computational problems so that separate parts (but still interacting) of each problem can be handled by the various arithmetic units. This is a major reorganization, but it gets around the limitations and leads to a further speedup and to computational problems that had to be deferred heretofore could be made tractable now. For example, problems in three dimensions.

This development has been described as <u>massively parallel</u>. Quite properly, some manufacturers have taken a more modest approach by introducing two, four and eight processors. This has more modest overtones in the software, or computational problem preparation, by clinging to age-old methods and making small modifications in the software.

It may come as a surprise to you that "serial" computers (as they are called because heretofore there has been only one arithmetic unit) with their blazing speed in doing a billion operations each second, could not solve every imaginable problem of interest. But it just isn't so. There are a lot of meaningful problems, not to mention more subtle and more sophisticated questions to be asked of the simpler problems. For example, the physical world around us has three space-dimensions and the mathematical interpretation of questions to be asked usually involves the dimension of time, making a fourth. The study of three space-dimensions will be a challenge for these massively parallel computers for a long time to come.

I might make reference (and promise to restrict myself from making any more references) to an issue of DAEDALUS devoted to these new developments in computational history. The issue was published early in this year. This issue is highly recommended, especially the three articles written respectively by Holland, Hasslacher, and Sokolowski; the others are good too. Maybe the problem of translating a learned article from its original language into a second or third language may be successfully revived, with the new capabilities at hand.

The prospects look good also for the so-called <u>soft</u> sciences, like economics, to become more tractable. But these subjects are very complicated and lots of infrastructure needs to be in place; there are many questions of foundations in each of these disciplines. Perhaps these new developments will help a little.

The time has come to ask the inevitable question about the future. Clearly efforts will go into parallel processing and its causes and cures. In particular, parallel processing will enable three space-dimensions in all their glory. There is the software development of the two forms of parallel processing, namely SIMD, single instruction, multiple data, and more generally, MIMD, where the first M stands for multiple, the rest is identical to the first. Another approach being developed here is networking; the team is led by Dr. Karl-Heinz Winkler.

Still others are wondering about sophisticated questions of reversibility of arithmetical operations and questions about minimal energies of operations, in an attempt to be more like the human brain. There are related questions concerning thermodynamic approaches. The efforts of Bennett, Fredkin, Chaitin, Hasslacher, and Toffoli are prominent. Nine years ago, the ubiquitous Feynman gave an interesting talk here concerning thermodynamic questions and Hamiltonians of computers. More recently, some far-out computer developments called collectively, nanotechnology, are emerging.

National laboratories are here to stay. The mushrooming effect of scientific and mathematical problems that are specific to the concept of national laboratories makes it unthinkable that they have a short half-life.

I would like to acknowledge the generous help that both Gian-Carlo Rota and James Louck gave to the preparation of this manuscript; their comments helped.

---

*Nicholas C. Metropolis came to Los Alamos in April 1943 from the Metallurgical Laboratory and the University of Chicago. In response to the computational challenges of complex systems, he was led to a career of computer developments and algorithms. He returned to the University of Chicago in 1946, then back to the Laboratory in 1965, oscillating between the two institutions in the interim. After his retirement in 1985, he became Senior Fellow Emeritus and continues his association with the Laboratory. He has been a member of the J. Robert Oppenheimer Memorial Committee since 1969.

Metropolis gave this talk as the Twenty-Second J. Robert Oppenheimer Lecture on August 3, 1992.

LOS ALAMOS, 1943
Arthur Wahl*

Arrival

Late in March 1943 Bob Duffield and I loaded Frank Oppenheimer's pickup truck with chemical and radiation-detection equipment from our Berkeley laboratory and drove to Santa Fe. On arriving at the outskirts of Santa Fe, we discreetly asked directions from a gas-station attendant to East Palace Avenue and received instructions for proceeding to 109 E. Palace. There, Dorothy McKibbin warmly welcomed us and told us how to proceed to Los Alamos. The trip up the hill was uneventful, except for trying all different driving speeds on the wash-board road from Pojoaque to Los Alamos to minimize shaking our detection equipment.

Arriving at Los Alamos late afternoon of April 1, 1943, and expecting desert, we were fooled, but were pleasantly surprised to find pine trees, a pond, boy-school buildings in an attractive setting, and laboratories and houses under construction. We were welcomed at supper in the lodge by about two dozen people, including Bob and Charlotte Serber, John Williams, Bob Wilson and the cyclotron crew, and Don Mastic, a chemist who preceded us from Berkeley by about two weeks to supervise construction of our future laboratories.

The first few weeks at Los Alamos were relatively relaxed compared to later times when pressures were high. Since laboratories were unfinished, we experimentalists could only make plans and check out our electronic (vacuum tube) detection equipment. We ate at the lodge and slept on screened porches at the Big House, since mess halls and dormitories were unfinished. Often in the evening Bob and Charlotte Serber would take small groups in their convertible to Santa Fe for dinner or a beer. We often ate at the Chinese restaurant on San Francisco street. On weekends we'd go on hikes or ride horses left from the boys school to enjoy exploring nearby mesas and canyons.

General Groves

One of the early experiments at Los Alamos was the determination of the average number of neutrons, v, per fission of ^{239}Pu induced by fast neutrons. Glenn Seaborg at the Metallurgical Laboratory in Chicago agreed to lend us, but for only a few days, 150 micrograms of ^{239}Pu, a sizable fraction of the world supply at the time. Having worked with plutonium at Berkeley, I was asked to prepare the source, a thin layer of plutonium on a one-inch platinum disk for measurements by John Williams, Joe McKibben, and their staff at the Van de Graaff.

The ^{239}Pu arrived late one afternoon. I first assayed a small aliquot by alpha counting and found only 130 micrograms, probably due to different alpha-counter calibrations at Chicago and Los Alamos. However, 130 micrograms was sufficient for the experiment, so I spent most of the night preparing the source by evaporating individual drops on platinum after precipitating plutonium fluoride in each drop. The measurements were made the following day, and the hoped for v value of about 3 was obtained.

Bob Wilson had devised a different experiment to determine v at the cyclotron, but needed the ^{239}Pu on the outside of a cylinder, so I spent the next night dissolving the ^{239}Pu from flat Van de Graaff source and mounting it a drop at a time on a platinum cylinder. Bob and his group obtained a value close to the Van de Graaff value, and everyone was pleased with the results. Bob returned the ^{239}Pu, still on the platinum cylinder, to Glenn Seaborg in Santa Fe.

Soon after the experiments were completed, Oppenheimer brought General Groves around to the laboratories to meet the scientists who had participated in the experiment. When they came to my laboratory, Oppie introduced me and explained that I had prepared the ^{239}Pu sources for the experiments. Expecting praise or some kind words, I was dumbfounded when General Groves looked at me, said "so you're the one who lost twenty micrograms of plutonium," turned, and stalked away down the hall.

First Plutonium Shipments

Before leaving Berkeley, I had arranged with my colleagues there to irradiate about one-half ton of uranyl nitrate hexahydrate with neutrons from the 60-inch cyclotron for several months to produce about 1 milligram of ^{239}Pu. There were two objectives: (1) to test the acetate separation procedure that had been developed at Berkeley and (2) to produce as much ^{239}Pu as possible for use in development of a plutonium purification procedure at Los Alamos.

The separations at Berkeley were completed during the fall of 1943, and the 1 milligram of ^{239}Pu was shipped to Lamy in about a liter of uranyl acetate solution. I rode to Lamy with an armed government man to pick up the valuable solution. I was still on crutches following knee surgery at Bruns Army Hospital in Santa Fe.

For separation of the milligram of ^{239}Pu from the remaining uranium solution, I enlisted the help of Bob Duffield, Cliff Garner, and Rene Prestwood. We worked in two twelve-hour shifts, Bob and I during the day, and Cliff and Rene at night. Not being very mobile, I worked at a desk developing and writing the procedures to be followed during the next 24-hour period. After about four days and nights, all uranium had been removed, and while the solution of purified plutonium was being evaporated in a centrifuge tube, the tube slipped into the water bath. Thus, we had to separate the plutonium from the water and crud from the bath, so our 12-hour shifts were continued for several more days and nights.

Several plutonium compounds were prepared during the next several months, but progress toward development of a plutonium purification procedure was slow because techniques for working with very small amounts (≈ 0.1 milligram) of plutonium had to be developed and considerable time was required to recover the valuable plutonium for reuse from the compounds made and residues created.

Early in 1944, about 1 gram of ^{239}Pu produced in the Oak Ridge reactor was received at Los Alamos, and subsequently other ≈ 1 gram batches of ^{239}Pu were received. This material allowed development of a purification procedure using convenient amounts (≈ 100 milligrams) of plutonium for experimentation. Also, a new plutonium recovery group was set up under the direction of Frank Pittman, so all efforts of my group could be devoted to development of a plutonium purification procedure. Of course, the larger amounts of ^{239}Pu required health-safety precautions, and respirators, rubber gloves, and protective clothing were worn.

---

*Arthur C. Wahl came to Los Alamos in April 1943 from the University of California, Berkeley, and was among the first radiochemists to study the fission and purification properties of plutonium, using microgram quantities produced at Berkeley. He left in 1946 for a position at Washington University and has been Emeritus Professor of Chemistry since 1983. He presently resides in Los Alamos and maintains an association with the Laboratory.

A SCIENTIFIC PHOTOGRAPHER AT PROJECT Y
Berlyn Brixner[*]

BEFORE THE BOMB

When I came to Los Alamos as a humble photographer during WWII, I had no idea what I had bumbled into. I never dreamt that brilliant people would take the trouble to extricate me from one tight spot after another. Nor did it occur to me that I would spend the rest of my useful life in Los Alamos.

In May 1943, when I received a surprise phone call from my boyhood friend David Hawkins, I was working in Albuquerque as a photogrammetric engineer with the cartographic division of the Soil Conservation Service updating maps of the southwestern USA for the U. S. Army Air Force. Before taking some brief training in cartographic engineering at University of New Mexico during the early years of the war I had for several years been the regional photographer with the Soil Conservation Service in Albuquerque. At the time David phoned, my cartographic work was nearing completion, and my draft deferment was running out; so, when asked if I was interested in a job as photographer with the U. S. Army Engineers in Santa Fe, I paused only long enough to inquire what kind of photography was needed. To find the answer, I had, like many another, to go first to 109 East Palace in Santa Fe. From there, with many cautions of secrecy, I was transported by bus to Los Alamos, where David met me and introduced me to Professor Julian Mack, my future boss and for four years my chief mentor. The job in question would be to run a high-speed camera, at that time still on the drawing board. After looking at the drawings I told Mack I thought I could learn to run the camera, and that was that.

Things at once began to happen. Mack started the paperwork for hiring me as a civilian photographer and told me I would be assigned an apartment so I could bring my wife and two children to the site. In Albuquerque my July transfer to the U. S. Army Engineers in Santa Fe for the duration of the war was quickly approved, and I had still time to complete my mapping project. The only apparent hitch was that during June I received a draft notification to report for physical examination, which to me meant that I would inevitably be drafted instead of embarking on an exciting new photographic adventure. However, that detail had also been taken care of. When I reported to the inspection center, my name was not called, and I was told that I should leave, that there had been a mistake; so I reported for work at Los Alamos during mid-July.

At first I lived in the "Big House," the dormitory of the former boys' school, and was assigned a temporary job, temporarily being done by a physicist, namely, running a blueprint machine and a photostat machine. Since I realized almost at once that orders for multicopy prints were coming in at a rate far too fast for one person to process, I thought up what I called the "check print" procedure. Instead of making all the copies requested, I made one blueprint while the customer waited and agreed to make additional prints on order if they were still needed. By that method I processed the pile of back orders fairly soon, and the procedure worked so well that it was adopted when a newly formed photo group took over the service—something over a month after I started on the job.

Since the high-speed camera was still in the process of being built, I was next assigned the job of making flashlight photos of a three-inch-diameter bullet as it was fired from a gun. Since the plan was to assemble in a gun a critical mass of active nuclear material for a bomb, the experimenters wanted to know whether smoke escaped ahead of the bullet. To make the flashlight picture I used the now famous "Microflash" invented by Harold Edgerton of MIT. Mack had already acquired one of these flashlights, which light up for no more than a few microseconds. I set up a camera shielded from the muzzle blast, synchronized the camera shutter with the gun's firing-pin action, and synchronized the shielded flashlamp with the emerging bullet. This last procedure I accomplished by inserting a probe near the end of the gun barrel. When the picture of the emerging bullet showed some smoke ahead of the bullet, the experimenters showed no surprise. After I had made ten or so pictures, I had worked out a reliable procedure and was able to turn the job over to a photographer in the research group.

Now I was free to begin studying the new high-speed, rotating mirror camera, the parts for which came out of the shop during September 1943. As I began to assemble, test, and debug the camera I found that the pyramid-shaped rotating mirror was the most troublesome part. The mirror, which was turned by an air-driven turbine invented by Professor Jesse Beams of the University of Virginia, was sensitive to any abrupt change in the air pressure. Such changes might cause the mirror, when rotating at speeds up to 1,000 rps, to jump off its seat. The problem was somewhat alleviated by installing a needle valve at the air supply.

Next, Felix Geiger and I, working together and at first using electronic strobe lighting, began to make test photographs with the new machine, which was a moving-slit-image type of camera built on the "photo-finish" principle used at horse races. Such cameras could see only objects that crossed the finish line, and this extremely high-speed version was to be used in the initial study of some implosion experiments. The experiments would use a cylindrical system that would be photographed in silhouette through the central hole. By January 1944, when the new camera had been installed at the Anchor Ranch site, Morris Patapoff and I were already using it to photograph cylindrical implosions.

Now another problem arose. The first photographs made with the new camera showed that the cylindrical implosion, contrary to expectations, was highly irregular and therefore unsatisfactory. George Kistiakowsky, who headed the explosion research section, was furious. He insisted the trouble was with the camera, which was recording optical illusions. Weeks were passing; the atmosphere was becoming unbearably tense; and then Walter Koski arrived in Los Alamos. Koski knew how to use the new explosive flashlight invented by A. W. Campbell, and together with him I succeeded in making a single submicrosecond snapshot of the implosion. This snapshot at last confirmed the pictures given by the slit camera. Kistiakowsky had to accept the results. Shortly thereafter Patapoff was running the new camera by himself, and I was confronted with new problems.

It was while I was still photographing implosions along with Patapoff, however, that I had my first and only workplace visit from Oppenheimer. Perhaps he came as a result of the optical-illusion controversy. Whatever the reason, he chose a bitterly cold day. Patapoff and I were both wearing our overcoats inside the Anchor Ranch bunker when the Director knocked and came in, followed by Niels Bohr. When we were asked how the work was going we told Oppenheimer that although the camera was working reliably the cold made adjustments difficult. He offered to send an electric heater and did so within a week.

As another footnote I should also mention that although the rotating-mirror slit camera continued to be used throughout the war because it gave the best available resolution, the resolution was still never as good as desired, and efforts to improve the camera never ceased. The weak part was the pyramid mirror on the Beams drive. Because the rotor of this three-faced mirror "hunts" in orientation and because it splits the image beam, detrimental irregularities in image brightness are sometimes caused. Once again I was able to borrow an idea from a superior brain. Mack suggested I see Ernest Titterton. Titterton then developed for us the electronic control needed to synchronize the explosion at a specified azimuth of a magnetized rotating mirror. Building on his work I was able to develop a rotating-vane mirror whose surface was parallel with the shaft of a commercial turbine drive mounted on ball bearings. Besides alleviating the above-mentioned difficulties, the vane mirror doubled the time resolution because at a given speed the image velocity was twice that of the pyramid-mirror image. In fact, the vane mirror even doubled the resolution once again because the sharper image produced by its undivided light beam stayed on its specified path along the film. The synchronized camera was an immediate success, and, this time with help from engineer Monroe Messinger, our group developed, by January 1945, a universal slit camera with lens-option interchangeability. These cameras continued to be used for several years before they were retired.

Now on to my next adventure, this time with dummy bombs. Workers at Los Alamos were making measurements of the ballistic characteristics of our bombs and wanted motion-picture photographs of the dropping bombs, starting when the bombs left the bomb bay and continuing until impact at the target. Photographs were to be made of dummy bombs dropped on the Muroc (California) Bombing Range. I was sent to Muroc to see if I could help get the desired pictures, even though I had no experience with motion-picture cameras. I was not the only photographer there. When I arrived I found that two Navy motion picture photographers were already taking pictures. At first I had some difficulty with my camera, a Mitchell 35-mm motion-picture camera. In order to show some detail as the bomb emerged from the bomb bay—nearly six miles above ground—the camera had a 24-inch focal length lens. This long lens unbalanced the camera and made it difficult for me to keep the bomb in the picture frame as I followed the drop. Fortunately, I found and borrowed a Martin machine gun turret mounted on a four-wheel-drive truck. By mounting the camera on the turret I was able to get a smooth pan-tilt head, and the turret's aiming control was so good that I could hold the bomb in the field of view until it was about 2,000 feet from the ground. To photograph the bomb in slow motion just before impact, I got another Mitchell (120 pictures per second). With these two cameras I got pictures that pleased the investigators.

That field operation in the desert was not without exciting incidents. A couple of them I observed as a bystander. At the first "Fat Man" drop, the dummy bomb went into a bad wobble and cast off its tail. As a result, several modifications of the tail and body had to be made before a stable fall was obtained. On another occasion the "Thin Man" bomb failed to release properly. The long bomb was suspended by two shackles, and at drop time only one shackle was released. Then, when the pilot finally got rid of the bomb, the bomb bay doors would not close. Although our modified B-29 bomber landed without accident, there was a delay of two months before we photographed another bomb drop.

Two of my scary adventures happened while I was still at the Muroc Bombing Range; a third, rather uncomfortable one, occurred later when the bomb-drop operation had been moved to the Wendover (Utah) Air Base. A week or two after the first "Fat Man" drop I got the camera truck stuck in the mud on the trail leading to the camera station and decided to run the cameras from the spot where I was, even though it happened to be at the bull's eye of the bomb target. Up to that time no drop had ever come close, so I thought I was safe. I walked to the station phone to give the ready OK, and then returned to my camera, where I got a shock. For some seconds after the bomb was dropped I could see only the bomb nose, which was heading straight at me. It seemed an age before a tail fin came into view, and the bomb, as usual, struck wide of target.

Another time I was walking along the railroad track on a hot afternoon searching for a survey marker that was thought to be close to my camera station. Suddenly the ground seemed to vibrate. I looked behind and had just time to jump down the embankment at the side of the track. A diesel locomotive, traveling at about 75 miles an hour, had been perhaps 100 yards away. As far as I could tell no one in the engine even saw me.

The incident at Wendover was less scary but longer and more uncomfortable. I had been pressed into service as an aerial photographer, taking pictures suitable for mapping from a 30,000-foot elevation. The mapping-camera mount at the tail gunner's position on the B-29 was outside the pressurized cabin. Though I was an experienced aerial photographer, never before had I worked at an elevation where the temperature would drop to perhaps 50°F below zero. In addition to a K-17 aero camera and a roll of film, I was fitted out with an oxygen mask, a pair of headphones, gloves, and a warm jumper. I could have used some electrical heating. A crew member gave me signals to start and stop photographing. I could also be seen from the cabin window, and I survived to tell the tale, but I was never so cold in my life. Soon after that I returned to Los Alamos, and bomb-drop photography was turned over to another photographer.

Back at Los Alamos, in addition to the long hours and hard work, there was some time for play. The weekly square dance, with accordion music by Willie Higinbotham, was led by base commander, Colonel Ashbridge. There were free movies at two theaters. A play production group put on well attended plays throughout the war, and I sometimes helped with set construction because my wife, Betty, who had some previous theater experience, was a frequent player. Some people in town owned horses and enjoyed riding, and, of course, there were numerous parties in people's apartments. Luckily there were also children around willing to be baby sitters.

At work we had fascinating lectures about nuclear theory in general and bomb theory in particular. Frequent colloquia gave us reports about the progress of the bomb builders, and also the setbacks. I particularly remember Dick Feynman. He was an enthusiastic young lecturer who was entertaining to watch because he gave such elegant mathematical demonstrations that the top theoretical people could not find flaws, not immediately, not even later. In addition, Feynman was a skilled lock opener. This hobby of his made him valuable to our group—among others—because Mack was one of those who frequently misplaced his keys.

THE BOMB

By the fall of 1944 experiments were being planned for testing the plutonium bomb, the "Fat Man," which was to be exploded on the top of a

100-foot tower. The uranium bomb, the "Little Boy," was to be used without prior testing, but there were doubts about the plutonium bomb because various seemingly valid calculations of the implosion gave vastly different explosive yields. At one point it had even been thought that the "Fat Man" should be detonated inside a large steel bottle, "Jumbo," so that the plutonium could be salvaged in the event of a dud.

A site for the bomb test was needed, and eight different sites were considered. One was as near as the Rio Puerco valley near Cuba, New Mexico, and another was as distant as sand bars in the Gulf of Mexico. On one occasion Ken Bainbridge, the bomb test director, took Julian Mack and me, along with others, to inspect a site south of Grants, New Mexico, that he was thinking of selecting for the test area. Immediately I began voicing noisy objections because the area was lava covered and construction and working conditions would be difficult. The surface was abrasive. There was no soil for road construction, and subsurface caverns were likely to cause heavy structures to cave in. A much better site, I suggested, would be the flat and desolate desert in the Jornada del Muerto (Journey of Death) region in the Rio Grande valley southeast of Socorro, New Mexico. For whatever reason, Bainbridge did select that site, which turned out to be in the remote northwest corner of the immense Alamogordo Bombing range; and by September 1944 field work had been started under the code name "Trinity."

Our group's job was to do the main photographic recording of the explosion. Mack had four concrete camera bunkers constructed, two at 800 yards from the bomb and two at 10,000 yards. My task would be to get the motion picture record. The initial plan to use twelve cameras quickly grew to more than fifty commercial cameras running at speeds up to 10,000 pictures per second. Ralph Conrad, our camera repairman and an amateur photographer, helped me do that enormous job.

As usual there were various hitches before the original plans could be carried out. To begin with, by February 1945 new calculations indicated that the 800-yard bunkers would not protect the cameras inside from the blast and radioactivity if the bomb yield reached the newly estimated maximum. These bunkers were supposed to contain a mixture of the highest speed movie cameras then available. To solve the problem I used only four Fastax cameras at each station and mounted the cameras on sleds. To protect the cameras I invented and had made two steel and lead bunkers. Each bunker contained four thick lead glass windows mounted above the sleds. These sleds could be pulled out of the radioactive area by a long steel cable; and because the viewfinders would not be accessible when the cameras were inside the bunker, I invented a special external viewfinder so that the cameras could be aimed accurately by means of adjustable mirrors above the windows. Although the aim was precise, the films received a good deal of fogging from radiation, presumably while the recovery tank was pulling the cameras out of the radioactive area. Nevertheless most of the film had images that could be printed and measured.

Each of the two 10,000-yard bunkers had an assembly of 16- and 35-mm movie cameras running at speeds from one to 650 pictures per second. Both black-and-white and color films were used. One Mitchell 35-mm studio camera and four Kodak 16-mm cameras were mounted for panoramic aiming in order to follow the rising ball of fire and the smoke cloud. All the cameras were started and stopped by signals from the central timing station. In addition, each bunker had several specialized cameras run by other members of our group.

During early 1945, a serious bottleneck developed at Trinity because the necessary timing signals were not available. Although the signal lines were strung and the relays were at the instruments, dry runs were meaningless without signals on demand. Alas, we could not get the signals at the specified times before zero. And then Joseph McKibben was put in charge of timing. He quickly solved the difficulty, and before long any desired sequence of timing signals was available, day or night.

During May we tested the capabilities of the large assembly of cameras and other instruments by piling up 100 tons of TNT and exploding them. Although I could get only half the cameras ready for the test, we obtained a satisfactory record.

A few weeks before the actual bomb test Bob Bacher, our division leader, told me he was anxious to get a good movie of the explosion, whatever the yield might be. I promised him my cameras would give him what he wanted, and then, around July 1, I got a cinder in my eye and feared I would not be able to run my cameras for the test. We had doctors with us at Trinity, but none of them could see the cinder in my eyelid, where I said I thought it was. The pain grew so bad that I could not work, and I wanted to be allowed to go to an eye doctor in Albuquerque. Instead, an ophthalmologist from Los Alamos, Dr. Jack Brooks, was brought to me. "There it is, on the cornea," he said at once, and after giving me time to rest my eye so that I could hold still, he swept a knife blade laterally across the cornea and wiped the cinder off. Soon I was able to get back to the work of camera installation.

July 16, 1945, came. By 3:00 a.m. we were at our camera stations preparing to photograph the "Fat Man" explosion on top of the 100-foot tower. When I reached our 10,000 yard north station, it was raining; and since the weather people did not think the rain would stop by the 4:00 a.m. firing time, a new time was set at 5:30. By 5:00 the weather was clearing, and shortly thereafter the countdown started. I removed the waterproof covers from the

Mitchell and other cameras on the roof of my bunker, sat down behind the Mitchell, and listened on the intercom to the countdown from the timing station at south 10,000. I shivered partly from thoughts about the expected explosion and partly from the wet cold desert air. Then, at minus 30 seconds the cameras began to run. At once I tried to look at the tower through the welding glass filter at the viewfinder but saw nothing until zero time was called, when I was blinded momentarily. The filter glass seemed to be lit up as bright as the sun. When I turned left and looked at the nearby Oscura mountains they looked brighter than by daylight; and when, a few seconds later, I looked once more through the camera viewfinder I saw a tremendous ball of fire rising at ground zero. Grabbing the aiming controls, I directed the camera to follow the ball of fire, which went out after perhaps twenty seconds. As had been expected, for about thirty seconds after zero the stupendous explosion was seen but not heard. Then, with a loud bang, the shock wave reached me, followed again by silence. If there were reverberations, I failed to notice them. The ball of smoke continued to rise, enclosed in a blue halo of ionized air caused by the intense radioactivity. For perhaps thirty seconds, the halo was visible. At sixty seconds after the start of the explosion a large photoflash bomb on the ground illuminated the dark smoke and enabled us to get a well-exposed photograph at that late time. At ten minutes the rising smoke cloud and column had moved towards the northeast, and part of it was beginning to settle on the desert.

My first thoughts about this fantastic display of explosive power were that the bomb had exceeded our greatest expectations, that the war would be quickly over, and that many American lives would be saved. But a reddish haze was settling on us, and Conrad and I began unloading the film from our cameras. While radiation monitors called for us to get into the evacuation vehicles, I quickly finished unloading the exposed film. The vehicles had no difficulty driving across the sandy desert to the main road, a few miles to the west. Afterwards it was determined from our radiation badges that Conrad and I had received a small amount of radiation from the settling haze.

From Los Alamos I took my 35-mm camera films to the Wendover Army Air Base for processing and back in Los Alamos projected the films at the next colloquium. Even I was amazed that I had made such spectacular pictures. Before the first bomb was dropped on Japan, General Groves asked for the Trinity movies, and when I delivered three Mitchell-camera films to him in Washington he sent me with the film to the Naval Motion Picture Laboratory to have duplicate negatives prepared for newsreel release. When I told the laboratory chief about the printing problems to be overcome in order to make good prints, he simply said, "Can do." Before long movie houses throughout the world showed the pictures of the spectacular Trinity explosion.

BEHIND TALL FENCES

Since the Japanese surrender did not come immediately after the first bomb was dropped on Hiroshima on August 6, a second atomic bomb was dropped on Nagasaki on August 9. On August 14, Japan accepted the surrender terms, and WWII was ended. The first reaction at Los Alamos was elation that our work had ended the war so quickly, but the mood changed as the realization grew that control of nuclear energy was a problem not easily solved.

Meanwhile many of the brilliant scientists who had built the bombs were preparing their final reports and getting ready to leave the laboratory. Julian Mack was one of these. He felt that he had trained me well enough during the war so that I could carry out most of the work of the optics group while he completed his reports. From this time on he no longer concerned himself with the work of the group.

All of us, with the war over and work going at a slower pace, had more time for outside activities, sometimes with unintended consequences. For instance, one Sunday morning my wife and I decided to attend a special church service, partly for the worldly purpose of displaying our two small daughters dressed in their Sunday best. But as is often the way with the best laid plans of proud parents, we ran into trouble on the way. Our eldest daughter decided to have a tantrum. Paying no attention to the gravel over which we were walking, she threw herself down on the path. A sharp stone cut a deep inch-long gash in her forehead, and since it was Sunday morning the doctors were all sleeping late after a party the night before. At the hospital a resourceful nurse put on a temporary bandage and sent out a call for the doctors, meanwhile preparing gallons of coffee. The coffee did the trick, and in less than an hour my daughter had been put to sleep. The stitching the doctors did was so effective that only a small scar—which quickly faded—remained. One more example of the excellent Army medical service we enjoyed.

A second adventure was pleasanter. During September Julian Mack organized a trip to Gallup, New Mexico, to see the Inter-tribal Indian Ceremonials. We were a large group. In addition to the Mack family (Julian, Mary, Newell, and Cornelia), there were Dick Feynman (his wife had died in Albuquerque of tuberculosis just as the war was ending), two other single young men, and the Brixner family (my wife and me, minus our daughters). At the hotel where we stayed in downtown Gallup, Dick, no longer obliged to hide under a wartime code name made the mistake of registering under his own name, Dr. Richard Feynman. In consequence he spent several nights being paged to give medical attention to various other hotel guests. In addition to enjoying Dick's dilemma, we also enjoyed our three days at the ceremonials and afterwards visited several other points of interest: the Navajo Agency Center at Window Rock, the Indian school at Ganado, the painted desert, and several trading posts.

AFTER THE BOMB

Although there was much debate about the future of the laboratory, Norris Bradbury, the newly appointed director, was one of those who predicted a bright future, and he was assembling a staff for continuing operations. Mack told me he thought I was competent to lead our group's activities, and after Bradbury approved me as group leader, I decided to stay. My main work during the next few years was photographing atomic explosions at Bikini, Eniwetok, and the Nevada test site, using techniques developed at Trinity. That photography was subsequently transferred to the firm of Edgerton, Germeshausen, and Grier.

Meanwhile at Los Alamos, where research continued on high-explosive shock waves, there was a demand for new cameras that would give better time and space resolution than could be obtained with the existing sweeping-slit-image and explosive-flashlight cameras. During 1950 our group took the lead in the development of turbine driven mirrors that could be run up to their bursting speeds. Since we were lucky in having in the group two engineers (W.E. Buck and R.W. Prichard) who were especially interested in mirrors of that type, we could soon make rotating mirrors of any desired size or shape. The fastest turbine drove a 10-mm mirror at 24,000 revolutions per second. For some years, however, we had difficulty with rotating mirror vibration, until in the 1960s, M.A. Winkler made a systematic analysis that helped us reduce the trouble.

It was during those early years that I modified and improved various existing cameras and even, in 1947, invented a new camera. This new camera—a simplified version of the sweeping-slit-image camera—gained for us a resolution of 10^{-8} second that could be used for a variety of explosion studies—including spectroscopy. Also, I helped develop the first megacycle framing camera at Los Alamos. It all started with A.W. Campbell's borrowed Bowen 76-lens framing camera that had a maximum speed of 400,000 pictures per second. The idea was to increase the speed of that camera. First we substituted a faster rotating mirror, thus increasing the speed to 1,500,000 pictures per second. Then, later, we substituted an even faster mirror and increased the speed to 3,000,000. Now, after that experience with an explosion-synchronized framing camera, I began to see a way to engineer a camera design of our own, one that would make larger pictures with better image quality and that would at the same time retain the megacycle picture rate. Within a year the new camera was built and soon became popular for explosion research. The camera was later widely copied and refined by camera manufacturers. For special problems we also made other models of the camera, some with speeds up to 15,000,000 pictures per second, some working at optical apertures up to f/4.0. For nuclear bomb explosions—which could not be synchronized with the rotating mirror—I invented a continuous writing camera that ran as fast as 3,500,000 pictures per second.

It was during 1950, also, that I ventured into the field of lens design. I had found it difficult to have manufactured to our performance specifications the special lenses needed for our new cameras. I would not have thought of designing my own lenses, however, without the invention by R.H. Stark and D.B. MacMillan of the now essential floating-decimal-point calculation procedure, a method that made it practical for engineers to make and use complex computing codes for their work. At that time, also, Stark and W.A. Allen made an easy-to-use ray tracing code for me; and then, with the aid of A.J. Lipinski, I was able to optimize lens performance by a simple graphic analysis scheme. In later years mathematicians J.C. Holladay and C.A. Lehman automated my earlier procedure, thus greatly increasing my designing capability. The result was that I was now able, with relative ease, to obtain lenses of my own design from commercial lens-fabrication shops. In addition, our group was soon designing special lenses needed for other projects at the Laboratory.

During the next twenty years the group continued to refine its engineering capabilities. We published a total of more than fifty scientific papers describing our methods and the capabilities of our work.

---

*Berlyn Brixner, an Albuquerque still photographer who had been documenting environmental conservation practices in the Southwest, came to Los Alamos in July 1943. His interest in scientific photography led him later to design and build improved high-speed cameras for photographing explosion experiments. He retired from the Laboratory in 1978.

THE FIRST IMPLOSION AT LOS ALAMOS
Charles L. Critchfield*

The original concept of using high explosives as a method of producing a critical mass of fissile material in a very short time was brought to the project by Seth Neddermeyer in the spring of 1943. In those days, for all one knew about how rapidly the material had to be assembled to avoid a fizzle it was thought that its assembly could be accomplished by using conventional artillery propellants and stopping the projectile inside its target where the system would be supercritical.

Seth's idea was to surround a hollow cylinder of active material whose dimensions were incapable of sustaining a fast neutron chain reaction, of course, by enough TNT to blow it into a solid cylinder in which the fast chain reaction would take place.

By July 4, 1943, O-Division (O for Ordnance) had been formed under the leadership of Captain W.S. Parsons, USN, and had acquired some TNT plus the primacord, etc., required to detonate it. On that Independence Day, Seth invited Captain Parsons, who was his supervisor, and Parsons's other scientific staff, which comprised Ed McMillan, Hugh Bradner, John Streib, and myself, to find a suitable place on South Mesa to demonstrate his theory. We took our explosives along with some ordinary kitchen stovepipe and some lengths of 2" cast iron sewer pipe to a spot near where Otowi building now stands. We packed the TNT around the sewer pipe, inside the stove pipe, equipped it with the detonating system including 50 yards of primacord to a sheltering rock where the six of us took cover and set off the experiment.

By coincidence this "haywire" experiment proved just the correct combination to blow the iron pipe into a solid mass and keep it that way. A lovely demonstration of Seth's idea.

Captain Parsons excused himself shortly afterwards because Martha, his wife, was a dedicated horse-woman and "Deak," as he was known, wished to drive over to Pecos to buy a saddle horse. After it was assumed that Deak was out of earshot, we loaded our remaining stove pipe with the remaining TNT and the five of us set off the biggest fire cracker we ever had in all our lives.

Deak conceded that Seth's experiment was interesting but regarded any pursuit of the idea to be a diversion of effort from the more urgent program of designing and testing the gun-assembly. Nevertheless, Seth persisted in his study and acquired an able staff whose work remained unnoticed until that autumn when John von Neumann visited Los Alamos and reported on recent results with shaped charges at Aberdeen Proving Ground in Maryland. He was impressed by the very high pressures which result in "focussing" high-explosive detonations and emphasized the possible importance of such systems in assembling the nuclear device.

It is strange that Seth did not accept the idea of compressing the active material during implosion. He believed in the advantage of merely forming a static critical mass. Deak held onto his conviction that the only reliable method of assembly was to use a gun. In fact he neglected even to mention the possible use of high explosives to General Groves. However, Oppenheimer quickly acquired the consulting services of George Kistiakowsky, director of the Explosives Research Laboratory at Bruceton, who later joined the staff at Los Alamos in February 1944.

When Groves learned of these developments he came here and addressed the entire Coordinating Council to the effect that he had tried to tell us that the best way to make a bomb was to blow a hollow sphere together with high explosives, and that he expected his field officer to keep him informed of such important prospects. It was evident that Captain Parsons felt severely reprimanded.

By April 1944 it became clear that the implosion was essential to the use of plutonium and its technical development was put under Kistiakowsky in a separate division, "X". Neddermeyer joined Don Kerst in the betatron program for x-raying implosions. He and Don had acquired serious doubts concerning their participation in developing the bomb, on moral grounds. They even turned down their invitations to the Trinity test which was to prove the validity of the implosion system.

Instead they drove up above S-Site and watched the flash from there, about 130 miles due north of the shot. That was the largest firecracker anyone had seen, up to that day, July 16, 1945, two years and twelve days after Seth's first implosion.

---

*Charles L. Critchfield came to Los Alamos in April 1943 to work on sabots, implosion techniques, and critical assembly problems. He left shortly after the war and taught physics at George Washington University, then was Professor of Physics at University of Minnesota from 1947 to 55, Director of Research at Convair from 1955 to 60, and returned to Los Alamos Scientific Laboratory in 1961, where he was prominent in leading its basic research programs and in developing relations with many universities. He retired in 1977, but maintained an active relationship with the Laboratory until his death in February 1994. He was a founder of the J. Robert Oppenheimer Memorial Committee.

RECOLLECTIONS OF PLUTONIUM METALLURGY WORK IN D-BUILDING
Edward F. Hammel[1]

Introduction

At Project Y, everyone came from somewhere else, and many of the staff had previously been involved in other parts of the Atomic Bomb Project. The following is an account of one such recruit's experiences as a wartime worker in D-Building.

On July 3, 1944, my wife, Caroline, and I were met at Lamy by a WAC driver, taken to Santa Fe where we were "processed" by Dorothy McKibbin, and then continued on via Espanola (still not knowing exactly where we were going) accompanied by a couple of other passengers who had been waiting for transportation at Dorothy's office. Not having been introduced while at 109 E. Palace, the conversation en route was relatively subdued until, more than halfway up the hill, at what is now called the Clinton P. Anderson overlook, Caroline surprised everyone by announcing, "I know where we're going. It's to Los Alamos. I've got a picture taken from this very spot." Most astonished was probably the WAC driver, who had been explicitly ordered to provide no information to anyone about our destination. Then Caroline explained. She had spent the summer of 1937 at Brush Ranch (near Tererro along the Pecos River) and one of their "field trips" was a visit to the Los Alamos Boys School and Bandelier National Monument!

After arriving at Los Alamos and surviving the customary "processing and familiarization procedures," we were taken to our apartment (the last Sundt at the western edge of town on Trinity Drive). Shortly thereafter, my new boss, Eric Jette, turned up to invite us to his place for the evening. With a fire burning in the fireplace (it had been cold and raining since arriving at Lamy), the Jettes' hospitality more than compensated for the trials and tribulations of getting ourselves out here.

The next morning at D-Building, I was introduced to the rest of Eric Jette's group (CM-8, Uranium and Plutonium Metallurgy), and filled in regarding my new job responsibilities, which were to take over the Plutonium Remelting, Alloying, and Casting Section from T.T. Magel.

Background

It is appropriate to interrupt these recollections to remind the reader that, until mid-1942, the scientific and engineering problems relating to the development of <u>atomic weapons</u> had been assigned the Metallurgical Laboratory (Met Lab) in Chicago and the direction of that program was the responsibility of Gregory Breit. Given the Met Lab's preoccupation with the production of plutonium, however, much of the actual weapons work was carried out by contractors, including a group led by J. Robert Oppenheimer at the University of California. In June 1942, Breit was replaced by Oppenheimer as director of this portion of the operation. Four months later, it became clear that an altogether new project would be required for the development of a nuclear weapon and in November 1942, Los Alamos was selected as the site of the new laboratory.

Before Los Alamos Laboratory became operational, one configuration of the weapon under serious consideration was a gun-like device in which two subcritical masses of fissionable material (one comprising the target and the other the projectile) would be rapidly assembled to produce a supercritical mass capable of sustaining a fast neutron (and hence an explosive) chain reaction. Another option simultaneously being considered, but at a lower priority, was the "implosion" device, in which supercriticality would be achieved by initiating a spherically-symmetric shock wave convergent upon a subcritical mass of active material. The resulting compression would yield a supercritical fissile core, also capable of sustaining an explosive chain reaction. The main difficulty with the implosion idea was how to design, construct, and detonate an explosive system capable of reliably yielding a spherically-symmetric convergent shock wave.

The Los Alamos Assignment

Regardless of the type of weapon built, the tasks facing the staff of the new project were daunting. Specifications and performance estimates for the weapon designs had to be determined or updated by the theoretical physicists, e.g. critical masses, predetonation probabilities, purity tolerances for the active material, efficiencies, damage estimates, etc.; the jobs of the experimental physicists were to obtain the necessary nuclear data, e.g. cross sections, neutron numbers, spontaneous fission rates, etc.; those of the chemists and metallurgists were to provide the necessary materials (in the sizes, shapes and purities required); and the ordnance experts were expected to develop the technology for creating the supercritical mass, to carry out the weapon's engineering design, and to ensure that its various components could be assembled into an operational weapon. Finally, the health personnel endeavored to minimize the hazards to which the staff was exposed and to treat any member of the Laboratory unlucky enough to have suffered exposure to radioactive or other hazardous materials.[2]

Among the events that occurred shortly after the establishment of Los Alamos Laboratory, one relevant to our story was a series of five lectures, delivered by Robert Serber during the first two weeks of April 1943. These lectures were designed to serve as an "indoctrination course" for the staff members recruited to get the project under way. Immediately, thereafter, Oppenheimer organized a series of conferences involving the senior staff at which a more detailed "Outline of Present Knowledge" was presented. The technical components of the Los Alamos R&D program were identified, remaining uncertainties and problems were discussed, relevant production schedules for the various Los Alamos programs were developed, and priorities were established for each major organizational entity of the project. Following this overview of the entire program, twelve more-specialized "Post Conference Discussions" were held during the week of April 27th, during which the most important topics were reviewed in detail by the individuals directly involved.

Chemistry and Metallurgy at Los Alamos

The chemistry and the metallurgy carried out at Los Alamos, one portion of which is the main topic of these recollections, had a somewhat controversial history. At the time Los Alamos was being organized, most of the expertise in plutonium chemistry resided at the Met Lab in Chicago and this body of information was constantly being upgraded and extended to optimize the plutonium extraction processes being carried out at Hanford and Oak Ridge. Attention was also being given at Chicago to the production and the properties of plutonium metal.

In view of this head-start, when Los Alamos began operation in March 1943, the division of labor between its chemical and metallurgical R&D programs and those under way elsewhere in the Manhattan Project (particularly those at the Met Lab) had not been agreed upon. The issue was not settled until May, when a special review committee appointed by General Groves and chaired by W. K. Lewis of MIT, recommended that the final purification of plutonium, reduction to its metallic state, determination of the metal's relevant physical and metallurgical properties, and the development of the necessary weapon fabrication technologies be carried out at Los Alamos. The reasons for this recommendation were not only that the Los Alamos Project would be responsible for the correct functioning of the weapon, but also that a considerable amount of plutonium reprocessing and repurification work would be an inevitable consequence of the research still to be carried out. This decision resulted in the most efficient organizational arrangement (from the standpoint of minimizing the time required for performing that research).

Minimizing the time spent to solve weapons R&D problems was a constant concern for the Los Alamos staff. Many of us had already participated in the costly isotope separation and plutonium production projects at sites X, W and their parent university laboratories, and we therefore knew that their engineering and construction phases were proceeding more or less on schedule, when their production phases were likely to begin, and what the expected production rates would be. Our current task was to make sure that, after enough active material had been delivered to Los Alamos to fabricate a weapon, that weapon could and would be built without further delay and then either tested or delivered to the Air Force for combat use. For the Chemistry and Metallurgy (CM) Division personnel, these concerns were intensified by the facts that: a) many important unanswered questions still existed regarding plutonium's chemical and metallurgical properties (these had to be answered before the metal could be fabricated into satisfactory weapon components), b) not until late 1943 did the first milligram quantities of plutonium begin to arrive in Los Alamos, c) the first gram amounts did not arrive until March 1944, and d) quantity shipments of Pu did not begin to arrive at Los Alamos until May 1945.

Concentrating now on the chemical and metallurgical activities, it is clear that the purification of plutonium would be receiving the most attention. Achieving the specified impurity limits was essential for the success of the project and it was expected to be a difficult task. The reason why the plutonium had to be so highly purified was that: a) the alpha particle emission rate for Pu is well over 1000 times that of enriched uranium, b) when these alpha particles collide with an impurity nucleus (especially with that of a light element) neutrons are created from (α-n) reactions, c) the resulting neutron background will (unless the impurities are reduced to the specified levels) increase the chance of initiating a fast fission chain reaction in the Pu well before the planned post-firing condition of maximum supercriticality is attained, and d) if that happens, the result will be a predetonation or a "fizzle," in which very little of the active material fissions before the entire assembly is blown apart.

Despite recognition of the impurity problem, little research was done on it at Los Alamos during the first eight or nine months because adequate supplies of plutonium were nonexistent during that period. One project undertaken almost immediately, however, was the design and construction of a facility in which the projected chemistry and metallurgy could be carried out with minimal contamination of the active materials being worked on by light element dust particles settling out from the air. This laboratory was designated "D-Building" and, after the decision of the Lewis Committee in May to construct such a laboratory, one of the important tasks of the senior CM Division staff was, in collaboration with the architect and, in particular, with C.A. Thomas,[3] the setting of specifications for the building, monitoring the design work and, subsequently, the construction phase. The result was a laboratory as nearly dust-free as the air conditioning technology available at that time permitted. Construction was completed and the building occupied in December 1943.

Concurrently, in temporary quarters and continuing through March 1944, when the division was more formally organized, the members of CM Division were engaged in a variety of tasks far too numerous to detail here. Most of them have already been described in other accounts of the Laboratory's early days. It may be of interest, however, to comment on the general *modus operandi* during the first eight to ten months of the Division's existence. April, May, and June of 1943 were spent primarily on the acquisition of personnel, equipment and materials, on organizational details, on getting highly specialized laboratories in operation, etc. J.W. Kennedy was appointed the Acting CM Division Leader and C.S. Smith served as an Acting Associate Division Leader for Metallurgy. The initial staff of chemists and metallurgists totaled about twenty professionals assisted soon afterward by roughly an equal number of technicians.* During this same period the functional structure of the division began to emerge. The two main organizational entities were obviously chemistry and metallurgy, but within those categories, small specialized groups were soon established. In the chemistry area, a clear need arose for expertise in radiochemistry, analytical chemistry, purification chemistry, and general or service-related chemistry. Then, in addition to synthesizing materials requested by other parts of the project, it was required that they be fabricated into various shapes with specified (and confirmed) physical and chemical properties. These last-mentioned tasks were carried out by the metallurgical and the analytical groups.

Because of the informality of the division's organizational structure, its early accomplishments were recorded in a series of LA or LAMS [Los Alamos or Los Alamos manuscript] reports, each dealing with a problem assigned to and reported on by an individual member or members of the division. Very brief semimonthly or monthly memoranda were also filed by the Division Leader summarizing the results of these topical reports. It is also worth noting that essentially all of the technical personnel in CM Division were experimentalists. As such, much of their work had, not surprisingly, a strong empirical content.

The Metal Reduction Program

One of the topics studied intensively from the outset was metal reduction. The Los Alamos approach to this problem was built in large measure upon the chemical and metallurgical research on uranium carried out at Iowa State University, Ames, Iowa, under the direction of F. H. Spedding on uranium and on up to milligram quantities of plutonium at the Met Lab in

---

*By July 1945 the CM-Division personnel had increased to 800.

Chicago, initially under the direction of G. T. Seaborg and later, also under J. Chipman. This inheritance included the technology of reducing uranium halides using an exothermic metallothermic (thermite) reaction, e.g. $UF_4 + 2Ca$ $U + 2CaF_2$ and, since this approach eventually turned out to be the most successful, it was finally selected as the reduction technology of choice for both the enriched uranium and the plutonium used in the weapon. For plutonium, however, a considerable amount of additional research was required to determine the optimal reduction conditions.

As noted in the first progress report on metal reduction, October 1943, the Los Alamos experimental program on the reduction of uranium was carried out "for the ... purpose of developing in detail methods that could be applied directly for the reduction of 25^4 [U^{235}] when it became available and to provide experience with a variety of methods, one or more of which would eventually be adaptable to work on 49." More specifically, the initial metal reduction work was focused on high yield reduction techniques and reduction techniques capable of producing extremely high purity product.

To achieve these objectives, five competing metal reduction technologies were investigated during 1943 and early 1944 using uranium as a stand-in for plutonium. These were metallothermic reductions, electrolysis of fused salts, hot wire reductions, reductions using atomic hydrogen, and reductions of the oxide with silicon and, later, with carbon. As noted above, of these, only the first-mentioned survived.[5] Most of the remaining discussion will therefore be focused upon that technology.

The first metallothermic reductions at Los Alamos (called bomb reductions) were carried out by R.D. Baker, involved the uranium halides, and were on the 10 and 100 gram scales. Mindful of the impurity and yield problems, these studies were focused upon a) finding a refractory which would neither react with the metal produced (thereby introducing impurities) nor be so porous as to absorb any of the resulting liquid metal or the molten salts, and b) finding that combination of process variables which would optimize the yield. For uranium, the most satisfactory initial results were found to be: reduction of UF_4 with Ca; use of 1/7 mole I_2 booster per mole of UF_4; use of about 25% excess Ca, –20 to +30 mesh, and free of oxide; and use of a MgO refractory fired at 2100-2200°C.

After resolving these "process" issues for uranium, another emerged, namely the existence of scale-dependent yields. In general, reductions carried out under the conditions described above yielded (on the 100 g scale) clean, relatively pure, well formed, coherent, non-porous regulae of uranium metal. On the 10 gram scale and especially on the 1 gram scale, however, a number of very low yield reactions occurred in which "only beads of metal formed" or, "the button was porous" or, "beads of metal were held in the slag" or, "only powdered metal resulted," etc. These results warranted further study to determine the cause or causes of such phenomena.

It had been expected that, since thermite-type reactions are strongly exothermic and since (at temperatures high enough to initiate the process) the added reaction heat should yield and maintain the products in their molten states, the metal produced in these smaller scale reductions would separate from the less dense slag and coalesce into a homogeneous mass at the bottom of the bomb's refractory liner in much the same way as in the larger scale reductions. As noted above, however, this did not occur and, after some analysis, it was recognized that the extent to which coalescence occurs was a function of the melting points of the metal and the slag, the viscosity of the slag, the surface to volume ratios of the metal particles formed in the reaction, the reaction rate, and the rate at which the reaction heat is lost to the environment.

Obviously, all reductions of both enriched uranium and plutonium would eventually be carried out on a large scale basis, but in early 1944 an immediate need existed for coherent, well defined specimens of metallic plutonium to permit the measurement of this new element's physical and nuclear properties. Hence, the importance of and the urgency for being able to accomplish satisfactory reductions of plutonium salts to the metal on the one gram scale as soon as such quantities became available.

Inasmuch as the optimal process variables had already been successfully determined for large scale uranium reductions (and those for plutonium were expected to be similar), taking additional time to determine new ones suitable only for small scale operations was considered an option of last resort. One alternative "solution," already successfully used for even smaller scale reductions at the Met Lab, was to increase substantially the probability of forming a single metallic button by replacing the gravitational coalescing force with an easily achievable and much larger centrifugal inertial force. To that end R.D. Baker constructed, in early January 1944, a centrifuge with a graphite rotor capable of accommodating two steel bombs. Magnesia and also thoria liners were used. When loaded with the usual 1 gram uranium stand-in charges and covered with lids of the same refractory material, the liners were inserted into the steel bombs (which were themselves securely capped) and placed in opposite cylindrical slots in the bottom half of the rotor; the top half was then bolted on. After placing the bomb assembly within a 4 inch diameter induction coil and attaching the rotor axis through a pulley and belt system to a motor, rotation was begun. When the desired rotational speed (yielding a centrifugal acceleration of about 50 G) had been obtained, the induction coil was turned on and the unit was heated at 3 kW until "firing" occurred.

BEHIND TALL FENCES

Between January 12 and January 31, 1944, Baker carried out 28 one gram scale UF_4 centrifuge reductions. For the first 15 he used MgO liners (with one exception) and the standard charge, varying only the rotational speed. The results were both mixed and erratic. In the remaining 13, the amount of iodine booster used was first doubled, then tripled and then quadrupled. Even with these changes, yields were uniformly poor and in only a few runs were coherent, consolidated buttons of metallic uranium obtained. Obviously, the centrifuge approach was not going to be "a piece of cake"! Furthermore, Baker's stationary bomb program still demanded an active research program: improving the purity of the reduced metal, further liner testing, reducing the melting point of the slags by adding "inert" salts to form lower melting eutectics, measuring ignition temperatures for different reactant charge ratios, etc.

Under these conditions, it became abundantly clear that additional, knowledgeable staff was urgently needed, and the most likely source was the Met Lab. Following a formal request in mid January, it was agreed that T.T. Magel and his assistant, N. E. Dallas, would transfer to Project Y as soon as possible. Both were active and highly regarded members of the Met Lab's metal production group, both had worked on small scale metal reduction problems, and both were familiar with centrifuge reduction technology. They arrived at Los Alamos on February 3, 1944, and made their first centrifuge reduction on February 11th using UF_4 and Ca (80 mesh) with an I_2 booster in a BeO crucible. During the next three weeks over 100 uranium stand-in reductions were carried out (~4 in each centrifuge run) in which different reductants, different crucible materials, different crucible and bomb designs, different amounts of reactants (i.e. different stoichiometries), and different firing conditions (times, temperatures, layering of reactants, reactant mesh sizes, etc.) were all carefully studied.

What emerged from this first series of experiments was the fact that, under essentially the same conditions, centrifuge and stationary bomb reductions yielded significantly different results. Specifically, UF_4 reduced with Ca (plus I_2 as a booster), which was the optimal charge for a stationary bomb, produced poor quality metal in the centrifuge. For the latter, Li was the reductant of choice for reducing UF_4, UF_3 or UCl_3. Furthermore, BeO (rather than MgO) was found to be the preferred refractory and no I_2 booster appeared necessary. Finally, when Pu became available it was quickly recognized that U was a poor stand-in for Pu. Because the melting point of Pu was so much lower than expected, satisfactory Pu metal was reproducibly obtained only when reduction temperatures were reduced by about 300°C.

By March 2nd, enough plutonium nitrate had been delivered to the Laboratory to enable the chemists to prepare sufficient pure PuF_3 to yield about 50 mg of the metal. Using the centrifuge, Magel and Dallas then made their first attempt to reduce that halide to the metal with Ca together with an I_2 booster[6]. The experiment was unsuccessful: "Only a grayish cokey mass was found in the tip of the cone; reduction appeared to have occurred, but no agglomeration." A second 50 mg attempt to prepare the metal was made with a second batch of PuF_3 on March 8th at a slightly higher temperature, for a shorter heating time, using Li as the reducing agent and again, with I_2 as a booster. This run resulted in a well-formed, clean, shiny 20 mg button. Although the yield was only 40%, it was the first unequivocal production of plutonium metal at Los Alamos.

---

[1] Edward F. Hammel came to Los Alamos in July 1944 from Princeton University, having begun work on the Manhattan District's P–9 (heavy water) project in mid-1941, to undertake studies of the properties of plutonium that would allow its alloying and fabrication into a form suitable for use in the bomb. He remained with the Laboratory at the end of the war to pursue a career in low temperature physics and superconductivity. He retired in 1979 and still maintains an active association with the Laboratory.

This article is dedicated to the memory of Eric R. Jette.

[2] The preceding paragraph mentions only the scientific and engineering personnel at Project Y. Clearly, the work could never have succeeded without the dedicated service of its support personnel: machinists, technicians, purchasing agents, "expediters," communications personnel, secretaries, custodians, etc. Many of the technical and the support personnel were members of the military [the Special Engineer Detachment (SED) and the Women's Army Corps (WAC)]. Other military personnel were responsible for the remaining services required at military sites such as Los Alamos.

[3] Research Director of the Monsanto Chemical Company who had been appointed by General Groves coordinator for all of the Pu purification work being carried out by the Manhattan Project.

[4] The code designation for ^{235}U was "25" and "49" for ^{239}Pu.

[5] Termed a "bomb" reduction because it was carried out in a sealed steel cylinder lined with a refractory (called the liner). Before firing, the air inside the bomb was replaced by an inert gas such as argon. The steel bomb was placed in an induction coil and heated by a high frequency generator capable of heating the bomb to a temperature of about 1400°C in 1 minute., e.g. which halide to reduce, at what temperature, how long a holding time at temperature, the rate at which that temperature was achieved, use or non-use of a so-called "booster" to react exothermically with excess reductant (thereby introducing additional heat locally to maintain the reaction products in a liquid state for a longer period of time, reducing the melting point of the mixed slag, and possibly helping to initiate the main reaction), amount of booster (if used), variations from strictly stoichiometric amounts of reactants, etc.

[6] Despite the fact that they had already convinced themselves that the preferable reductant was Li, so many Los Alamos reductions had successfully used Ca and an I_2 booster that they were probably "persuaded" to try this combination first.

TIMING ON THE TRINITY BOMB EXPLOSION
Joseph L. McKibben*

On April 23, 1945, I was approached by Robert Wilson, P-Division Leader, and John Williams, my Group Leader. They had an urgent job for me. They wanted me to get involved in timing for the two tests at the Trinity site. In these tests it was essential that all the observational equipment be activated in coordination with the ignition of the explosion, so a complicated timing system was under construction.

The first test was scheduled for May 7, when 100 tons of TNT were to be exploded. The primary purpose of this test was to calibrate the shock-wave measuring instruments. It was also to be an exercise in using the cameras and other diagnostic equipment, and for that they needed the timing equipment to be in operation. E.W. Marlowe, who had been hired to do the timing, had just requested that the test be postponed two weeks so he could get his equipment into operational condition. But the Trinity test was on a tight schedule and other requests for delay of the 100-ton shot had been turned down. I was pointedly requested to see to it that the equipment was assembled and installed on time at the test site. The explosion was to take place on schedule, and that was only two weeks away.

Marlowe was expert in relay equipment and had obtained equipment from Union Switch and Signal. This company made signaling equipment for the operation of railroads so their relays were of the highest quality. The basic units of this equipment were four 32-position stepping relays. The many individual relays of each 32-position assembly were in a well-sealed box of moderate size. A stepping relay was advanced one step when the 5-mA DC current in the twisted-pair line to it was reversed. A particular piece of operational equipment was to be activated by a stick-polar relay, and these were also in well-sealed cases. If it was to be activated at the time associated with step 11, then the relay got a current from the stepping relay when it arrived at position 11, which closed it. A stick-polar relay stays closed until it is opened by a signal of the opposite polarity and vice versa.

Bunkers for observational equipment were located at S10,000 yards, W10,000 yards and N10,000 yards from the place where the explosions were to take place, and a relay station was to be located at each bunker. The fourth relay station was to be located at W800 yards and it turned on observational equipment near ground zero and relays for detonating the explosion in a safe manner. The timing signals were generated by equipment located at S10,000.

At the time I became involved in this project, Marlowe had just received the relays and the wooden boxes to put them in. He had two SED assistants to assemble them, namely Walter Treibel and Roger Moore. I was alternate group leader of P-2, which operated the two Van de Graaff accelerators. I made technicians out of several members of the group; some were Ph.D's. Marlowe was kept quite busy supplying the wiring diagrams.

Marlowe did not have a device to generate the timing signals, so Clarence Turner and I designed a timing drum. The drum was to make one revolution per second starting at minus 45 seconds. Two rows of pins were placed on the drum to activate a pair of microswitches. These operated the stick-polar relay that reversed the current in the twisted-pair lines to the four stations. Turner went to our little machine shop and built the device on schedule.

Four days before the 100 tons of TNT were to be exploded, we loaded the equipment onto a weapons carrier and took off for the test site. At the assigned gas station in Albuquerque, we became aware that one tire on the weapons carrier was failing rapidly and we had no spare. So Sgt. Walter Treibel took the jeep we had along and went to Kirtland Air Force Base. He soon returned with a tire. I have no idea of the story he told to get that tire.

The next morning Marlowe and his two assistants went to the outlying sites and installed equipment there. I stayed at S10,000 and wired it up. I did not have time to go and see the 100 tons of TNT stacked up. We only had time to do a small amount of checking up on the operation of our equipment. The 100-ton test presented us with a few failures, but with such a tight schedule that was not unexpected.

The reactions of Marlowe and me to these failures were quite different. I believed that we had excellent equipment, but some more work was needed to assemble it into reliable operating condition. For example, Marlowe had designed each station to consist of three separate boxes connected together with multiple-prong plugs. To use such plugs in a region with a large amount of fine gypsum powder present was foolish. Several of the twisted-pair lines between the bunkers were not continuous and we had no time to locate the faults. We needed a few dry runs so the overall system could be checked out.

Marlowe was aware of a much more elaborate system that was used on some railroad operations and which was also made by Union Switch and Signal. The system, upon command to carry out a particular operation, responded with a message that indicated whether it had succeeded or not. He obtained permission to purchase this equipment—I was not consulted. However, the use of it required sending radio-frequency signals over a heavy copper wire. Installation of the heavy wire in the short time left would have been quite a chore. I was also afraid that learning to use it and getting it together properly would require more time that we had available. Besides, I did not believe its use would significantly improve the reliability of our timing operation. In the meantime, I was informed that the full responsibility for the timing on the so-called Gadget shot was mine. After a meeting in which Marlowe's method was explained to those users that came, I decided not to use it.

The relay equipment of each station was then packaged into single long boxes. The three bunker stations were designed to stand vertically while the W800 station was designed to be placed horizontally in a shelter dug into the ground. Output switches, pilot lights and user names were placed on each of the boxes. Also posted on each station was a sheet listing the users and times of all 32 steps. After assembly, the equipment was connected together as it would be at the test site, and the fact that it operated correctly was demonstrated. I also wrote an operating procedure for the overall timing operation. We started installing equipment at the test site in late June. I was assisted in the above work by SEDs Treibel and Moore. Lester Guttman also assisted me at Trinity.

The use of a few high-speed cameras to observe the fireball required the generation of three signals starting at minus 0.100 seconds before the pulse that detonated the bomb was sent out on a coax cable. These signals were generated electronically by Ernest Titterton of the British delegation. His chief assistant was Val Fitch—who was to win a Nobel prize in particle physics in 1980.

There were numerous dry runs using the timing equipment before the Gadget was installed in the tower. On one of these dry runs there was a lightning storm between S10,000 and the tower. A consequence of this storm was that the thyratron in the detonator circuit ignited prematurely. The early ignition was observed as a voltage drop on a meter connected to the detonator voltage supply, which was located on the timing meter panel. After considerable discussion, it was decided to connect a twisted-pair line in series with the line between the W800 station and the coils of the arming relays. A switch on this twisted-pair line was then installed in a locked box at S10,000 and therefore provided additional safety. During the countdown period Don Hornig, who had developed the detonation circuit, watched the detonator voltage and could have prevented these relays from being closed—and the bomb being detonated—and would have if he saw this voltage drop prematurely. The fact that all four of the arming relays were closed was guaranteed by sending the signal to Titterton's timer through series contacts on the relays.

At approximately 9 PM on July 15, Ken Bainbridge informed me that he, George Kistiakowsky, and I would be spending the night at the base of the tower to make certain that no one tampered with anything. I had been working very hard that day and was quite tired, so about 2:00 AM I lay down on the floor under the tower and went to sleep. However, we had a drizzle as it was a rainy night, and I awoke once, dreaming that Kistiakowsky was sprinkling the bomb with a garden hose. Bainbridge woke me up a while before we were to set off the bomb so that I would be alert.

When it was finally determined that the weather conditions were satisfactory to proceed with the detonation, Bainbridge announced, using the radio at the base of the tower and coded language, that we were arming the bomb and intended to detonate it at 5:30 AM. He then opened the locked box at the base of the tower and closed four switches. We next went to the station at W800 yards. Using an ohmmeter, I determined that all the outgoing lines were still continuous except the line that closed the arming relays, which was open inside a locked box at S10,000. I then closed the switch on each of these lines. We then went back to the base of the tower and Bainbridge announced over the radio that we were starting to drive to S10,000. We arrived there at minus 20 minutes, just in time for the first timing switch to be activated. We needed to get the test off by 5:30 AM because the Voice of America came on at that time and could have seriously interfered with our radio.

Sam Allison was the announcer on the radio and gave the countdown. He had a wonderfully senatorial voice. When I turned on the automatic timer at minus 45 seconds, a bell chimed every second to assist in the countdown.

The amount of light that came in the back door of the bunker was impressive. I did not see the fireball until about 13 seconds after the explosion, as I had to activate a timing switch at plus 10 seconds. When I saw the highly colored and turbulent fireball, felt the shock wave and heard the many echoes off the neighboring mountain peaks, I began to believe that the war would be soon over. I knew we had two bombs almost ready to use.

I wish to thank Walter Treibel for helping me recall some of the details and making suggestions on this story.

*Joseph L. McKibben came to Los Alamos in April 1943 from the University of Wisconsin and continued work on accelerator development and fast-neutron measurements began there. He remained at the Laboratory after the war, where he continued his career in nuclear physics. He retired in 1980 and continues to pursue his scientific interests.

THE MAKING OF THE BOMB
A Personal Perspective
Hugh T. Richards*

My involvement in the A-bomb project began during my graduate student days at Rice University during the period 1941–42.

In 1941 papers about uranium fission were conspicuous by their absence in physics journals. Hence an obvious implication was that a fission bomb was under consideration. I was therefore not completely surprised when sometime in January 1942 H. A. Wilson sounded me out on the possibility of undertaking (with Bennett) an OSRD project to measure energy spectra of fast neutrons.

Apparently Wilson had been at an earlier secret conference with Compton and others (probably at the U. of Chicago or in Washington). I suspect that Bonner also attended since he was the recognized expert on fast neutron energy measurements. Wilson told me that intelligence reports indicated that the Germans were working on a fission bomb. Perhaps a bomb was not feasible, but if the Germans could even produce large amounts of radioactivities, the military shock possibilities of dropping these on troops or cities might be important. Hence we must carefully explore the possibilities. I conjectured that Bonner believed that his radar work was more important and that Bennett and I could adequately handle the neutron measurements.

We accepted. Since the end of the first semester was near, I would devote full time to the project second semester. I had plenty of research results for my Ph.D. thesis and could use evenings to write up the material. Although I wouldn't formally receive my Ph.D. till June, I became a Research Associate at the then munificent rate of $2700 per annum. The schedule left me almost no free time, but I had already survived several years at Rice with minimal social life.

The new job triggered a security clearance investigation and required a birth certificate. I was born November 7, 1918, on a Colorado ranch without professional help. Dr. Tucker from Elkhart, Kansas, didn't arrive until it was all over, and apparently had neglected to file a birth certificate! However, my mother and Dr. Tucker were still alive and could file a late certificate even after a gap of 23 years and two months; hence the certifying doctor's signature is dated <u>January 22, 1942</u>! Dr. Tucker did stretch the truth by certifying that he attended the birth. My mother's handwriting fills in the family details on the certificate although her statement that my father was born in Coudey Co, Missouri, disagrees with all our other records. It should have been Nodaway Co, Missouri. In fact there is no Coudey Co, MO!

Professor Gregory Breit of the University of Wisconsin was then in charge of the fast neutron studies. Although he was our boss, we only dealt through H. A. Wilson who administered the Rice project. Many felt Breit was too security conscious. When he resigned in May 1952, Oppenheimer was chosen to replace Breit.

Our first task was to measure the energy spectrum of neutrons from $^{12}C + {^2H}$. Only later did we learn that the Minnesota group was using this reaction as a source of fast neutrons to measure important scattering cross sections; if the neutrons were not monoenergic, the measurements would be hard to interpret or useless. Since it was important to detect any low energy group of neutrons, the cloud chamber technique was our method of choice. (The range of a recoil in the gas of the cloud chamber is of course long compared to the range in the dense emulsion.) The geometry correction for recoils leaving the illuminated volume of the chamber is similar to the one I derived for the photographic emulsion case but was considerably more complicated. Bennett and I finally just solved it numerically for five different track lengths and then interpolated between them. We indeed found the neutrons to be monoenergic: our secret report was declassified after the war and published in the Physical Review, 71, 565, (1947).

Our next task was to measure the spectra of neutrons from the fission of ^{235}U. To this end Breit had arranged for a small (r about 3 cm) sphere of ordinary uranium to be manufactured to our design. We used the $^7Li + H$ source at a proton energy giving neutrons below that which would fission the ^{238}U isotope. Since the only known measurements were crude and especially inadequate for the low energy part of the fission neutron spectrum, again a cloud chamber with a hydrogen containing gas (e.g. ethane) was our technique.

The uranium sphere came in time to start on these measurements in July 1942. Although the general continuum shape of the spectrum one learns rather quickly, the cloud chamber technique was not practical for the high energy part of the spectrum. This later required my photographic emulsion method. Nor is it easy to deduce the true original ^{235}U spectrum since the fission neutrons can be inelastically scattered in the sphere and/or cloud chamber, and some of the higher energy fission neutrons will fission the ^{238}U isotope. To sort these effects out requires use of a smaller and/or enriched sphere. So fission neutron spectra would occupy my time for much of the next couple of years.

With Oppenheimer replacing Breit, we learned (at the end of the summer) that various separate OSRD contracts such as ours were to be consolidated into bigger projects with the goal being one central laboratory. To this end we were asked to go in October to the University of Minnesota to help them finish up various measurements of fast neutron scattering cross sections. Fortunately with my new salary, I had splurged and bought a low mileage second hand 1940 Plymouth two door sedan for $750. I kept this car for 13 years; then sold it to a UW grad student for $20! New cars were of course unavailable because of the war. With the uranium sphere in the glove compartment of the car, I took off for the north. The first leg of the trip was to the Met Lab at the University of Chicago where we were briefed by John Manley and Edward Teller.

Manley indicated the need for our helping finish the Minnesota fast neutron cross section measurement so we could all be assembled at a central location for bomb design. He wanted me also to continue on the spectrum measurement of fission neutrons.

Teller was (and is!) an intelligent and enthusiastic person with great imagination. Only later did I learn proper skepticism about his enthusiasms: e.g. in a postwar visit to Madison, he bewailed the fact that everything the physicists had tackled had worked! He noted that a 10% return on an investment is very good: he argued that we should be less conservative and push more far-out projects. By contrast, in political matters I realized even in this first 1942 contact that he was ultraconservative, e.g. he told me about his disappointment with the (to me far from radical) Chicago Daily News. Other Met Lab people attributed his political paranoia to his early experiences in Hungary with the Bolsheviks after WWI.

Platteville, Wisconsin, was on the way from Chicago to Minneapolis so I stopped there to visit my invalid Aunt Florence who was in a nursing home. I stayed at Judge A.W. Kopp's home. His wife was a good friend of my mother's and they lived only a block from our old Mineral St. home.

When I arrived in Minneapolis, Professor John H. Williams, head of the local effort, arranged for me to stay in the faculty guest rooms of the Coffman Memorial Union which was only a block from the physics building; there were also an underground garage for the car and a faculty dining room.

The U. of Minnesota electrostatic accelerator (completed just prior to WWII) was a _huge_ homemade vertical type (financed largely by the Rockefeller foundation) and housed in an outdoor steel cylinder (18 foot diameter!) to contain the pressurized insulating gas. The control room and labs were underground beneath the accelerator and connected to the physics building. Despite the large physical size, the peak terminal voltage (about 3 MeV) did not equal Herb's smaller (6.5 foot diameter) horizontal machine at Wisconsin; however, the sparks from the terminal (9 foot diameter) to the wall made an impressive sound! The large outdoor container resulted in both pluses and minuses: 1) access for servicing was through the bottom and one need not remove the hoops since one could climb up inside the hoops and insulator support system; 2) the temperature changes of the accelerator system followed the outdoor Minnesota temperatures despite a radiator installed in the bottom of the cylinder. One consequence was that the wax which sealed sections of the vacuum tube became brittle enough when the outdoor temperature dropped to < -20°F that a vacuum leak invariably opened up! Maintenance work inside the tank at these temperatures was impractical so we worked on other projects until the outdoor temperature rose to > -20°F and the leak sealed itself!

Professor John H. Williams, who (with Rumbaugh and Tate) had built the accelerator, was a pusher who thought big and worked hard. A Canadian by birth, but with a Ph.D. from Berkeley, he came to Minnesota in 1933 after an NRC fellowship at Chicago. Probably because of the project he became naturalized in 1942. He had a down-to-earth manner and philosophy, hence got along well with colleagues, service personnel and students. I was therefore not surprised that he later headed the electrostatic accelerator group at Los Alamos, was in charge of all services at the Trinity Test, and postwar served a term on the AEC [US Atomic Energy Commission]. He was a sports enthusiast and introduced me to college hockey. After his death of cancer in 1966, the University named their sports arena after him.

The rest of the local group consisted of three students: Carl Bailey, Thor Bergstralh, and Richard (Dick) Nuckolls. Hence the addition from Rice of Dr. Bennett and myself was a considerable expansion of the effort.

The main effort was measuring the total fast neutron cross sections of H, ^{2}H, C, and O as a function of neutron energy (up to about 6 MeV). For neutron sources we used ^{7}Li(p,n)^{7}Be, ^{12}C(d,n)^{13}N, and ^{2}H(d,n)^{3}He. In addition I exposed photographic emulsions to fission neutrons and continued with the spectrum measurements. The neutron scattering cross sections measurements were declassified after the war and published in Phys. Rev., 70, 583, (1946), and 70, 805, (1946). (Postwar at Wisconsin Professor Barschall and students extended and improved such total fast-neutron cross section data.)

The department chairman, J.W. Buchta, was very cordial and helpful: he claimed to remember my application to Minnesota for graduate work and was sorry I had not accepted their offer. Professor Al Nier, the mass spectroscopist already famous for first separating ^{235}U and demonstrating that it was the isotope undergoing fission with thermal neutrons, I found most impressive both as a physicist and a person. His talented student Bob Thompson later came to Los Alamos, but finished his degree at MIT with Rossi in cosmic ray studies. Melba Phillips (of the Oppenheimer-Phillips explanation for (d,p) and (d,n) reactions) was helping out (temporarily) with physics teaching. A very bright young spectroscopist, Dr. John Radar(!) Platt, particularly intrigued me: he held a Rockefeller Foundation fellowship and was clearly going to do well in the future though I didn't expect his later switch to non-physics fields (mental health and environmental studies).

At that time we knew that before the end of March we would close down our project and move to a new location. We had a U.S. map on the lab wall and sold pins to be placed where one believed the new lab would be. Rumor was that Oppenheimer had a ranch in Arizona so the pin density was high there, but of course his ranch was in New Mexico!

The move also required that we have physical exams and for security reasons that we move our bank account to our hometown bank. I opened a joint account at De Ridder, LA, with my mother. I had considered selling my car, but fortunately decided against it. Our directions were to have the steering and brakes checked and in good shape before the move: very wise advice for the then primitive road to Los Alamos!

The Manhattan Project requisitioned most of our lab equipment and tools. An army inspector came to sign for and supervise the packing. He was of course completely baffled by most of the items and could only write down what we told him, but when it came to small hand tools, he beamed and insisted on more details, e.g. pliers had to be identified as slip-joint gas pliers!

Just as the frigid Minnesota winter ended (and the snow was gone!), I again packed my car and left Minneapolis on Sunday, March 28, for the trip to Santa Fe. I spent Monday night in Denver and arrived at 109 E. Palace, Santa Fe, the next day. There I received a pass signed by Oppenheimer. Since housing was not yet available at Los Alamos, early arrivals had temporary lodging at dude ranches near Santa Fe. As I recall, most of the early arrivals were from California and a group from Princeton. At the dude ranches I remember meeting Feynman and also the J.E. Mack family who, though from Wisconsin, had come via Princeton where Julian had been a visiting professor.

Since the last 12 miles (of the 35 mile Santa Fe to Los Alamos trip) went from the Rio Grande River's 5500 foot elevation to 7200 feet via a narrow mountain road with hairpin turns, I now understood the advice on checking the steering and brakes on the car! We had our choice of the shorter (35 mile) route via a quite primitive road to Pojoaque and to the Otowi bridge over the Rio Grande, or via a longer (45 miles) route crossing the river at Espanola. I was therefore pleased when they let some of the bachelors temporarily stay at the site in an old ranch school building, "The Big House".

(Although Feynman was not a bachelor, his wife was in the hospital in Albuquerque so he stayed there with us also.) It was later in April when we could move into the first newly completed dormitory.

According to Manley, neutron physics was the bottleneck in 1942 when he and Oppenheimer took over from Professor Breit: a central lab such as Los Alamos would solve the problem of the nine separate contracts (Washington, Rice, Minnesota, Wisconsin, Purdue, etc.). Though originally planned for about 100 scientists, this estimate was already inadequate in April 1943: the cyclotron and electrostatic accelerator scientists and theoreticians already there were a major portion of the planned 100. The Los Alamos review committee in May recommended a doubling in personnel. Subsequently there was a doubling every nine months!

Early in April the military were not yet in evidence at the old Los Alamos Ranch School for Boys. Security was by Hispanic guards who only casually glanced at my pass from Oppenheimer. Construction of the dorms was under way but much of the technical area was nearing completion. J.H. Williams temporarily served as acting director at the site while the project office was still at 109 E. Palace. He asked me to worry about the facilities at building W in the Tech area as this was to house the Wisconsin accelerators when they came. They and the Wisconsin crew arrived about the middle of April. By dedicated hard work we had the "long tank" installed and operating by the middle of May and the "short tank" a month later.

Oppy chose Prof. J.H. Williams for the electrostatic accelerator group leader. Besides Williams, Bennett and myself, students Carl Bailey and Dick Nuckolls also came down from Minnesota. The Wisconsin crew included four post-docs: Joe McKibben (who headed the Wisconsin group and who had designed and built the short tank), Al Hanson, Dick Taschek, and Clarence Turner (who had helped Prof. Herb design and build the long tank). In addition there were seven talented, hard-working, Wisconsin grad students: Morris Blair, Dave Frisch, Jim Hush, Bob Krohn, Rolland Perry, Rolf Peterson, and Worth Seagondollar. Hence we had adequate staff for round the clock operation of the accelerators.

In early April Oppy and Condon (then associate director) arranged for Serber to give a series of lectures to summarize the theoretical considerations, and fast fission data. Although H.A. Wilson at Rice had done some back of the envelope calculations on bomb size, etc., when we started work in 1942, this was the first time I'd seen detailed serious treatment of the problems. It was of course both fascinating and sobering. Becoming acquainted with these impressive theorists (especially Bethe) gave me much more confidence that our work might really result in something practical for the war effort.

BEHIND TALL FENCES

The entire facilities of the Ranch School had been taken over including horses and camping equipment. Access to these encouraged occasional excursions in the nearby Jemez Mountains. By conserving gas ration stamps we could also accumulate enough to visit neighboring points of interest: e.g. Indian Pueblos, Taos, Santa Cruz, and Chimayo. Hence those of us with cars (or who had friends with cars) had no reason to feel sorry for ourselves.

Fortunately most of the newcomers were married or there would have been little social life since almost the only single females among the very early arrivals were a couple of nurses (Sarah Dawson and Harriet Peterson) and Oppy's secretary Priscilla Green. Having a car did give me advantage over some of the other bachelors, e.g. I had a couple of dates with Sarah: swimming in the Santa Cruz reservoir and a visit to Chimayo (where I bought a nice hand woven blanket), but no romance developed. (All three females later married Los Alamos residents.) As the lab expanded, there were of course more single female employees though never an equal ratio.

Early in the summer of 1943, Cyril Smith, head of metallurgy, brought out a new secretary, Mildred Paddock, who had been a librarian at the National Research Council. I was attracted and we started dating, horseback riding (the horses from the Ranch School were still available), and hiking in the Jemez Mountains. Cyril let her take time off to go on our group's vacation trip to the Pecos. In the fall we also went with some friends (who included Dave and Rose Frisch) for a weekend at Eagle's Nest Lake. Dave Frisch was encouraging our romance. Somewhat later I'd learn on pretty good authority that Niels Bohr was coming to the lab but of course it was highly secret and he would come under the alias of "Nicholas Baker." Subsequently Dave and I were doing maintenance inside one of the accelerator tanks and I told him if he could keep a secret, I had something interesting to tell him. When I told him about Bohr, disappointment was obvious: he had been expecting me to announce my engagement to Mildred! He had to wait until late in December for that announcement.

Courting Mildred was of course auxiliary to my main Los Alamos activities, namely fast neutron measurements. As indicated earlier we had both Wisconsin electrostatic accelerators operating satisfactorily by June 10, 1943. With proper choice of nuclear reactions, these accelerators could then provide monoenergic fast neutrons whose energies could be varied from a few thousand electron volts (keV) to several million electron volts (MeV). Our priority activities related to the number of neutrons emitted per fission event for both ^{235}U and ^{239}Pu, the energy spectrum of fission neutrons, and the dependence of the fission cross section on the energy of the fast neutrons. All these data are of course crucial for calculating the critical mass for a fast neutron reaction and the efficiency of the gadget.

For a couple of weeks in July our group had the world's supply of plutonium, a barely visible speck (a few hundred micrograms) prepared by cyclotron bombardment at Washington U. (St. Louis). We compared the neutrons emitted from our small Pu sample to a known ^{235}U sample by measuring only neutrons of energy greater than those we used to produce the fissions. Simultaneously we recorded the number of fission fragments and then in a separate experiment we determined the relative fission cross sections for the particular energy bombarding neutrons. To check the results we simultaneously used a thorium fission detector whose threshold was above the primary neutron energies used to produce the ^{235}U and ^{239}Pu fissions.

This was in fact the first experiment completed at Los Alamos and everyone in the group had devoted all free hours to the project. It earned us the earlier mentioned R & R camping trip to Pecos Valley.

These were important measurements: they showed that the number of neutrons emitted per plutonium fission was, in fact, larger than that for ^{235}U fission. Subsequent measurements have never materially changed the results.

Bennett and I had summarized the pre-Los Alamos status of the fission neutron spectra in LAMS-1. Our Rice cloud chamber data indicated a higher average energy than the Liverpool photographic emulsion data. At Stanford, Staub and Nicodemus were using pulse size distribution of proton recoils in an ion chamber to infer a spectrum. Their preliminary report disagreed strongly with both other measurements and gave a much lower average energy. Indirect measurements of mean fission neutron energies obtained from absorption measurements in water (e.g. at Liverpool and Chicago) were also discordant. All direct measurements had suffered from being made with large masses of dilute material which enhanced the inelastic scattering problems. The Rice and Liverpool data suffered from low statistics and large corrections needed for energetic recoils escaping the detector. The Stanford data on the monochromatic d-d spectrum indicated the difficulty of differentiating an integral pulse height distribution to give a reliable spectrum. The Stanford modulation scheme may also have favored including a large number of delayed neutrons (of lower energy).

The decision at the lab was that I should continue with the photo emulsion technique especially as better ^{235}U and ^{239}Pu sources became available. To this end I was allowed the full time services of an army WAC, Pvt. Lyda Speck, whom I trained in the measuring techniques. Besides Lyda, I also trained Mary Fisher and a number of scientist's wives to measure tracks in the emulsions e.g. Ilse Perlman, Nora Rossi, and Betty Greisen. Our group's secretary, WAC Sgt. Margaret Swank, occasionally helped when she had free time.

BEHIND TALL FENCES

The high beam currents available from the short tank were crucial for a number of our experiments, but its peak voltage of 2 MeV limited severely the neutron energies available from the ^{7}Li(p,n)^{7}Be reaction. McKibben, who had designed the accelerator, had suggestions how this limit could be overcome. To this end, we rebuilt the accelerator during the fall of 1943 and indeed by December we could use it at 2.5 MeV. This was my second experience helping rebuilding an accelerator: the first was at Rice in summer of 1941. McKibben's success on the tank rebuilding reinforced my earlier admiration of his ability, judgement, and creativity in things mechanical and electrical. Hence in 1945 I was pleased that for the Trinity test, McKibben was in charge of signals for the test and equipment: these would function correctly!

The name most commonly heard over the loud speaker paging system in the tech area was J.J. Gutierrez. The spelling is probably wrong, but I recall that he was a Hispanic in charge of the janitorial staff. However our electrostatic accelerator group hired a talented Indian from the San Ildefonso Pueblo to help us as a technician. We taught him how to run a lathe, etc., and he was of immense help in the rebuilding of the short tank mentioned in the paragraph above. His name was Po Povi Da; he was the son of Julian and Maria Martinez, famous for their black San Ildefonso pottery. Po himself was a gifted watercolor artist. I bought three of his paintings for my 1943 Xmas gift to Mildred.

Our electric power was produced locally at a plant run by the Army Engineers. It was erratic enough that we finally got a small diesel electric generator installed outside the accelerator building so that we didn't have to shut down work when the power went off.

Even when using power from the army-run plant, we had problems with the frequency dropping appreciably below 60 Hertz. The generating voltmeters monitoring the dome high voltages on the accelerators had synchronous drive motors. Hence the output signal of the voltmeters was frequency dependent. J. H. Williams complained vigorously to the army engineers. Thereafter the frequency exceeded 60 Hertz, which was equally bad for us. When Williams again complained, the army engineers explained that they were purposely running the frequency high so that it should be at 60 Hertz by the time it reached the lab!

During the spring or early summer of 1943, John Manley came around to ask my advice on whether the labs should recruit H.H. Barschall who was then an instructor at the University of Kansas. I was enthusiastic because I'd recently seen a paper coauthored by Barschall. The article dealt with removing background fog grains from photo emulsions: I saw an opportunity for him to take over the photo emulsion measurement of neutron energies, and thus free me for more interesting experiments. Hence, when later Manley told me Barschall was coming, I was quite pleased but then disappointed when he added that Barschall would work with him on the Cockcroft-Walton accelerator! Later I suspected Manley was less interested in my advice than in setting up a possible transfer in case Barschall did not work out well in Manley's group.

The visit by the great Niels Bohr, about which I earlier swore David Frisch to secrecy, occurred in December 1943. Bohr of course gave one of our weekly physics colloquia.

The meeting hall was packed to hear the great man. Bohr was famous for being hard to understand because he tends to swallow the last syllable of each word. Consequently the audience was very quiet and attentive so as not to miss any word of wisdom. I recall Ed Teller sitting on the front row and leaning forward to grasp every word that Bohr spoke. I was a couple of rows back but seated directly behind Enrico Fermi. Fermi also listened with great attention.

Bohr's talk dealt only with qualitative considerations. Being aware of Fermi's insistence on numbers and quantitative reasoning, I was not surprised that in the question period which followed, Fermi unsuccessfully tried to pin Bohr down on how big various quantities were: what would be estimated numbers, etc. Fermi's frustration was starting to show: When Fermi sat down he turned to his seat mate, and I overheard him say: "People come to hear Bohr like they go to church: not that they will learn anything, but only that it is the thing to do." Clearly, Nobel laureates may have orthogonal styles and still make important original contributions.

In general, we found the Los Alamos weather quite delightful except for the springtime which tended to be very dry and windy. Usually there was negligible precipitation until the Indians did their rain dances in June! The summers were sunny but not hot and humid, and the occasional afternoon thundershowers sometimes spectacular. In the fall the aspen painted the nearby Jemez mountains with golden light, and far across the Rio Grande valley to the east were the spectacular Sangre de Cristo (Blood of Christ) mountains. Throughout the year the dry thin air and clear skies resulted in large temperature fluctuations between night and day. As soon as the sun set, it turned cold!

A Christmas card from a Minnesota friend came with a note: "We suppose that you are enjoying the sunny southwest, but you must miss the snow and cold of Minnesota. P.S. We haven't had any snow and cold yet this year." When I received the card, we were going around in snow up to our knees, and the temperature was dropping to -20°F at night! Most people don't realize the effect which the 7500 foot elevation has on weather although the snowfall can be variable: two years later lack of snow produced a serious water shortage, and in 1943 I noted in a letter home that it snowed on May 9 and with the largest snow flakes that I'd ever seen. Of course this May snow melted almost immediately on the mesa but the nearby Jemez mountains remained snow capped for a longer time.

Periodically there were minor epidemics of diarrhea ("Los Alamos-itis"). People questioned the water supply, but the Army assured us that the chlorination excluded that. After Feynman had a bout with the "itis", he got a microscope and demonstrated living organisms in the water. Things improved but periodically there were still problems. Live worms ("hair snakes") were occasionally seen in some glass cooling coils of a distillation unit in the tech area. I had a bout of the "itis" which took me to the hospital for a day of so. After that I drank only boiled water and had no more problems.

Feynman made a big effort to keep his life as simple and efficient as possible. To this end one set of clothes and a jacket sufficed for most occasions. I admired him for this life style, but one of my friends with a sensitive nose felt the style resulted in an excessive period between washings. To this person Feynman's wife being in the Albuquerque hospital might explain but did not excuse the result.

Second only to Fermi, Feynman was my favorite as an all around physicist and person. He was just my age and like me had finished his Ph.D. also while working on the project but before coming to Los Alamos. However, he was obviously so much more talented that sometimes it was quite depressing. I suppose that was the reason that I almost gloated when in checking some calculations he had done for one of our projects, I discovered an error of a factor of ten. Of course if it had been an important calculation, I'm sure he would have checked and caught it himself.

One weekend shortly after we were engaged, Mildred and I were driving to Santa Fe to worry about wedding arrangements and we took along Dick Feynman who was hitchhiking to Albuquerque to see his wife in the TB hospital. He congratulated us on our engagement and then volunteered the following sage advice: "The single most important thing for a successful marriage is that each of you is always wholly and completely honest with each other." It is interesting that my mother wrote us a wedding letter in a similar vein: "Here's my last word to you—always be absolutely truthful with each other i.e. be assured that you can rely on each other's word. Never let any circumstances swerve you from this path."

Getting married at Los Alamos under the tight secrecy and censorship had both pros and cons. No family could be present; in fact neither of us ever met the other's family until August 1945, and by then we had a three month old son! The Episcopal minister in Santa Fe, Reverend Kinsolving, tied the knot February 11, 1944. We had friends from the Hill for the ceremony and for a reception afterwards at the La Fonda Hotel.

The next morning (Saturday) we caught the small airplane from Santa Fe to Albuquerque and then on to Carlsbad. It was also the first airplane ride for each of us. The plane, a Lockheed Lodestar, after taking off from Albuquerque, had to struggle to clear the Sandia mountains. The view of the New Mexico country side was of course terrific, but the low altitude at which the plane flew made it subject to all the updrafts and down-drafts as we crossed the numerous mesas and canyons. While our stomachs got queasy, we did avoid any upchucking.

Carlsbad, near the Texas border, has one of the lowest elevations in New Mexico: about 3100 feet. New Mexicans liked to tell vacationing Texans that New Mexico was larger that Texas if one correctly considers the volume above sea level: Texas is just spread out thinly!

The Carlsbad Caverns were properly impressive (including the bat flight from the cave), and the time we had allocated reasonable. Refreshed (and now a well bonded married couple), we flew back on Tuesday to Santa Fe and then drove our car to Los Alamos.

Shortly after Mildred and I were married, Cyril Smith told me that to have a happy wife the husband should keep her "barefoot and pregnant." Though following half of his advice indeed made Mildred happy, Cyril was not so keen on losing his crackerjack secretary.

Cyril's views on children were that they shouldn't be born until they were two years old. Failing to achieve this, the father should be careful <u>never ever</u> to change a diaper or feed the baby. I'm sure Cyril's bark was much worse than his bite: he was probably an exemplary father.

Cyril Smith's handwriting was notoriously illegible. By necessity Mildred became rather proficient at deciphering it. Hence the lab workers often asked her to transcribe the handwritten notes or directions which he had given them.

The best story however relates to his dictation. Mildred was good at taking shorthand and Cyril usually dictated from notes that he had prepared. However his notes were only written for himself, not for others to read, so the note writing had developed into a sort of a private shorthand with just a few first letters and a squiggly line to remind him of his thoughts. Early one morning he called her in to take dictation. Obviously he had worked hard the evening before preparing extensive notes. He took out his notes and studied them quite carefully for a long time, then gave up and said, "If I could only get the first word!"

After Mildred went on part time work, she occasionally got calls to help out in other offices. The most memorable time was when she substituted for Bethe's secretary. He had a lot of dictation for her, but she had never encountered anyone whose dictation was so smooth and flawless. He slowly paced back and forth while he dictated at a steady rate, with perfect grammar, with no changes or corrections. It was hard to believe that he wasn't reading from a polished manuscript. I therefore find credible the story I once heard that our famous Bethe's Bible (his April 1937 article on Nuclear Dynamics in the Reviews of Modern Physics) was simply dictated during a few weeks time.

The main activities of the electrostatic accelerator group during this period included studying (as a function of incident neutron energy) the neutron number per fission and important cross sections such as fission, scattering, and capture reactions.

The area where I had primary responsibility was still the measurement of the energy spectra of fast neutrons, especially fission neutrons. To this end I exposed the special Ilford Halftone emulsions to fast neutrons from various sources. After the emulsions were developed and processed, then I supervised my crew of technicians whom I had trained to use high resolution microscopes in the tedious work of locating and measuring the ranges in the emulsion of the recoil proton tracks resulting from elastic collisions with the fast incident neutrons. I also analyzed the resultant data and wrote the technical reports.

A compact neutron source whose spectra approximated that of fission neutrons would improve the accuracy of many important integral or semi-integral tests of materials or assemblies where traditionally Ra-Be neutron sources had been used. The Ra-Be neutron source suffers from having a distinctly higher average energy than fission neutrons. To help design such a mock fission neutron source, we had been measuring neutron spectra from polonium alpha particles bombarding various light elements.

Otto Frisch came to Los Alamos in December 1943 with the first of the British scientists. One of his early tasks at Los Alamos was to check the large geometry corrections which I had calculated for the probability that long range recoil protons would leave the emulsion and hence not be measurable. I was unaware that he was working on the problem until one day he came around and told me that he reproduced my calculations!

Otto was an exceptionally gifted and interesting person: not only did he play classical piano pieces over the local Los Alamos radio station, but he was also interested in topology: I remember a fascinating lecture he once gave on trying to decide whether a tangle of strings was just a tangle or a knot. He called the lecture "When is a knot not a knot?"

After the war Frisch held an important named professorship at the University of Cambridge. During my first visit to Cambridge I tried to look him up but found that to preserve his privacy he had made access very difficult. However I finally did manage to enter the building and get to his office. He was glad to see me, and I learned he was planning a trip to America later in the year. I persuaded him to include the University of Wisconsin in his itinerary and give a physics colloquium. He came in January and of course gave his usual fine talk. We took him for lunch at our student union which is on Lake Mendota. That this huge lake was frozen and many ice fishermen populated the surface, he found incredible: he insisted on walking out on the lake and having us photograph him on the ice so he could prove to his children that "he could walk on water".

Several times at Fuller Lodge, Mildred and I happened to eat at the same table as Niels Bohr and his son Aage. Niels Bohr always extended himself to entertain and make small talk. He particularly liked to tell jokes, but with his accent and his swallowing the last syllable of most words, he was sometimes very hard to follow. Fortunately, Aage always laughed at his father's jokes so even when we missed the point, we got along OK by cueing our laughter to Aage's.

By the beginning of 1945 the urgent cross section and other physical parameters which were the responsibility of our accelerator group were in relatively good shape. Hence we and the other groups of the Research Division were recruited to help with the testing of the plutonium implosion type bomb.

No test was deemed necessary for the gun method of assembly of the ^{235}U material. However, the high spontaneous fission rate of ^{240}Pu (produced concomitantly with the desired ^{239}Pu in the Hanford production reactors) made the gun assembly method too slow for a plutonium weapon: the difficulty is that neutrons from the spontaneous fission of ^{240}Pu have a chance of triggering the chain reaction just as the assembly barely becomes critical and hence blow it apart before an appreciable fraction of the plutonium can fission.

The implosion method was devised at Los Alamos to achieve a converging spherical shock wave to assemble and compress rapidly the plutonium to a highly supercritical mass which could then explode with high efficiency when triggered by a neutron burst generated by the shock wave mixing of Po and Be in an initiator at the center. Plutonium production rates at Hanford were large enough to permit the needed testing by the middle of the summer of this radically new method of assembly and still have sufficient material for subsequent military use.

Although plans for the test had started by March 1944 and the Trinity site was selected by September 1944, the big push came in 1945. By March 1945, Oppy formed a new division, TR, headed by Ken Bainbridge, for the Trinity tests. Most of the personnel came from the old Research Division. Our accelerator group leader, J.H. Williams headed group TR-1 in charge of all the services and he also served as Bainbridge's alternate. J. L. McKibben headed the crucial TR-1B group handling all timing and remote control signals. Bob Wilson was in overall charge of TR-3 (Nuclear Physics Measurements), with Fermi and Weisskopf as consultants.

I was in charge of group TR-3B which was assigned the neutron measurements. Group TR-3B consisted of seven other people mainly from our old accelerator group: J.M. Blair, Dave Frisch, Jim Hush, Ernie Klema, Bob Krohn, Rolland Perry, and Clarence Turner.

Our planned neutron measurements were of two kinds: 1) number of neutrons as a function of distance from the explosion and 2) neutron intensity as a function of time at several locations.

Ernie Klema assumed major responsibility for the first type of measurements. He employed the radioactivity induced by the bomb's neutrons in sulphur and in cadmium covered gold detectors at various distances from ground zero. The reaction in sulphur is $^{32}S(n,p)^{32}P$. The resultant radioactive phosphorous has a half-life of 14 days and results only from the prompt neutrons since the effective neutron threshold energy for the sulphur reaction is approximately 3 MeV and thus discriminates against delayed neutrons whose energies are about 0.6 MeV. The reaction in the gold detectors is $^{197}Au(n,gamma)^{198}Au$, and the resultant radioactivity of ^{198}Au (half-life equal to 2.7 days) is proportional to the total neutron flux of both the prompt and the delayed neutrons. The neutron capture in gold occurs almost entirely after the prompt and delayed neutrons have both been slowed down to very low energies after many collisions with air nuclei.

While I had major responsibility for the time record of the neutron intensity, Blair, Frisch, Hush, and Krohn were essential and important collaborators. For this measurement we designed a "cellophane catcher camera" where a motor pulled a cellophane tape rapidly between two ^{235}U coated plates. Neutrons from the explosion would produce fission in the ^{235}U. Some of the resulting fission fragments will escape from the ^{235}U surface and be caught on the rapidly moving cellophane tape. The subsequent measurement of the radioactivity of these fission fragments caught on the tape gives the desired time differentiated neutron record.

We constructed three such cameras: one was to be airborne on a tethered balloon 300 meters out from ground zero and 300 meters above the ground. Having it airborne was to simplify the interpretation of results. The other two cameras were located in little "dog houses" at 300 meters and 600 meters from ground zero. The "dog houses" were constructed of aluminum. Their design had to be a compromise between shielding the cameras from the blast wave and avoiding undue absorption of neutrons by the structure.

We were aware that if the test bomb exploded with high efficiency, some or all of our cameras might be destroyed. However, if the efficiency was low, the cameras should survive and their measurements might be important for diagnostic purposes.

A 100-ton calibration and rehearsal shot was scheduled May 7, 1945. Because there would be no neutrons to measure from this test, it would not be a calibration of our neutron detectors. However, by installing the equipment at a "scaled-in" distance we could test whether it would suffer blast damage and whether the signals to turn on the equipment functioned properly. I was excused by John Williams from this test because our first child, David, was born on April 15.

As group leader of TR-3B, I and 18 other group leaders and/or consultants for the Trinity test attended a weekly meeting chaired by Bainbridge. The meetings lasted one or two hours and served to correlate work and scheduling. Possible new experiments were examined and progress reports given. J.H. Williams, in charge of all services for the test, wisely insisted that all information of general usefulness be circulated to the personnel of the Trinity groups. He did a remarkable job of coordination, and Bainbridge rightly stated that the successful completion of the TR project owes much to Williams' superior judgement and long hours of hard work. Joe McKibben and his TR-1B group in charge of all timing and remote control signals also deserve accolades for stellar performance of these vital functions under quite adverse field conditions.

As mentioned earlier, Williams had excused me from the May 100-ton calibration and rehearsal test so I spent relatively little time at the Trinity site until several weeks before the July 16 test. For this last period I lived at the base camp. Our time was partially spent in setting up the "dog houses" at 300 m and 600 m from ground zero, installing the catcher cameras and signal leads, and then checking and double checking that everything worked. The catcher camera on the tethered balloon occupied the rest of our spare time. Bob Krohn painted his wife's name BARBARA ANNE on the balloon and assumed major responsibility for that part of the program. Since we ran into no major problems, we were able to meet schedules without any overtime.

When odds for the success of the implosion method were not high, a 214-ton steel pressure vessel named "Jumbo" was ordered that would contain plutonium in the event of a real fizzle. By the time Jumbo was delivered to the test site, confidence in the implosion technique was much higher and the liabilities re measurements and interpretations were so great that use of Jumbo had been abandoned. However, a week of so before the test, Jumbo was erected at a point 800 yards from its original location. It was an impressive thing to see in the desert!

The base camp was considerably south and west of the old McDonald Ranch. When we arrived it was certainly dry dusty desert country, and the designation on the ancient maps as the Jornada del Muerto valley seemed entirely appropriate. The water from the wells contained much gypsum and was so "hard" that they issued us special hard-water soap. Even then washing and showering left much to be desired. But a couple of weeks before the test summer thundershowers started and some were quite severe. A dried up reservoir at the ranch filled with water and suddenly that night the air was filled with beeping of thousands of frogs. It is easy to understand how the ancients came to believe in spontaneous generation! Emilio Segre (group leader to TR-3C concerned with measurement of delayed gamma rays from the test) was incredulous. I doubt if he found the July 16 test as incredulous! I too was impressed by the number and variety of wild life which surfaced in this seeming desert.

At Trinity I became acquainted with Segrè and found him a truly delightful personality. He made a great effort to learn American idioms, etc., but sometimes these came out slightly fractured. My favorite is when he came to me about some problem and said, "Richards, I've got a chicken to pick with you."

I was at Base Camp, 9.7 miles from ground zero. The shot was scheduled for 4:00 AM July 16. However, around 2:00 AM a heavy thunderstorm hit the base camp area and on advice of the meteorologist, the test was postponed until 5:30 AM to let the bad weather pass the area. It was indeed a bit frightening that lightning might prematurely start the test! The electrical disturbances would at least complicate the timing and signals to turn on equipment.

We had been issued dark welding goggles to shield our eyes and had been instructed to lie down away from ground zero. We followed the countdown over a loudspeaker: 10, 9, 8, 7, 6, 5, 4, 3, 2, 1. At time zero the first thing I noticed was that although facing away from ground zero, it felt like someone had slapped my face; it was of course the heat radiation from a most successful test. The neighboring mountains were vividly illuminated, and I turned around, took off my welder's goggles and watched the luminous fireball change color, expand and rise majestically upward.

Of course we had not yet heard anything: it would take about 40 seconds for the sound and shock wave to arrive at base camp. Fermi was a bit in front of me and I was intrigued by the experiment he was performing: during the passage of the shock wave, he was dropping paper chaff from about a six foot height and measuring on the ground the nearly 8 foot displacement (by the shock wave) of the paper chaff. He then took out his slide rule and calculated the efficiency of the explosion. His crude experiment implied about a 10,000-ton TNT equivalent. The strength of the shock wave was still impressive at this 9.7 mile distance from the explosion. After the passage of the shock wave, reverberations of sound from the distant mountains continued for a surprisingly long time.

Euphoria was my first reaction after the years of hard work and increasing tension: the long war would soon be over. But of course the experience was also very sobering. I realized that the explosion signaled irreversible changes in the world. Would these changes be for better or for worse? By nature I'm basically an optimist: but of course the final verdict will never be in. Nevertheless, over the past scores of years I believe a case can be made that the explosion has made world war an obsolete way of settling disputes.

After the test, our first job was to recover our "catcher cameras" as soon as authorities would allow us into the area. Dave Frisch and I were then allowed to drive a jeep in but we were instructed to limit our radiation exposure to 5 roentgen (one year's allowed exposure). We quickly got to the 600 meter "dog house" station and saw that it had suffered considerable blast damage. However, we were able to extract the "catcher camera" which although also suffering blast damage was still intact. We brought it back and our total radiation exposure did not exceed the allowed 5 roentgen. Since the blast damage would not have occurred until after the cellophane tape had recorded the initial burst of neutrons, we were hopeful that we could still retrieve some of the data. Such indeed was the case and our results are shown in Fig. 4, p. 50, Trinity, LA-6300-H and the results discussed on p. 45–46. For pictures of the damaged "dog house" and camera, see *Through Los Alamos, 1945: Memoirs of a Nuclear Physicist* by Hugh T. Richards, © Medical Physics Publishing, Madison, WI 53705.

As we had expected for such a successful explosion, our cameras at 300 meters, both the balloon borne and the ground station one, were completely destroyed and hence no data survived.

To help interpret the Trinity neutron measurements we also performed an experiment with a mock fission neutron source in a large container filled with liquid air. Since the density of liquid air is about 1000 times that of atmospheric air, the distance to a 600 meter detector in air would scale to an equivalent ≈ 0.6 meter in liquid air, and thus we could simulate the effect of the atmosphere on the fission neutrons.

After we had written up our reports, many of us were allowed to take early vacations in early August to unwind. I believe it was Saturday, August 4, that Mildred, our 3-1/2 month old son David, our dog Sange, and I drove north from Los Alamos via Taos to Fort Garland, Colorado, and then east over the scenic La Veta pass to Walsenburg and on to the cattle ranch where my sister Tally and her family lived. My mother was also coming from Louisiana, and my elder sister Hila and her family would be there. I suspected that the first bomb might be dropped about August 6, so when some of us went to meet the train, I told Mildred to keep Tally's radio on for a possible interesting announcement. The announcement about Hiroshima indeed came on this trip, but Mother had already heard it on the train. So our secret was out. The second bomb over Nagasaki came on August 9 while we were still at Tally's. We all expected the war soon to be over, but it wasn't until August 14 as we were returning from Walsenburg to Los Alamos that we learned of the Japanese surrender.

People on leave from universities and corporations were of course rapidly returning home and reestablishing their former activities. Now that I had family responsibilities, my interest shifted to long time career activities. I had feelers and/or offers from a number of places (including Princeton, Illinois, and Westinghouse) but Wisconsin seemed the most promising to me since I had been impressed both by their accelerators on loan to Los Alamos and by the Wisconsin personnel (including students and post docs) with whom I had worked at Los Alamos. Other Wisconsinites at Los Alamos included Joe Hirschfelder, Julian Mack, and Stan Ulam, as well as the foreman of the laboratory shop, Gus Schultz. In addition I knew that Professor Ray Herb and Gregory Breit would both be returning to Wisconsin from other wartime projects.

Hence I was glad to accept a Wisconsin offer, but I insisted that initially I be full time research because I wanted to get a good research program going before carrying a heavy teaching load. Meanwhile, Los Alamos had negotiated the purchase of the short tank from Wisconsin and only one of the two accelerators would be returning to Wisconsin. My Los Alamos boss, John Williams, helped me out by putting me in charge of returning the long tank to Wisconsin.

---

*Hugh T. Richards came to Los Alamos in April 1943 from Rice University via the University of Minnesota and continued work begun there on measurements of fast-neutron cross sections. He went to the University of Wisconsin after the war and was Professor of Physics until his retirement in 1988. He is presently Professor Emeritus and continues his association with the University.

This is an abridged version of <u>Through Los Alamos, 1945: Memoirs of a Nuclear Physicist</u>, Hugh T. Richards, © 1993, Medical Physics Publishing, Madison, WI, 1993.

EARLY SUPER WORK
Foster Evans*

Several years ago my wife, Alice, and I were walking through the Smithsonian Museum in Washington, DC, when we came upon an exhibit describing the ENIAC computer and showing some of its hardware. I commented to Alice that I had put one of the first problems on this computer. With some hint of pride, I said that it was too bad they didn't have an exhibit of the Princeton computer, because I had put the first big problem on that. As we continued our perusal, we walked around a corner and to our surprise discovered a similar exhibit of the Princeton computer. This occurrence in the environs of a museum led me to feel that I had been a part of history. I realized that in the course of my career at Los Alamos, I and my colleagues had participated in a revolution in the ability to do numerical computations. We had witnessed the development of computers from the old mechanical desk Marchant that went "klunkey-klunk" as it slowly ground out a simple arithmetic operation to the modern day high-speed electronic computers. This revolution has made it possible to investigate by numerical approximations the mathematical complexities of non-linear physics problems that are much too complicated to treat analytically. My participation in this arose primarily from several years work on the Super problem beginning in late 1946. The following is an attempt to give a non-technical account of some of this work and how its progress paralleled that of the development of computers.

The Super was conceived as a possible nuclear weapon that makes use of thermonuclear reactions—the same process that generates heat in our sun. In the case of the Super, reactions between isotopes of the hydrogen atom (H); namely, deuterons and tritons (D and T), are involved. The nuclei of these isotopes have the same electric charge as does the single proton that comprises the nucleus of H but with one neutron added for D and two for T, so that a D has twice and a T three times the mass of an H. When a D combines with a T or another D, energy is released. Because these nuclei carry like electric charges, they repel each other and it is necessary to overcome this "Coulomb" force before a nuclear reaction, or fusion, can take place. Enough energy to overcome the Coulomb repulsion can be obtained by heating the material to a very high temperature approximating that of the sun's interior. Hence the term thermonuclear. (If "cold fusion" in deuterium is indeed possible as a practical source of energy, it must involve some as yet unidentified mechanism for avoiding the Coulomb repulsion.)

Let's suppose we have some deuterium heated to a temperature that will initiate thermonuclear reactions. If the material is in the shape, say, of a cylinder, the Super problem is to calculate whether the energy released in these reactions will in turn heat the adjacent cold material sufficiently to initiate reactions there, so that the reaction process will propagate along the cylinder. At these temperatures the deuterium atoms will be ionized, and the heated gas becomes in effect a mixture of two gases composed of the deuteron nuclei (deuterium ions) and the electrons, one per atom, that have been stripped in the ionizing process. Such a material is called a plasma.

An immediate complication arises from the fact that the energy released in a reaction is not deposited locally at the place where the reaction occurred, but instead is manifest in reaction products that move at high velocity through the plasma. These consist of positively charged nuclei and uncharged neutrons. In order to distinguish between the high energy nuclei that are created as reaction products and low energy nuclei that are a part of the plasma gas, the former will be referred to as fast nuclei and the latter as thermal nuclei. A fast nucleus distributes its energy to the plasma along its path as it is slowed down through Coulomb interactions with the thermal nuclei and electrons. A fast neutron loses its energy through successive elastic collisions with thermal nuclei, which in turn exchange their recoil energy by the above slowing down process. Because the fast nuclei lose their energy at different rates to thermal nuclei and electrons, these gases will acquire different temperatures, and therefore the process of energy exchange between the two gases must be taken into account. An especially important reaction product in deuterium is the next heavier isotope mentioned above, tritium. There are two reasons for this, one is that a D has a higher probability (cross section) for reaction with a T than with another D, and second, one product of the DT reaction is a very high energy neutron. Thus the presence of T noticeably increases the rate of the thermonuclear process, and since the high energy neutron deposits its energy over a large range, it may contribute significantly to forward propagation. When a fast nucleus loses essentially all of its energy, it becomes a thermal component of the plasma. The deuterium is constantly being depleted and displaced by thermalized reaction products, and as the concentration of the D's decreases, so does the rate of the thermonuclear reaction. Of course, a fast nucleus or neutron may escape the system taking what remaining energy it has with it.

The thermal nuclei and electrons are in constant agitation, and as an electron moves in the vicinity of a nucleus, its velocity is changed causing it to give up energy in the form of radiation called Bremsstrahlung (braking radiation). The photons that comprise this radiation lose, or gain, energy as they are scattered by electrons and eventually may escape carrying their remaining energy with them. Actually many of them escape with more than their initial energy, because most of them are emitted at very low energies, so that when scattered by an electron, the photon very likely picks up additional energy from the electron. Thus, Bremsstrahlung can give rise to considerable loss of energy, and since the immediate loss is to electrons it contributes further to the difference in temperature between thermal nuclei and electrons.

The temperatures of the plasma gases will vary considerably from place to place as the reaction proceeds, and energy will flow from hot to cold regions by thermal conduction. In particular, energy will be lost this way to the colder outside. Temperature variation causes hot regions to expand and cold regions to compress so that density and temperature of the plasma are continually changing over space and time. All of the above described physical processes in turn depend strongly on temperature and density so that each is dependent upon what is going on in the others. This brief description of some of the physics in the Super Problem indicates its complexity and the difficulty encountered in attempts to obtain a coherent picture of the net result.

During the early days at Los Alamos, a group under the leadership of Edward Teller investigated the basic physics involved in a number of the individual phenomena, and some thought was given to a schematic conception of a thermonuclear weapon. The primary work of the laboratory, however, was devoted to the design and construction of a fission weapon, and major work on the Super was postponed until after the war. Teller continued his interest and was a major contributor throughout.

I became familiar with the problem through applying analytical and simple numerical methods in collaboration with Rolf Landshoff and Frank Hoyt. At the time there was a pretty general consensus that the high energy neutron produced in the DT reaction contributed the primary means of transmitting energy ahead of the main reaction in a manner necessary to sustain its propagation. Some aspects of this process were treated analytically, and together with numerical hand computations, attempts were made to draw some conclusions about the feasibility of a Super. Early in 1948, it became evident that no conclusion could be reached in a finite time without considerably faster methods of numerical computation.

At this point the program got a tremendous boost when Johnny von Neumann, the genius mathematician from the Institute for Advanced Study at Princeton, entered the picture with his deep interest in both computers and the Super. This happenstance was not only indispensable to the Super program, but also fortunate for me personally, because it led to a long association with Johnny.

There was considerable interest during the early forties in the possibility of building high speed electronic computers, which was stimulated in part by the demand of war work. Johnny was a principal innovator in the logical design of computers and in 1945 began plans for building his own machine at the Institute for Advanced Study in Princeton, New Jersey. By

1948 this work was well under way, and with Johnny's help we at Los Alamos began to plan a formulation of the Super problem that could be executed at Princeton as soon as the computer was ready.

We divided the problem into two parts: "hydrodynamics" and "particle physics." In the particle physics part, all of the thermonuclear reaction products and the photons were treated by Monte Carlo (a statistical sampling method) to determine where and at what rate the particles exchanged their energy in the plasma. In the hydrodynamics portion, the resulting heat exchange and motion of the plasma was calculated. As mentioned earlier, all of these processes take place continuously and simultaneously. But in a numerical calculation, one approximates this by dividing time duration into small but finite intervals and space into small zones. One assumes that conditions such as temperature, density and thermal particle composition are uniform over each spatial zone and constant during a time interval, but will vary from zone to zone and one time interval to the next. Consequently all differential equations are replaced by difference equations. In a hydrodynamics cycle the plasma conditions are known at previous time intervals, and using the known energy exchanges that had been calculated in the previous particle physics cycle, new plasma conditions are computed. These results are then used to determine how many reactions take place, and in the subsequent particle physics cycle, the photons and the various types of thermonuclear reaction products that were produced are represented by samples large enough to approximate their average behavior. Each particle in the samples, plus each that survived the previous cycle, is traced for the duration of the time cycle along its trajectory, which may cross several zones with different plasma conditions, and the energy exchange is recorded for each zone traversed. Using the totals of these energy exchanges, one continues to the next hydrodynamics cycle, and so on. These calculations must be repeated for each zone, each time interval, and each particle in the samples. It is apparent that various computations are repeated very many times, and this involves millions of arithmetic operations. In addition, all the data that are relevant to each zone must be stored in the computer's memory for at least two time cycles. Thus the capacity of the memory limits the number of zones one can use. This in turn determines how finely the space can be subdivided, which, together with limits on the shortness of the time interval, determined in part by considerations of machine speed, are important factors in how closely the calculation models what goes on in the real world. Thus, in addition to adapting a description of the physical phenomena to a mathematical form that can be treated numerically, it is evident that a lot of give and take goes into organizing the bookkeeping aspects.

It became apparent that the Princeton computer would not be ready as early as had been anticipated. So work on the Super was temporarily put aside, and we began to examine aspects of the much simpler problem of how to initiate the process. It was thought that by making a number of simplifying approximations, this problem could be handled on the ENIAC, and after several months of detailed planning, the calculation was done during the summer of 1950. At about the same time, Stan Ulam together with C.J. Everett started a hand calculation on the same problem, but necessarily with many approximations. Everett, with slide rule and desk computer, would estimate how the reaction proceeded during a cycle, and then Ulam would sit back and "guess" how the energy was distributed to nearby zones, and in turn Everett would compute another cycle. Gamow quipped that this calculation was done single-handedly by Ulam, and the single hand was Everett's. The results indicated that more than the expected amount of tritium would be needed. Although these types of hand calculations had limited usefulness at the time, they in no way constituted "proof," as some have since claimed, that the original idea for the Super as conceived by Teller could not work.

The ENIAC (Electronic Numerical Integrator and Computer) had its origin in the demands placed upon the Ballistic Research Laboratory (BRL) at the Aberdeen Proving Grounds in Aberdeen, Maryland. At BRL calculations were made to determine the manner of aiming artillery so as to hit a target at a specified distance, and tables were compiled to anticipate a variety of firing conditions. Presumably at least some of these results would be tested by experiments on the proving grounds. In the early months of the war, BRL was swamped with requests for firing tables, and the primitive computing facilities in existence were woefully inadequate for keeping pace. As a result people began to seriously consider the possibilities of electronic computers. In 1943, BRL contracted with the Moor School of Engineering at the University of Pennsylvania to build the ENIAC. Actually it was not completed until after the war when, in 1947, it was transported to Aberdeen where it began to fulfill its primary function of computing firing tables. For each set of problems, it was necessary to reset many plugs and relays making it impractical for more general use. Various people, however, recognized the machine's potential and worked out a scheme to convert it to a stored program computer. Nick Metropolis participated in this process and, together with Klari von Neumann, executed the conversion. I remember Nick's patient explanation of the mysteries of how one entered a program into the computer by means of coded instructions. Now, it is difficult to picture how marvelous this was to us, then, to be able to have a sequence of operations carried out automatically and repeatedly at a previously unheard of speed. Although by present standards the ENIAC was an extremely primitive machine, it was an exciting adventure to plan a computation and go to Aberdeen to carry it out on what was then one of the most advanced computers in the country.

Aberdeen was hardly more than a crossroads on the Pulaski highway named in honor of a Polish nobleman who served in the American Revolutionary army, and the site where we worked was, appropriately, a military base. We stayed in a nearby motel called the Flying Clipper, which was bordered on two sides by railroad lines, and since we were allowed only the graveyard shift on the computer, our unfamiliar attempts at daytime sleep were not helped by the noise of passing trains. There were positive aspects, too, aside from the excitement of observing the results of our calculation, such as evening drives in the lovely Maryland countryside for relief from the humid heat. Not the least of our pleasures was making sorties to neighboring restaurants that prepared delicious dishes of fresh seafood. The ENIAC itself, though a miracle of its day, was by modern standards a monster. It was a conglomeration of electrical hardware the most conspicuous of which was a roomful of radio vacuum tubes. When the computer was turned off or the power failed for any reason, restarting inevitably resulted in the failure of a number of these tubes, and it was a major operation, which sometimes took days, for the engineers to locate and replace them. We observed approaching thunderstorms with apprehension in anticipation of power outages and long delays in our calculation. To put it in perspective, modern hand-held computers can calculate more rapidly and more reliably than that roomful of tubes. The ENIAC had very limited internal memory, and the external memory consisted of IBM punch cards. As the calculation proceeded, the results would be punched out on cards that would be fed back in providing initial data for a new cycle. It was, relatively speaking, a slow process and consumed many, sometimes monotonous weeks. As the calculations wound to a close, my thoughts turned poetic as I searched for an appropriate description of the Aberdeen experience. The result was inscribed on an IBM card and mailed back to Los Alamos to announce our departure, and with apologies to the Bard is here reproduced.

> And so at last we leave the Clipper room
> To point our course upon Pulaski's way.
> And yet for one last look we pause and turn
> To contemplate: This crossroads in the East;
> These cottages surrounded by steel rails
> Whereon great monsters trumpet to the morn;
> This seafood paradise; this seat of brass;
> This testing ground of parabolic death;
> This parent of computers yet unseen;
> This humid home; this heat; this Aberdeen!

As mentioned earlier, a large number of simplifications were necessarily made for the ENIAC calculation, so the results could not be taken as definitive. Nevertheless it was a learning exercise, and in the subsequent detailed preparations for the Princeton calculation, we worked to include as much as possible of the relevant physics. Research on the Super was always made difficult by the fact that a successful outcome was marginal, so even physical effects that contributed very little one way or the other had to be considered.

In 1952, the computer was ready, and the following year we went to Princeton where the long, arduous task of coding was completed. (Nowadays the term is "programming," but then we spoke of "coding.") In this early stage of electronic computers the instructions involved very elemental operations; software such as Fortran did not yet exist. At various times a number of different people assisted with this work at Aberdeen as well as Princeton. These included my late wife, Cerda, who was a colleague throughout, Klari von Neumann, Marshall and Arianna Rosenbluth, David Liberman, Jack Calkin, and Herman Goldstine, who had worked with Johnny on computer theory. Once the coding was completed and entered in the computer, we proceeded through the program order by order and checked each branch against a hand calculation; a procedure unheard of in this day and age. We did this not only to confirm our accuracy in the still novel process of coding, but to check that this new computer was doing what we had told it to do. And, indeed, we uncovered a few remaining engineering bugs. There still remained the possibility that as we ran the problem, novel demands would be made that might confuse this untested computer, or that blips in the electronics might cause errors, so at various intervals we repeated the calculation to see if the results would duplicate. A sufficient number of non-duplications was encountered to justify the precaution. Johnny estimated that in the course of running this problem the number of arithmetic operations that had been executed by the computer approximated the total number performed in all of history up to that time. (Imagine what the total must be for all the computations by the many computers that have been operating during the forty intervening years!)

All of this consumed several painstaking months, but the Princeton environment was very stimulating for a physicist. There was, for example, the opportunity to hear lectures by such notables as Bohr and Dirac, and I even achieved an on-campus nodding acquaintance with the colorful Einstein. But most rewarding of all was the almost daily contact with Johnny and the good company of both von Neumanns.

Two examples were examined, and both gave negative results. It is evident that there were several weaknesses in the computation; for example, limitations in memory capacity required rather large hydrodynamic zones, much too large to resolve a shock wave or a detonation wave. Calculations with more modern equipment that have made it possible to include these and other physical effects indicate that propagation may indeed be possible. However, interest in this "Classical Super" decreased considerably following what is commonly referred to as the Teller-Ulam proposal of a different approach, which led to the development of the thermonuclear weapon now called the H-bomb.

It is a remarkable tribute to Johnny that although computers with much greater speed and memory capacity have been made, they have largely evolved from the Princeton computer and the logical designs that originated with him. What is amazing to me is that it has all happened in such a short period of time.

I should like to acknowledge the support to my effort on the Super problem that was given by Carson Mark, who was then Division Leader of the Theoretical Physics Division. Also, his report LA-5647-MS (1974), "A Short Account of Los Alamos Theoretical Work on Thermonuclear Weapons, 1946-1950," was very helpful in recalling the sequence of some of the events and adds some names of people who contributed to this and related work.

---

*Foster Evans came to Los Alamos in 1946 from the University of Colorado having received his Ph.D. in physics from the University of Chicago in 1941. He was among the first to recognize and implement the newly acquired power of the computer into solving complex problems in hydrodynamics, transport theory, and nuclear physics encountered at the Laboratory. He retired from the Laboratory in 1982.

FIRST FUSION NEUTRONS FROM A THERMONUCLEAR WEAPON DEVICE
Two Researchers' Personal Account
John Allred and Louis Rosen*

From the outset of the Los Alamos Scientific Laboratory (LASL), there was speculation about the possibility of producing a nuclear explosion by the fusion of light elements—a reaction discovered by Rutherford in the early 1930s.

Because of spontaneous fission and other sources of neutrons in the environment, the atomic bomb (A-bomb) is limited in size and power. The critical mass imposes a limit on the total amount of fissionable material that can be employed. There is no spontaneous fusion of light elements, however. Thus, it was thought, and correctly so, that the explosive power of a fusion device is virtually unlimited. Early speculation was that if a fission weapon could be made to work, the energy resulting from its explosion could be used to heat deuterium to such a high temperature that a fusion reaction would be initiated which would be self-sustaining. The device discussed in those early days was named the Super. The naive thinking, before design studies could be seriously made, was that once one had a successful fission device all one would need to do would be to get a supply of deuterium, and the rest would be straightforward. As is frequently the case, however, the design of the hydrogen bomb (H-bomb) turned out to be much more complicated than the first ideas about it.

Any scientific endeavor that has to do with atomic energy, and particularly with weapons, is so intimately intertwined with and influenced by politics that it would be misleading to discuss such an endeavor in terms of the science alone. It is therefore necessary to recall the international circumstances dominant in the 1940s and early 1950s in order to appreciate the attitudes of those of us who participated in weapons design and testing.

The United States, with its allies England and France was attacked in 1939-41 by Germany, Italy and Japan, the Axis partners. The Western Allies fought for their lives and won. The possibility of using nuclear energy to produce weapons was recognized by Leo Szilard and Albert Einstein in Einstein's famous letter of 1939 to President Franklin D. Roosevelt; this possibility was equally well-known to German scientists. The German effort, directed by Werner Heisenberg, never amounted to much. Nonetheless, the U. S. effort was launched, since at that time it was believed that the Axis partners might be the first to develop this terrible weapon.

Our alliance with Soviet Russia led to curiously mixed feelings and especially to mixed postwar reactions. The exhaustion of Hitler's armies on the Eastern Front against the Soviet Union was doubtless a large factor in his defeat. The defection to the U.S.S.R. of Klaus Fuchs with the 'secrets' of the A-bomb was an enormous shock to the Western scientific community, even though, as has often been said, the real secret of the A-bomb was the fact that it could be made. When the threatening posture of Soviet Russia was discovered, and it became known that persons privy to the secret councils of the British and United States governments had taken their knowledge to the Soviet Union, the question of the possible manufacture of a hydrogen bomb by the United States loomed with immense importance.

The U.S.S.R. exploded its first A-bomb on August 29, 1949. On January 31, 1950, President Harry S. Truman instructed the U. S. Atomic Energy Commission to determine whether or not the H-bomb could be made and, if so, to proceed.

At that time, the Los Alamos Scientific Laboratory was the only laboratory in the United States which could readily undertake such a task. At the end of World War II, although most of the original scientific staff had by then returned to their academic posts, many continued to be consultants to the Laboratory, and behind them they had left a first-rate cadre of younger scientists to continue the work.

Discussion among scientists in the Laboratory centered on the problem that the proposed new weapon—if it could be made—might unleash the possibility of unlimited destruction of people and property. It could bring war to homes, women and children in the most terrible way. A few of the scientific staff even decided that they could not participate in the development of such a weapon and left the Laboratory.

On the other side of the argument, the point was made that if the H-bomb could be made, and if it were first made by the Soviet Union, the threat of its use might well bring the Western Allies and the entire world under the domination of the U.S.S.R. Those who took this view believed it essential that Los Alamos carry out President Truman's order, and they remained at the Laboratory to participate in the development of fusion devices. We were among the latter group.

The Formation of the Experimental Team

Among the scientists to arrive at Los Alamos in 1944 was Louis Rosen, then in his mid-twenties. He joined J.L. Fowler, who had arrived the previous year, in a program of studies of the interaction of explosives with materials. In 1945, Fowler and Rosen assembled a group to reactivate the cyclotron after the departure of R.R. (Bob) Wilson and most of his group. This was the 42" cyclotron from Harvard, which had somehow wormed its way through Box 1663 onto the high mesas. The two experimenters soon began nuclear physics experiments with the 10-MeV deuteron beam.

Allred arrived at Los Alamos in September 1948 as a graduate student and joined Fowler and Rosen in their experiments. A year later, his dissertation was completed at about the same time the first Soviet A-bomb was exploded. A short time later, the President gave his order and the Los Alamos Scientific Laboratory teams moved into high gear to develop a fusion weapon, if indeed it could be done.

Rosen asked Allred to join him, in what would be described today as a postdoctoral position, to assist with some measurements needed for the weapons design program and in the later diagnostic measurements which would determine how well theory would correspond with experiment. For organizational purposes, Rosen became a Group Co-Leader in J-Division (the Weapons Test Division) with William E. Ogle. Rosen and Allred were joined by a third colleague, Donald D. Phillips, Sr., who had come to Los Alamos from the University of Texas.

Experimental Techniques

In order for two nuclei to undergo fusion, their colliding energies must be sufficiently high to overcome the repulsive electrostatic Coulomb potential between two positively charged nuclei. Prior to building the hydrogen bomb, high collision energies for fusion reactions were obtained by accelerating beams of light nuclei, such as deuterium, and bombarding stationary targets of other light nuclei.

The crucial experiment that we were to perform was to determine if an observable amount of nuclear fusion reactions could be obtained by energizing light nuclei with the heat produced by an A-bomb explosion. If this was the case, we would observe the neutron spectrum characteristic of fusion neutrons. The distribution of the neutron intensity as a function of neutron energy should show a sharp peak at 14 MeV. Our detectors were to be a series of nuclear emulsions, using techniques we had developed in our experiments with the 42" cyclotron.

In the late 1940s, the nuclear emulsion technique was primitive, but advancing rapidly. Rosen became interested in this field, mainly because the cyclotron was so unreliable that there was an enormous bonus attached to accumulating and recording a large amount of data with a small amount of cyclotron time. He devised numerous camera systems with which he could measure spectra and nuclear distributions from interactions of charged particles or neutron spectra from various sources. As an example, he made one of the best measurements to date of neutron intensity versus energy for fission neutrons from uranium-235, using nuclear emulsions as his detectors. By 1948, Rosen had established the Nuclear Microscopy Laboratory at Los Alamos and soon thereafter became its Group Leader.

In our method, neutrons are first made to collide with protons in a 'converter' target; emulsions are placed some distance away from the target. The direction and range of the recoil protons from neutron-proton collisions are measured and the neutron energy deduced from these two measurements. However, in this experiment we have used a target of polyethylene (CH_2), a hydrogen-rich plastic with a density of 0.93 g/cm^3.

As is the case with all experimental tools, nuclear emulsions have their advantages and disadvantages. One important advantage is that they are, like photographic film, continually sensitive. They also require no source of power, a significant feature when considering their use on a Pacific atoll, the proposed testing site of the thermonuclear device. All other diagnostic experiments relied to some degree upon electronic equipment. Depending upon the type of emulsion, there can be extremely high sensitivity to radiation. One disadvantage of nuclear emulsions is that they can be blackened by exposure to even moderately high temperatures, such as 40-50˚C. A second problem with emulsions is that they do not have time resolution: no determination can be made as to when events on the emulsion were recorded.

It may seem a curious choice to select—as your principal measuring instrument—delicate glass microscope slides, covered with thick and radiation-sensitive emulsions, to protect from and be exposed to the rigors of the environment near an atomic or thermonuclear explosion. That the choice was a good one is borne out by the experiment's results which gave unequivocal evidence of the success of the operation. By the same token, our choice dictated a rigorous series of preliminary tests to ensure that the effects of fast and slow neutrons, gamma radiation, thermal radiation, blast, fallout, and other related problems would not destroy the experiment. We dealt with the combination by taking the problems one by one. There being no way to 'mock up' a full-scale bomb explosion, we subjected our instrumental apparatus to various agents, one at a time.

Testing the Experimental Apparatus

From the very beginning we knew that somehow we would have to collimate the fast neutrons so that they would enter the detector chamber more or less parallel. However, neutrons cannot be collimated similarly to charged particles (by using stopping power); they required nuclear interaction. Various experts pointed out that the collimation of fast neutrons would modify their energy spectrum, severely limiting the usefulness of the energy measurements we had planned.

Our simple calculations showed that this would not happen; thus we proceeded to construct a three-hole test collimator using steel cylinders bored to about a half-inch diameter; limonite concrete was poured around the cylinders.

We then placed the test collimator in the thermal column of the Water Boiler Reactor in Omega Canyon at Los Alamos. To be more precise, we removed the reactor's thermal column and replaced it with the collimator. As a result, both slow and fast neutrons struck the collimator face. From this test we learned that the cavities where the nuclear cameras were to be located would quickly fill with thermal neutrons, and that the resulting (n,p) reactions with the nitrogen in the emulsions and (n,γ) reactions in the iron collimators would blacken the emulsions. We therefore had to take special steps to exclude thermal neutrons from reaching the interior of the shield where the emulsions resided.

To 'mock up' the gamma-ray dosage which the cameras were expected to receive, we placed our trial collimator in front of the 20-MeV Betatron, the first built by Donald Kerst and brought earlier to Los Alamos by him from the University of Illinois. A few days of running showed that the shielding design of the collimator was adequate to protect our nuclear emulsions from the anticipated maximum gamma-ray dose in the weapons experiment.

Reciprocity failure was another concern. We knew that exposure time must be increased nonlinearly to make photographs if incident light levels are very low (which is another way of saying that emulsion sensitivity is affected by radiation intensity and exposure time). To investigate this effect we made arrangements to use the microsecond X-ray flash machine at the General Electric Laboratories in Bloomfield, New Jersey. Alice Armstrong, Kay Froman and Allred went to New Jersey where they exposed nuclear emulsions to microsecond X-ray bursts. Our results showed that we need not have been concerned that the brief, intense burst of gamma radiation from an exploding fission primary which is used to trigger a fusion reaction would overexpose our emulsions, as compared with the radiation dose from the betatron test.

Testing the Effects of a Blast

How would the blast affect our instrumentation? A simple calculation showed that the over-pressure in the shock wave at a distance of a few hundred yards from the test device would be equivalent to the over-pressure produced by a few hundred kilograms of high explosive placed a few meters from the face of our collimator system. We trucked our collimator to an isolated site where high explosives could be detonated and did the experiment. The front face plate blew off; we redesigned it.

Physicists who work with heavy equipment soon learn to appreciate riggers. Our gadgets weighed up to several tens of tons. It takes real skill to lift and place into position such loads, where high precision of location is required. During all our preliminary experiments at Los Alamos, we had the help of a superbly competent rigging crew, led by Louis (Hoss) Rojas, later Sheriff of Los Alamos County, New Mexico. We learned a lot about rigging from Hoss and his men, although we never actually rigged a sling or touched a crane.

Probably the most serious error a crane operator can make is to drop a load. The rule is that a load is to be dropped if and only if the safety of the crane itself is threatened, e.g., when the crane begins to topple. Hoss and his crew therefore thought we had lost our minds when we decided we should hoist our 30-ton load to the top of the crane and "let 'er go." The object was, of course, to test the ruggedness of the collimator system, especially the cameras which it contained, should the blast of the bomb cause the collimator to roll or tumble. Dropping a load on purpose was something the riggers had never done before. They did it. Our instruments survived, the cable on the crane was ruined, but nobody was hit!

Soon we were almost ready for our experiment in the Pacific, but one more check was needed. The behavior of the neutrons in the device to be exploded was reasonably well-understood at energies of 14 MeV and below 3 MeV where monoenergetic neutron sources were available. But 14 MeV neutrons in a thermonuclear device soon degrade from this energy. A nagging concern was the interaction of 6-12 MeV neutrons with thermonuclear fuel. Knowledge of these interactions would also be essential to proper analysis of our experiment.

This concern mounted as time for the test neared. We were finally persuaded to devote some effort to answering these questions. Unfortunately, we had no source of neutrons in the energy range 6-12 MeV. What we did have was Gregory Breit who convinced us that if we provided him with p-D (proton-deuteron) and p-T (proton-triton) differential cross sections, he could calculate their neutron counterparts, that is, the n-D and n-T cross sections. We did not have, at LASL, any source of protons beyond 3 MeV. However, there was such a source at the Berkeley 60" cyclotron. A brief discussion with Ernest Lawrence resulted in our obtaining 'beam time' on that machine, in competition with many other users. We measured the p-D elastic scattering differential cross sections there and passed them on to Breit, who factored them into his calculations.

Soon thereafter, we headed for the Pacific and Eniwetok, a coral atoll of about 40 islands at the northwest end of the Ralik chain of the Marshall Islands: the site of our experiment.

Latitude 11° 30' North, Longitude 162° 15' East

A coral atoll is topologically a circle, except for an occasional break in its outer reef. Eniwetok Atoll is about 80 kilometers in circumference and lies geographically north of the doldrums. A continuous trade wind blows from the east at about 15 knots. The air is saturated with moisture, as might be expected. During the day the temperature rises to about 85° F, and at night may drop by about 10°.

The main military base and airstrip was located at about five o'clock on the circle on Eniwetok Island. To the east was Parry Island, the scientific base. One of the most popular spots on the island was Rosen's lab, which had a photographic laboratory and darkroom: the only air-conditioned space within several thousand miles (VIP space excepted).

To reach Eniwetok Atoll, one flew from Los Alamos, by way of Albuquerque and Los Angeles, to Honolulu; there one changed to military aircraft, continued on to Johnston Island, stopped again on Kwajalein Atoll, and then finally landed on the tiny airstrip of Eniwetok Island—a distance of 6,000 miles and, in 1951, more than 20 hours of flight time. It's a long way to carry a Leitz Ortholux microscope, especially when it's the only one you'll have, and you want to protect it by taking it aboard as cabin baggage. There are no shopping centers nor scientific supply houses on Eniwetok; all tool needs must be planned months ahead, and some tools must be shipped by surface vessel.

Rosen had designed our collimators and negotiated their manufacture in Los Angeles. They were shipped empty of their concrete shielding and arrived as large and intricate steel boxes, that had been disassembled into sixths and weighed perhaps a fourth of what they would ultimately weigh once filled with limonite concrete.

Limonite is $2Fe_2O_3 \cdot 3H_2O$, a brownish iron ore. Many physicists now know that if you mix limonite, cement, steel nuts, bolts, punchings, and water, you get a superior shielding concrete. Its density is about three times that of the densest concrete made with ordinary aggregate. Of course, it does not behave anything like regular concrete in the mixer. A third of a load is all the mixer can manage. The mix is extraordinarily sensitive to the amount of water in it, turning to soup when the water is too much by a spoonful—or so it seems. Test pourings at 500 lb/ft^3 brought exclamations of disbelief from our concrete superintendent, who was accustomed to judging the strength of concrete by its mass density.

Rosen sent Allred to Eniwetok to supervise the filling of his collimators. Allred was told to be present when any collimator was being filled to be sure the mix was wet but not soupy, that the machined tops would fit and that there was no overfilling.

It would be fun to know exactly who and what was expected of the concrete expert shipped to them from LASL by the superintendents in charge of the Holmes and Narver, Inc., construction contract at Eniwetok. Having poured a total of about one-third cubic yard of limonite concrete in his entire career, Allred was probably not precisely the expected type. But the tremendous good nature of the men, together with their capability to improvise solutions to problems, overcame any surprise they might have had. Besides, they were not altogether sure what to do with the hundreds of barrels of limonite and steel junk which were waiting for them. At least Allred knew that too much water made a bad mix, and what to do about it if it happened. As with our rigger friends, the construction men proved to be a great resource. Their term on the atoll was 18 months. They had great internal fortitude, worked well together, and were willing to take suggestions.

Some months later, one of the island superintendents, Bing, volunteered to go with us on one of our instrument recoveries—mainly so that he could see what an A-bomb did to the bunkers his crew had spent months building. He thought nothing could tear down these structures and was vociferously astonished and amazed when he saw the wreckage. Bing, like many of his fellows, was a gratifyingly erudite and graceful man—an indispensable help to our experiment.

Entertainment on the Island

Eniwetok is a monotonous place with a monotonous climate. While we were there, one of the construction men started to swim home and was not heard from again. Little entertainment was available: a snack bar, a limited liquor bar, nightly movies, monthly get-togethers.

On our first visit to Eniwetok, we were invited to a special entertainment: the combined monthly get-together of the island and construction superintendents. Uniform of the evening was aloha shirt, shorts, and sandals—the most formal attire ever worn at Eniwetok. We were served cocktails, elegant Polynesian hors d'oeuvres (by the head chef of the construction contingent, Mr. Ng) and a delicious buffet. We then sat down to the *piece de resistance*—an evening of nude movies (of pristine innocence compared to today's adult fare). Imagine our feelings when the audience (ourselves excepted) began to cheer and whistle at every slightly suggestive movement. These otherwise sober and sagacious men, upon whom our experiment depended, behaved like college sophomores! Perhaps we were too puritanical; after all, we had not spent a whole year at Eniwetok as they had.

     We sometimes played penny-ante poker. Edward Teller, a frequent visitor, joined us on a few occasions, usually forgetting his money and borrowing some, and losing that. He was distracted by other thoughts. None of us was enthusiastic about poker—it was our alternate pastime on evenings when the movie was not attractive to us.

     We wondered initially how useful the presence of the military on the island would prove to be. After a monsoon, fallout from a weapons test, a tsunami alert, submarine sightings and a better understanding of logistics, the necessity of the support of the Armed Forces became clear. This support was provided by Joint Task Force Three under Lt. Gen. Edward (Pete) Quesada, USAF. Alvin Graves, Allred's friend and mentor, and a fellow Texan, was the Scientific Deputy Commander.

H-Bombs

     As with the A-bomb, the major secret about the H-bomb is the fact that it can be made. The trick is merely to choose the right fuel and heat it to a high enough temperature for it to burn before it flies apart—which is the same problem researchers in controlled thermonuclear reactions face today. Clearly, scientists in the U.S.S.R., the United Kingdom, the People's Republic of China, and France have recognized and solved this problem in their weapons research.

     Most of the details concerning the design of thermonuclear weapons remains classified at this time, including the details of the device involved in our measurements, which was in no sense a practical weapon but merely an experiment to confirm ideas about principles. However, such details need not concern us here. The important information is that, by 1951, LASL had measured many of the necessary basic properties, and had a number of educated guesses, a lot of theory and many calculations of how a thermonuclear burning might proceed. Thermonuclear burning occurs inside the Sun and other stars, where the nuclei are confined by the enormous gravitational forces. However, an actual thermonuclear burning had never been seen on Earth, and it was not certain whether we understood things well enough to make it happen. What was most needed at that time was a full-scale nuclear experiment to find out whether or not things occurred in the way the calculations said they would. If the hoped-for thermonuclear burning took place, we would see energetic (14 MeV) neutrons. Our apparatus, and that of several other groups, was designed to detect and measure these neutrons from the thermonuclear test device.

Our experiment is described in detail in the paper written at the time. As noted above, our detector had no time resolution—but it had no dependence on electric power, either.

Experiments and Experimenters

Our colleagues Herbert York and Hugh Bradner, from the Berkeley Radiation Laboratory (now Lawrence Berkeley Laboratory), designed an experiment to detect neutrons by time-of-flight. Their neutron detectors were fairly close to the test device and were destroyed tens of microseconds after detonation. The data had to be recorded remotely.

Harold Stewart, from the Naval Research Laboratory, looked at (n,γ) reactions in air with a series of collimators and electronic counters. His bunker was several hundred meters from the 61-meter test tower, far enough away to survive the blast.

William Ogle's group measured neutron fluxes with threshold detectors which were activated through $(n,2n)$ or (n,p) reactions. This group from LASL included Clyde Cowan, Wendell Biggers, Leon Brown, and Martin Warren. Clyde realized that an atomic explosion ought to give off a large radio signal. To test the idea, he improvised an antenna which worked and soon became one method of remote detection of weapons tests.

A Final Rehearsal

With his unerring instinct for detail, Rosen insisted upon a dress rehearsal. We had to load nuclear plates and polyethylene radiators into our cameras; evacuate the cameras; put them into our LCM; take them to the test island; insert them in the collimator blocks; remove them; return to our darkroom, and develop the plates. We did all this—and the plates were ruined! This might have been the fate of our million-dollar experiment and, more importantly, of the priceless data which was to come from it!

We quickly found what had gone wrong. Somehow, our finely powdered hypo (sodium thiosulfate—the photographic fixing agent) had gotten into the air. Some of it landed in our developer trays, spoiling the solution. We mixed new solutions more carefully and had no further trouble. We thought we were ready; as it turned out, we were.

Fusion Neutrons Observed

In our earlier experiments we had often 'seen' the tracks of 14 MeV neutrons by finding the recoil protons of that energy. We were therefore acquainted with them in a familiar way. They are almost exactly 1 mm long in emulsion and once seen are unmistakable.

After the George shot (the name for our test), we recovered our cameras within hours by boat, truck and helicopter. The plates were developed the same day. Rosen put one on the microscope stage. We saw the tracks we sought—and thus knew that fusion had occurred.

Before long we found Edward Teller. "Edward, it worked!" "I believe you, but I want to see for myself," was his reply. So, in our lab on Parry Island, Edward shared with us the first direct evidence for thermonuclear fusion.

On that day Teller committed the only 'breach of security' to which he will admit—and even this he blames on Louis Rosen. Teller and Ernest Lawrence had placed a bet together on whether or not fusion would occur in the device we were testing (the George shot). After seeing the profusion of 14 MeV protons on our plates, Teller dashed to the airstrip—a nonsecurity area. As Lawrence was about to take off aboard the plane, Teller stopped the aircraft and handed Lawrence a five-dollar bill. By that action Teller paid the bet he had just lost and, without speaking, told Lawrence that the device had worked—in a public unprotected area!

Addendum

The successful George shot in 1951 was followed on October 31, 1952 by the explosion of a very large thermonuclear device. Although this was still not a practical weapon, President Truman's order had been carried out. Beginning with the tests conducted in early 1954, including detonation of the first practical weapon, the H-bomb arsenal of the United States began to accumulate.

It was at that time that serious analysis began on the effects of the detonation of multimegatons of thermonuclear explosives. It is indeed a sobering thought to know that Man holds the key to his own destruction. It is also sobering to realize that each sword has two edges, and that the attacker cannot survive his own attack.

One of the great concerns shared by many scientist has been the proliferation of nuclear arsenals among numerous countries in the world. Herb York, who participated in the George test experiments, has been an eloquent expositor of the dangers of continued escalation. The dangers are real, and involve all thoughtful people. These concerns have led to treaties banning weapons-testing in the atmosphere and in space, and to the Strategic Arms Limitation Talks.

Hindsight appears to us to say that those of us who elected to remain at Los Alamos and develop the H-bomb made the proper choice. Had this not been done, we might very well now have much less to talk about with other nations—if indeed we were allowed to talk at all.

On the positive side, there have been no nuclear exchange and no world war since 1945. It may be that those of us who hoped through our actions to help preserve peace have succeeded. Beyond that, thermonuclear explosives are the only means yet discovered to produce energy from light elements. Project PACER, a means of using underground thermonuclear explosions to provide electric power as well as fissionable material, has been studied extensively at LASL and was seriously supported by then director, Harold M. Agnew. It is conceivable, and perhaps very fitting, that what started as weaponry should be considered as a candidate for the solution of the energy problem.

The ambiguity in our purposes of research is perhaps best illustrated by an anecdote from Louis Rosen. Earlier in his career, he promised the Director of LASL, Norris Bradbury, and the Technical Associate Director, Darol Froman, that he would devote half his effort to basic research and the other half to applied, or weapons, research. From that work, over a span of many years, came 100 papers. Rosen now cannot tell, as he looks back at the early papers, which were intended to be basic and which were intended to be applied. One topic which he selected as being absolutely 'pure' was immediately found to have applications in weapons!

We suppose that the lesson to be learned from this story is something that all men know, but of which few like to be reminded: that Nature is neither inherently good nor evil, neither a friend nor an enemy. Scientific knowledge is man's single way of controlling Nature. What he does with that knowledge is not science; but it should, and does, concern scientists along with every citizen. It is one of the many threads in the fabric of the world in which we live.

*John Allred came to Los Alamos in September 1948 and completed his Ph.D. dissertation awarded in 1950 by the University of Texas, under the direction of J. L. Fowler and L. Rosen. He joined Fowler and Rosen to assist with measurements needed for weapons design and diagnostics. Most of his career (1956-79) was spent at the University of Houston where he rose to Professor of Physics and Biophysical Sciences and to Vice President and Dean of Faculties. In 1979 he returned to Los Alamos where he is consultant to the Laboratory.

Louis Rosen came to Los Alamos in July 1944 with a Ph.D. from Pennsylvania State University. He joined J. L. Fowler to study the interaction of explosives with materials, and later to lead the cyclotron group in nuclear physics experiments. Recognizing the need for a medium energy accelerator for basic and applied research in nuclear physics, he was instrumental in establishing the Los Alamos Meson Physics Facility in 1965 and was its director from 1965 to 1985. He is presently Senior Fellow Emeritus at the Laboratory.

A MAVERICK VIEW
J. Carson Mark*

Asked to say something reflecting my thoughts concerning the Lab's history and present prospects I can offer only an account of events starting from the time of my first arriving at Los Alamos. The matters referred to are, then, those seen from a quite limited point of view. By now, of course, I am aware of many things which affected the Lab but with which I was not directly in contact at the time. These could better be discussed by persons on that particular scene.

I came to Los Alamos only in May, 1945—before Trinity, but much too late to have had any part in the Lab's spectacular war-time success. However, for the two years preceding I had been a member of a small section directed by George Placzek at the Montreal Laboratory. This laboratory was the British-Canadian project managed by the National Research Council of Canada for the purpose of designing a heavy water pilot plant for the production of plutonium—the reactor subsequently built at Chalk River, Ontario. Though not directly part of the Manhattan District (MED) operation it maintained a close liaison with the MED under the direction of the Tripartite (U.S.-U.K.-Canada) Combined Policy Committee. The procedures for information control adopted by the committee for the Montreal Laboratory were, of course, the same as those applying in the MED. This meant that though some limited exchange between the Montreal Lab and the Metallurgical Lab at Chicago was allowed, no distinctive Los Alamos information was permitted to reach either Lab. Though rather simple approximations to the solutions of the neutron transport equation were sufficient for most problems met in the design of a moderated reactor, Placzek was well aware from discussions with colleagues in pre-MED days that much more accurate solutions to that equation would be necessary for fast-neutron problems of the sort arising at Los Alamos. He had consequently put a small group to work on developing means to obtain more accurate numerical solutions for the neutron transport equation. By sometime in 1944 this group had succeeded in outlining an approach which, though quite cumbersome to apply, would be capable of providing numerically accurate solutions to some types of problems of interest. Word of this was welcomed at Los Alamos and some application of the method was made there.

In early 1945 Placzek finally received his U.S. citizenship papers, which enabled him to plan to transfer from the Montreal Laboratory to Project Y. He arranged that two members of his Montreal sub-group should transfer with him. As a result, Placzek, Bengt Carlson, and I came to Los Alamos within a few weeks of each other, with my own arrival being in the second half of May. That was an exciting time; but it wasn't a particularly favorable time for getting down to work. Everyone was either rushing to complete preparations for Trinity or breathlessly awaiting the outcome. It was no time for setting ignorant newcomers on the track of problems needing attention.

After the resounding success of the Trinity test and the closely following end of the war, Los Alamos entered on a period of rapid change and uncertainty. A large fraction of the most senior and knowledgeable staff made plans for an early return to their pre-war posts, and the large contingent of enlisted personnel, about 50% of the technical staff in mid-1945, waited only for discharge from the army to resume civilian life. As of October 1945, it was expected that the size of the staff would fall to one-third by March 1946.

In addition to the uncertainty consequent to individual plans for departure, there was much uncertainty of an institutional nature. The MED was a war-time organization with a war-time mission. It typically wrote its contracts—as that with the University of California—to expire at some time (like six months, say) after the cessation of hostilities. This was on the supposition that by some such time there would be national legislation establishing some authority to take over the atomic energy enterprise. In the meantime the MED would renegotiate extension of contracts as necessary to ensure that what it deemed to be essential activities were continued while avoiding, as far as possible, long-range commitments that might limit the freedom of action of its successor without being aware of the existence of the tremendous project on atomic energy until after the bombing of Japan. It took Congress some time to pass legislation to create a successor and to specify its nature and powers and responsibilities. Until this was done, the Lab could only speculate as to whether it would be expected to continue its activity along the existing line, and, if so, whether under civilian or military auspices, and whether it would continue at Los Alamos or at some other less out-of-the-way and easier-to-maintain location. As it turned out, the Atomic Energy Act was passed only in August, 1946, with the actual transfer of authority from the MED to the new and yet to be formed AEC to be effective on January 1, 1947.

The Atomic Energy Act was passed by the 79th Congress in August 1946. Naturally it required some time for President Truman to locate and sign on a suitable group to fill the very important and novel positions of commissioners in the new AEC. By the time he had made his appointments it was so late in the year that the confirmation hearings had to be held over till after the off-year election of 1946 in which the Republicans gained control of both houses. The actual hearings, then, were conducted by the 80th Congress which assembled only in January, 1947.

After January 1, 1947, though the AEC was nominally responsible for the conduct of the atomic energy program, it lacked a firm mandate for decisions until the appointment of its members should be confirmed by the Senate. Major decisions on many matters were urgently needed, some of which bore directly on the generally felt need for strengthening the national security and on the nuclear weapons program in particular. Until these decisions could be made, the activity at Los Alamos was left without a clear directive. Though well aware that progress on those matters affecting national security would not be possible until the AEC should be confirmed, a powerful group of prominent senators apparently had no difficulty in setting these considerations aside in favor of mounting a concerted campaign to defeat the confirmation of David Lilienthal, Truman's appointee as chairman of the AEC. Some members of this group were, incidentally, also unreconciled to major provisions of the Atomic Energy Act itself, such as those for civilian control and government ownership of facilities. There followed one of the more disgraceful episodes in the history of the U.S. Senate. By endless and repetitious recitals of their reasons for dislike or disapproval or disagreement with David Lilienthal, based on past actions or reported opinions or unfounded allegations or calumnious interpretations of such items, the group sought to extend the hearings or promote a Senate refusal to confirm. This effort failed of its purpose—and it must be left as an exercise for the reader to wonder what would have happened had it not—but even so it was April 9, 1947, before the Senate by a vote of 52 to 38 confirmed Truman's appointees to the AEC.

Only then could the AEC get down to business. Only then, also, could the Lab be assured that the program it had supposed it should work on was the program which was wanted. In the Lab's view, an early series of tests of improved weapons was high on the list of things needed. It soon became clear that the AEC, and also the President, favored such tests, and already on June 27, 1947, without public notice, Truman gave his formal authorization to prepare for a test series in the Pacific in April 1948.

In addition to the extended period of not knowing what the shape of the post-MED atomic program would be, there were some extraneous events which cut into progress or raised serious uncertainty. However, by the time the AEC finally got into action these were things of the past.

One of these events—the famous water shortage—which appears trivial in retrospect, was quite disturbing at the time. On a cold night in December, 1945, the pipeline from Guaje Canyon [which serviced Los Alamos] froze solid. Other sources were insufficient to meet domestic needs and the needs of several Lab sites. A water trucking operation was rapidly put in motion whereby surface or near-surface water from the grazing land on the bank of the Rio Grande was brought up the hill and put in the distribution system. The hastily mobilized carriers from the surrounding region had evidently previously been engaged in transporting various flavors of fuel oil, and for biological protection the water delivered was so generously treated with chlorine that it acted as an effective bleach if splashed, for example, on ladies' stockings. For several weeks the water available was minimally adequate for domestic needs and operations at a few sites had to be curtailed. Undoubtedly some individuals, undecided as to whether or not to stay with the project, were moved by the discomfort and disruption to leave Los Alamos. On the other hand, by a letter on January 4, 1946—almost immediately after the water emergency struck—General Groves assured Bradbury that trucking of additional water sufficient to supply continual service to all housing and sites would be maintained as long as necessary, while construction, to be initiated promptly, proceeded on a new system to assure a year-round supply. In addition, Groves reported that planning was already underway for building at least some satisfactory permanent family housing. Thus, even in advance of the legislation which would determine the pattern of the post-MED operation of the project, this major new government investment in the facilities at Los Alamos encouraged many in their assumption that the Lab's activity would continue, and would continue at Los Alamos.

In connection with the Lab's postwar work on weapons, two matters were obviously of the greatest importance and called for whatever immediate attention the Lab could put on them. One was to complete new and improved designs and prepare for testing them, since they seemed to promise better performance and better use of fissile material. The other was the need of re-engineering the components of the Trinity device so that teams of enlisted personnel, after training by members of the Lab staff, would be enabled to assemble and check out a complete weapon. In the fall of 1945 the Engineering Division of the Lab, which would handle both the work on the components and the training mission, was in the course of moving from Los Alamos to new quarters at Sandia Base near Albuquerque where the military personnel involved would be stationed. At about the same time as the water shortage struck, a far more serious disruption of plans was declared. The Lab was informed from Washington that it would be technically responsible for firing two or three devices in a series already approved by President Truman and planned for mid-1946 at Bikini Atoll in the Pacific. It was (it was said) chiefly for the purpose of seeing the effects of atomic explosions on naval vessels, though from the plans for observers it was evidently also to be a public demonstration of the power of the atom. Given the circumstances, it would be necessary to use a proven device—which meant an unmodified Trinity-type assembly. Such a plan required a large team of Los Alamos personnel mainly from the Engineering Division in the field, since the original device had been put together more like a large and very complicated piece of experimental laboratory apparatus than as an engineered package. It was also necessary to obtain diagnostic data sufficient to establish whether or not the expected performance had been realized, and to do this under firing conditions quite different from any previously used; and this required personnel from other divisions of the Lab. Operation Crossroads, then, had extensive effects on the Lab's planned activity, in that the full attention of the Engineering Division was preempted for a period of about nine months and major attention from other sections of the Lab was also required, though for shorter periods.

For its particular purposes the operation would appear to have been successful. It provided some data of interest to the Navy; and it provided a colorful several-week Sunday-outing for a swarm of idle curious: there were several ship-loads of observers—Navy and other brass, congressmen, foreign delegations, and a whole ship full of ostensible journalists. There was rather little in way of technical return to the Lab in compensation for its setback in planned work beyond the fact that so far as it was possible to tell, all four of the Trinity-type devices which had then been fired had given generally similar performance.

The other major unsettling event (so far as forming a clear picture of the Lab's prospects was concerned) occurred at about the same time as the Crossroads Operation came up. This was the Administration's announcement in November 1945 that it would propose to the United Nations that work on atomic energy be put under international control to ensure that the atom would be used only for peaceful purposes. Proposals to this effect were prepared in Washington during the succeeding months with little or no public discussion and were laid before the United Nations Atomic Energy Commission (UNAEC) on June 14, 1946—two weeks before the first test of Operation Crossroads—by Bernard Baruch. In most respects the U.S. proposals were favorably received by 10 of the 12 members of the UNAEC but they were adamantly opposed by the USSR on the particular matter of the Veto as laid down in the U.N. Charter. It was not publicly known at the time that the USSR was already heavily engaged in a project to obtain nuclear weapons of its own. Many concluded early that the proposals would never go anywhere, though active debate continued till the end of 1946. The Baruch proposals were not formally withdrawn; but after Baruch's resignation as U.S. representative at the beginning of 1947 further discussion of international control petered out and no longer affected the Lab's activities.

Leaving aside now the discussion of external events which affected the Lab, I turn to some comments on internal events, and particularly those which concerned T-Division, since those are the ones of which I was most directly aware. Though changes of similar interest and significance impinged on every section of the Lab, they could best be recounted by persons closer to the scene.

One early notable event, of course, was Oppenheimer's resignation as Lab Director on October 15, 1945. Oppenheimer and General Groves had persuaded Commander Norris Bradbury to take over that responsibility. This he did, for a maximum of six months, or until legislation should establish the post-MED status for work on atomic energy. Even on this basis, Bradbury faced an awesome challenge in that the war-time leader of every technical division had plans to leave Los Alamos within less than four months. Fortunately for the Lab, and fortunately for the country, Bradbury decided to extend his time at Los Alamos for a period much longer than six months—quite possibly because the job was confronted by such hopelessly heavy seas. He retired only after 25 years of outstanding service as Director of the Lab.

Early in December 1945, Hans Bethe, war-time head of T-Division, announced his decision to resign from the Lab in order to return to Cornell at the beginning of 1946. Bradbury then asked Edward Teller if he would take over T-Division. Teller replied that he would be willing to do so on condition that the Lab would undertake to work aggressively to improve fission bombs to the extent of conducting at least a dozen tests per year. Even Teller, weak as he may have been in gauging the time and effort required to carry out new and exacting mechanical operations of any kind, must have realized that such an undertaking was totally impossible under existing conditions and that Bradbury had no choice but to refuse any such commitment. In the event, Teller left Los Alamos near the end of January, 1946, to join the faculty of the University of Chicago, though as a consultant he continued to give very generously of his time to the Lab. On Bethe's departure, Bradbury appointed George Placzek as his successor.

Because of ill-health, Placzek had to get away from the altitude of Los Alamos, and early in the summer of 1946 he left the Lab and returned to the east coast where he later became a member of the faculty at the Institute for Advanced Study in Princeton.

In the fall of 1946 Robert Richtmyer was appointed to succeed Placzek as T-Division leader. At about this time Teller (back at Los Alamos as a consultant) sketched out a possible new pattern for a thermonuclear device which came to be called the "Alarm Clock." Over the next year, Richtmyer, with a small group, assessed the performance of several configurations of the Alarm Clock type. Since, in the parlance of the time, a "thermonuclear" device was practically synonymous with "multi-megaton," the examples considered were all of that sort and, with the techniques for assembly then known, all were vastly too large and too heavy to be of any practical interest as weapons. Later, with the new insights developed in 1951-52, this came out differently, and a weaponizable device of the Alarm Clock type—the TX-14—was successfully tested in 1954 with a yield of 7 megatons. Early in 1947, a new type of experiment involving thermonuclear reactions was proposed by some members of T-Division which, after extended discussion and important modifications proposed by Teller in September, 1947, became known as the "Booster Experiment" or "booster." After several years of work on details, but without basic change in pattern, this was successfully tested in the Item shot of May 1951. In May 1947, Stanislaw Ulam proposed the Monte Carlo scheme of calculation to John von Neumann who immediately responded by preparing a draft of the first paper giving prescriptions for the application of the Monte Carlo method, which paper was expanded and put in final form by Richtmyer.

In the fall of 1947, Richtmyer came to the conclusion that in order to obtain worthwhile estimates of the behavior of a system in which fission and thermonuclear burning interacted it would be essential to have a detailed picture of the progress of a fission explosion. The calculation required was of unprecedented size and complexity and the only computing machine which appeared to be capable of handling such a problem was the IBM SSEC then nearing completion at the IBM Building on Madison Avenue in New York City. He decided to undertake this enormous calculation (which came to be known as "Hippo") himself; and, since ready access to the machine would be necessary, this entailed transferring his activity to New York City, where he would have the great additional advantage of easy access to von Neumann who was based in Princeton, New Jersey. Once it was settled that he would take his work for the Lab to New York City (about November, 1947) he resigned as T-Division leader and I—who by that time, had spent most of the preceding two years on the nuclear design of devices of the type proposed for full scale test in Operation Sandstone—became responsible for T-Division.

Richtmyer's project took longer than had been expected at the start; but results were available early in 1950—in time to be useful in connection with devices involving thermonuclear burning in the Greenhouse Operation of 1951. One unanticipated but extremely important byproduct of "Hippo" was the proposal by Richtmyer and von Neumann that a "viscosity treatment" for calculating the progress of shocks would make such calculations feasible on automatic calculating equipment. The viscosity method was so advantageous that it was rapidly adopted for almost all calculations—implosion, as well as explosion—involving shock hydrodynamics.

To go back in time somewhat: by July, 1946, all the war-time group leaders in T-Division had left the Lab with the exception of Donald "Moll" Flanders who was scheduled to return to Chicago early in September. Flanders' large group carried out computations primarily to meet requirements arising in T-Division, and also studied improvements in computational methods. In view of his experience in a similar role at the Montreal Lab and his prior experience in numerical and statistical methods at Yale, Bengt Carlson succeeded Flanders in September, 1946. As group leader, Carlson had the assistance of Max Goldstein, who had been his assistant at the Montreal Laboratory following pre-war experience at the Mathematical Tables Project in New

York, and who had come to Los Alamos from Montreal in the late spring of 1946. Goldstein stayed on as Carlson's alternate for about eleven years. He then returned to his home town where he joined the computing staff of the Courant Mathematical Institute of N.Y.U.; and, after various assignments there, he became director of the Computing Facility of the Courant Institute. The wartime computing equipment at Los Alamos, which consisted mainly of an early version of a card-programmed calculator plus a large number of hand-operated desk calculators: Burroughs, Marchants, and Fridens, was replaced by larger and more capable machines. The computing capability of the Lab was augmented many-fold in 1952 when the Los Alamos-built MANIAC came into operation in a new group under Nicholas Metropolis. Carlson's group continued to expand as generation after generation of top-of-the-line commercial equipment was brought in. The requirements of the technical divisions other than T-Division grew from a sporadic component to a steady stream of major problems originating from every field of activity in the Lab. The computing power of the equipment assembled at Los Alamos—which was always large compared to most other computing centers in the country—kept on growing. The Lab's computing activity remained in the form of a couple of groups in T-Division until 1968, at which time it was separated off as a new major technical division of the Lab—C-Division.

Throughout his time with the computing group Carlson had maintained his interest in devising convenient means of obtaining accurate solutions to the transport equation. Along with a few talented collaborators a series of progressively improved computing schemes were developed, partly on the basis of new insights and new algorithms and partly on the basis of adaptations to improvements in automatic equipment. Increase in accuracy and flexibility and economy of calculation time were immediate benefits to the Lab in weapons neutronic calculations, but also to the wider community of persons working on nuclear reactors as full transport theory solutions of neutronic problems became possible and began to be required. Though the nature of problems of interest to the Lab was highly classified, the mathematical methods of obtaining solutions to the transport equation were free of classification restrictions. Consequently the solution methods developed at Los Alamos gained attention and came into fairly general use throughout the country, and even abroad. For example, it came as a surprise that the Lab Library received an unsolicited copy of a bibliographical booklet prepared and published in 1966 by a staff member of the Atomic Institute in Bucharest, Rumania, entitled "The SN (Carlson) Approximation to The Neutron Transport Equation." After the formation of C-Division, Carlson remained with T-Division as head of a small new group concerned with Transport Theory.

Now from these accounts of particular and early post-war personnel changes in T-Division, and leaving aside other changes in T-Division as well as many similar changes in other parts of the Lab, we turn to consider, in sketchy outline, the progress of the Lab's post-war weapons program. There are, of course, other programs which could warrant discussion, and among these are some which may in the future outweigh the weapons program; but as the oldest, most distinctive, and largest single program and the one most subject to change at the moment, only the weapons program will be referred to here.

By the end of 1946, the Engineering Division had completed its move from Los Alamos to new—though still inadequate and temporary—quarters at Sandia Base. The division was also free of its extraneous involvement with the Crossroads Operation. During 1947 it designed a new assembly of the non-nuclear parts of a weapon (designated the Mark IV) with components suitable for mass production and testing and simplified assembly procedures. The Mark IV system was ready for full-scale test in the Sandstone Operation at Enewetak in April-May 1948. The Lab also had ready several new nuclear designs embodying features which, right from the time of the Trinity test in 1945, had appeared likely to provide improved performance, though the fact of improvement was not guaranteed, nor the amount of improvement established, as there had been no previous opportunity to test.

The Sandstone results were entirely satisfactory. For Z-Division it marked the end of the day of the atomic device as a piece of complicated laboratory apparatus rather than a weapon, and provided a sense of accomplishment and confidence. The resulting increase in industrial and military orientation led within a year to the separation of Z-Division from the Los Alamos Lab (and from the University of California's contract) to become the nucleus of the Sandia Laboratory under Western Electric (AT&T) management.

The results from the new nuclear designs were also quite satisfactory. The improvements in performance were in reasonable agreement with expectation and, more importantly, it was shown that U-235 could be used effectively in an implosion system, either by itself or in conjunction with plutonium. Since U-235 had previously been used only in the Hiroshima gun-assembly system, and since a gun-assembly system requires something like a couple of times more fissile material than a system of implosion type, the number of units which could be made from the existing stock of plutonium and uranium could be increased appreciably merely by refabricating the fissile parts of the weapons in hand.

The successful experience in Sandstone was also of great importance in another way in that it provided the Lab with a first firm footing for the consideration of a range of possible variations in design patterns such as devices of reduced size and weight, or reduced cost in fissile material, or for meeting the specialized requirements of the first test objects aimed at exploring the behavior of thermonuclear fuels—as, in particular, for the Item and George shots of the next following Pacific operation, set for April-May, 1951.

Beyond the stage reached in the Greenhouse Operation, the Lab's progress in the weapons program has often been described, so it need not be followed here in detail. The principal highlights were demonstration in principle for a method of achieving very large thermonuclear [TN] explosions (Mike shot, 1952); proof tests of several large TN devices in weaponized form (Operation Castle, 1954). Although proof in principle of boosting had been obtained in the Item shot of 1951, this was in a form unsuitable for weaponization: successful demonstration of boosting in the weaponizable form which has been used ever since it was obtained at about the time of Castle. From 1956 to the present, with preliminary experience in both TN models and boosters in hand, and with Livermore beginning to participate after its first successful tests in 1955, a very large number of tests have been conducted. A wide range of variations and refinements has been explored in these tests which has made it possible, for example, to adapt warheads to meet the requirements imposed by many new and smaller carriers. The success of such developments has, of course, required continuing improvements in the nuclear design aspects of warheads, along with great advances in computing capability needed to realize such design improvements. But it would not have been possible without the extraordinary advances made at the Lab in a number of other special fields. These include advances in chemical explosive technology, in mechanical and electronic engineering, in the understanding of material properties and in material handling, in neutronic, nuclear, and atomic data, in radiochemical technology, in a great variety of sensitive and rapid detection and recording equipment, and other fields as well. Out of these developments the country now has a very impressive spectrum of options as to weight, size, shape and yield of environmentally qualified weapons. It also has these in awe-inspiring numbers—although the Lab, happily, has had nothing to do with that aspect of things.

In purely mechanical terms, a nuclear weapon, whether large or small, has the one and only capability of imposing damage on an adversary. No doubt there are people who equate national security with the ability to impose damage. For these, there may be no limit to the number or types of nuclear weapons which can contribute to national security. There are, of course, others—probably a much larger number—for whom national security consists of being free from having damage imposed on us by an adversary having a nuclear stockpile. For these, weapons in numbers or types beyond what may be necessary to ensure that objective do not contribute to national security. For these, the Lab may already have reached the boundary of what it can contribute to national security by further work on weapon development. Indeed, the fact that the U.S. Administration has already withdrawn some types of weapons from deployment, and favors reduction in the number of other types, may reflect such a view.

It is difficult at this time to say much about the role of the Lab in the future, since that depends strongly on the picture held by members of the Congress and the DOE of the nature of the Lab and its proper relationship to problems of national importance.

The Lab is frequently and popularly referred to as a "weapons lab"; and to many this conveys the idea that its primary capability consists of making and testing new weapons. If no new weapons are required, the cost of operation and funding should, then, decrease proportionately. But that, of course, is not how things really work since there are aspects of weapons activity quite apart from work on new developments in which even those who wish for the termination of work on new weapons and testing would not intend that there should be any cutting back. Such aspects probably include the maintenance and surveillance of the existing stockpile to the extent necessary to ensure deterrence; the technical means of detecting or inhibiting proliferation; the means of detecting and tracking down stolen or diverted weapon material; devising the most favorable procedures for the dismantlement of weapons to be retired and the proper disposition of recovered fissile material. Such types of weapons activity will continue to require attention even after it may have been decided that no work on new developments is desired. Events of the recent past suggest that we may be approaching such a regime; but we are not yet securely established in such a position. That will require that the present turmoil in the major states of the former USSR should be resolved and that credible agreements along with acceptable procedures for verifying dismantlement, disposition of recovered material, for verifying existing stockpiles and production of new materials, are all in place.

At least several years will be needed to complete such a transition—though it is conceivable that our government, anticipating a favorable outcome, might declare an end to work on new weapons before that. However, should the situation change in such a way that work on new weapons is called for, then, from being known as the original weapons lab, the country would certainly look to the Lab to respond to the new situation. It would be assumed that the Lab would start with about the level of proficiency which has been built up at present; that is, that all the necessary specialties would be brought to bear with today's capability. For this to be true, of course, it would be necessary that attention to these various specialties had been continued up to the time they were called on, since in many cases once such work were laid aside it might require considerable time to reconstitute a group with the knowledge, skill, and experience—as well, possibly, as assembled and tuned equipment—to reestablish today's status. At least some of the specialties referred to are multi-purpose, and with a growing number of technology transfer projects taking shape it is quite possible that continued attention at the frontier of at least some of the special fields referred to will result from such activities; but it is improbable that all will be covered in that way.

The important point is to maintain the capability of taking up work on new designs from close to the present position. This is a clear obligation for the DOE, as well as for the Lab. Care will be needed to decide just which specialties will require ongoing support in order to meet such an objective. For example, though testing is essential in connection with a new weapons design, it may not be necessary to maintain any activity or organization on that aspect of things, as witness the several occasions the Lab has put together adequate diagnostic teams starting with little or nothing in hand adapted to the specific needs (e.g. Trinity, Greenhouse, and Mike). Also, this needed capability to resume need not be thought of as something geared up to bat out a sudden response, as to meet a "crisis" or "emergency"—though these words have sometimes been used in this connection. After all, even when a weapon has been fully designed and tested it will still require a year or so for the production complex to turn out enough units of a new model to make any decisive difference to an existing stockpile. In any case, the obligation to maintain the capability to resume work on new weapons remains; and its needs should be met until there is a reasonably firm assurance in place that further work on new weapons will no longer be needed.

It is true that statements at least generally consistent with the point of view indicated above have been made to congressional people on a number of occasions by representatives of the Lab; and no doubt there are a number of congressionally related people who understand the Lab's continuing responsibilities. Still, the Lab's message on this point may require reiteration since the DOE does not seem to be making much of it.

The other major player in the Lab's role in the future is the DOE. At present the DOE would appear to be busily trying to sell off choice slices of the Lab for industrial cooperation. It will be good for the Lab and will also be a public good if the early cooperation ventures are successful. Similar projects would certainly follow. But to sustain a program of this sort a policy concerning ongoing research and support of such research will be needed. A more diverse range of activity is likely to be called for, and this will need to be foreshadowed in the research program and in DOE's policy respecting individual research projects. A new and more flexible policy will be needed—one which more clearly recognizes the value and nature of research rather than considering it as a sort of commodity to be gauged and accounted for and doled out as a favor by the clerks and bookkeepers on DOE's staff—an approach, in short, which carries the notion of collaboration in an effort of common interest rather than the present grudging approach whereby research proposals may be submitted for "review" and possible "approval" by a Department staff which, for the most part, lacks adequate means for making sound judgements on such matters.

*Carson Mark came to Los Alamos in May 1945 from the Montreal Laboratory managed by the National Research Council of Canada having received his Ph.D. degree in abstract mathematics from the University of Toronto in 1938. He was Theoretical Division leader from 1947–73, which included the tumultuous period during which the H-bomb was developed. He retired in 1973, but has maintained an active relationship with the Laboratory and served on numerous government advisory boards and commissions. He is a past member and present honorary member of the J. Robert Oppenheimer Memorial Committee.

LOS ALAMOS BLUES

Unknown G.I.

Some folks live in the city.
Some folks live in a town.
Some live out in a suburb.
But we—well, listen now:

We're just a P.O. number.
We have no real address
Although we were selected,
I wonder—for the best!
We're not like other people,
No one knows what we do:
So, P.O. Box 1663,
Here's to you.

They put us on a mountain
Outside of Santa Fe
Where the only sign of wild life
Is GI wolves at bay.
We're on a secret mission
And secret work we do
Where we're not to tell folks what we know.
But I don't know, do you?

And when this war is over,
Down from this hill we'll roam.
We'll ride down from this Shangri-la
Right to a Veteran's Home.
So heed my word, you children,
Of brilliance do not boast
Or you'll end (as we have)
A genius up in Los Alamos.

THE ROBERT OPPENHEIMER I KNEW
Charles L. Critchfield*

It's a pleasure to be here and to have guests who were here at the same time I was during the war. They told me before the meeting that you'd keep me honest.

I don't want to give so much an assessment of Robert Oppenheimer as to tell you about the personal contact I had with him, because next year we're going to have the 50th anniversary celebration and we're going to hear a lot about Los Alamos and Robert Oppenheimer. Of course, he's now in the history books and a good bit of that, naturally, is wrong. It usually is. I thought it would be refreshing for me, and I hope for you, just to talk about personal contacts that I had with him.

My friendship with Robert got off to a very doubtful start. I applied for a National Research Fellowship and wrote him in as my master. I had contacted him, of course, and he agreed that I could come to Berkeley. But during that year I got to working on some theoretical problems with Eugene Wigner at Princeton University, so I wrote to Robert and asked him if it was OK for me to change from Berkeley to Princeton. He very graciously agreed to that and found a substitute for his post-doc. What I didn't realize was that these two guys were not speaking to each other. It had something to do with Europe. I never asked either one about it. But when I went to Princeton to work, I got word by the grapevine that the man who took my place at Berkeley was doing a problem that I'd already done but never published. This man who had told me the gossip said, "Now you can scoop the guy and publish before he does."

So I wrote it up and took it to Wigner, told him the story, showed him my work and said, "Now, Eugene, what do I do? Do I publish this or do I write to Robert and tell him that I have already done it?" Eugene very coldly said, "I can't help you with that. That's your decision." So I sent my work to Robert with a letter telling the story—except I didn't tell him about Eugene—and said, "If this can be of any help to you, please feel free to use it."

It turned out that Joe Weinberg, the man who took my place, had done the problem by a completely different method but got exactly the same results. So he published it and acknowledged my letter and very graciously thanked me. From then on we were friends. I got passed up.

The next time I saw Robert was when I took my first defense job at the Geophysical Laboratory in Washington. Robert Oppenheimer and Edward Teller came to see me in the laboratory there and asked if they could talk to me out on the lawn. This was in December 1942. They said, "We have a very important project and we want you to come and join it. If it's successful, it will end the war and put an end to all wars. But, it's located in a remote part of New Mexico. You have to be in uniform and your family can't live there." "Forget it," I said, "because my job here isn't finished and we're planning a home in Maryland." We had a three-month-old child, and I had no desire to go to New Mexico. Well, they went away.

But that March, the director of the laboratory where I worked got notice that I was going to New Mexico. I got a military priority on a DC-3 to take me to Albuquerque and arrived here in April 1943 in time for the conference where we were briefed by Robert Serber.

They had decided by that time that we didn't have to be majors in the Army and that there would be houses for us when they got built. So we moved here in June 1943 and lived down in Bandelier at Frijoles Lodge along with the Tascheks and Hemplemanns and some others. That's how we got started in Los Alamos.

Incidentally, yesterday was the 49th anniversary of the first implosion, the main event I remember of that summer. Seth Neddermeyer had brought up the idea that instead of shooting pieces of uranium together to make a critical mass, you could pull them together with high explosives. A very repulsive idea to the military. He had Oppenheimer's and Dana Mitchell's approvals to get some TNT, some primacord, blasting caps and things—all that you need to make an explosion. On the 4th of July, 1943, Seth invited Robert (who was on travel so he wasn't there), Deak Parsons, our boss, and a Navy man who headed the Ordnance Engineering Division, and Ed McMillan to go out on South Mesa. We were going to make an implosion.

Seth got some two-inch sewer pipe and several lengths of ordinary stove pipe. We put the sewer pipe into the stovepipe, packed it with TNT, and got the primer for it—about 30 yards of it—down to a big rock. We all got behind the rock and blew it up. It was just about perfect. What you read in the books is right: the sewer pipe just condensed right into a solid mass and stayed there. So that was a great success.

But Deak Parsons, the military man, didn't believe in this blowing things together. He thought it was nice, but he had to go over to Pecos to buy a saddle horse for his wife, so he left. When he got out of sight, we took the rest of the stovepipe and packed it with TNT, put a primacord in it and got behind that rock again, and we had a 4th of July explosion. It was the biggest firecracker we could ever have. I don't know if either Deak or Robert found out about that, but there are some records of that first implosion.

CHARLES L. CRITCHFIELD

We were pretty crowded in those days. Parsons, Ed McMillan, myself, and Parsons's secretary, whose name was Hazel Greenbacher, each had a desk in a room about 12 by 12 in the U Building, which was a physics laboratory until we got our office buildings built. They were called A and B buildings. A building was Oppenheimer's and B building was Parsons', or Administration. My office wound up in A Building just a few doors from Oppenheimer's. This was when I really began to get acquainted with Robert Oppenheimer. Our relationship had always been cordial and in this case, Robert was quite informal. He kept his door, the hall door and his secretary's office door open, so when you went by, he would greet you if he wasn't busy. Sometimes he would say, "Do you have a minute? I'd like to talk to you." That's me. I don't know what he did with other people. So I'd go in and he'd close the office door to the secretary and to the hall. Then he would start discussing—maybe things about work—but it always wound up in a lecture of some kind. Of course, he was a professor and he liked to talk and he desired to have somebody to talk to. There were just the two of us. Of course, I was two degrees lower and 10 to 12 years behind him in my education, so I was a student. Incidentally, he got his Ph.D. in Goettingen in 1927 when I was a junior in high school and he was 23 years old. My Ph.D. came 12 years later, so I was very much a captive audience.

But he didn't talk about weapons or physics. He talked about the mystery of life. He had a special way of lecturing. He liked to walk around the room. Of course, his room had the conference table and plenty of space. He would rub his palms together and look to the side. He was talking to himself; he wasn't talking to me. The reason I remember this is not so much because of what he said but because I didn't really understand what he was talking about.

He kept quoting the *Bhagavad Gita*, the Hindu sacred writings, and he kept talking about the mysteries as recondite [re kaun´ dite] significance of some things. Of course, I never pronounced that word that way. It's recondite [rek´ un dite], the way I pronounce it. It's the same word as *escondido* in Spanish. But he was talking about the mysteries, the secret things that are so important to life. This reference to the *Bhagavad Gita*—let's call it the *Gita*—indicated that he had this mystic streak. He was very interested in theological terms, but the setting for the *Gita* is strictly reincarnation and caste system and so on. He couldn't possibly be believing in that, in my opinion.

So I got acquainted with this side. This happened about once a month for the year that I was in that same building with him. I was enjoying it, and I wish I had kept notes because the only reason I remember it now is because of that "re kaun´ dite" stuff.

I decided before I gave this talk that I should read the *Gita*, a copy of which is in our library. I didn't see any "re kaun´ dites" in it, so I borrowed the public library's two copies, which are more recent translations. It was written in Sanskrit and Robert read Sanskrit, as probably everybody knows. Well, no "re kaun` dite," but the word "unmanifest" is very prominent in one of the books. So I reckoned that what Robert was getting at was a grasp of theology, which is very similar to Paul Tillock's concept of the relationship of the individual to the universe. So I copied the translation in Edward Arnold's version. Edward Arnold was a British poet and journalist about 100 years ago. This translation, I think, is relative to what Robert had in mind. It's called *The Book of Religion by Devotion to the One Supreme God*.

In discussing the recondite aspect of this relationship, God was portrayed in this poem as Krishna. Ordinarily, Krishna is thought of as being an avatar of Vishnu in the trinity of the Hindu mythology, but in this poem, he is the supreme god. He's the creator, the destroyer, the redeemer. What he says is, "This is that life named the "unmanifest"" and this was my clue to the recondite thing: "The infinite. The all. The uttermost. That light is mine and I am theirs." So you see this is the eternal bliss that the Hindu people, including Buddhists, aspire to. Life itself is just misery, and you have to get out of it, and you do that by being good. The rest of the book is mostly Krishna telling his soldier who doesn't want to fight—the hero of the poem, actually—what he has to do for eternal bliss. That's what it's all about. Robert was such a mystic, poetical and complicated guy himself that he was searching for this, and he was making me listen to it, which I enjoyed.

I had read the *Gita* myself when I used to read Plato, Piccard and things like that. I thought it made a lot of sense because the idea was that if you wanted to adjust your life to the rest of the world, the thing to do was to grow up: pay your debts, keep your word, and such things. But Robert saw much more to it than that. As I say, I enjoyed it.

There was another aspect of Robert that came to light, and it's one that John Manley mentions in his review of the book *Day One* by Peter Wyden. He had a great sense of the dramatic. He loved to make statements that were completely absurd without any warning if they were supposed to be funny or whether they meant something that you could take seriously. This streak he had—you might call it a weakness—proved his undoing because he made some remarks to Louis Strauss and Edward Teller and others that worked against him later on. But he could make these remarks, like the one you may have read in this Wyden book: When he first met Harry Truman, who was then president, Robert came in and said, "I have blood on my hands." Later Truman told his aides, "Hey, let's keep that guy out of here. I made those decisions. I gave the orders." That's according to Wyden. I don't believe much of the stuff I read in books. It's hard to read histories of Los Alamos; I always make my own.

Another one of Robert's favorite words, after the bomb was shot or dropped on Japan, was "sin." He would say things like "Physicists have known sin." Well, what does that mean to a man like Robert Oppenheimer or to any of you? To him—and I figured it out, too, from reading these translations that I got from my own library. In order to sin, in order for the soldier to sin (for example, he didn't want to fight) was to refuse to fight. After all, he was one of the soldier class. If he didn't want to fight and kill his relatives who were in the other army, it would be a sin. The way Robert figured was that the physicists took credit for the bomb (they deserved only about a fourth or a third of the credit, of course) but they shouldn't do that, because if it's a sin, it's a dishonor to work. It's all right to work, but you shouldn't take any pride in your work. You shouldn't gloat about it. And that was my interpretation of Robert's idea of sin.

Another one you may have read, but very few people have heard is that several times, when we were talking about the progress of the work at the Lab, Robert had a little prayer he would say: "May the Lord preserve us from the enemy without and from the Hungarians within." Now obviously, that was funny. But I called it to the attention of Edward Teller a few years ago, and he said he'd never heard Robert say that. Edward said, "He must have been talking about Leo Szilard." That is very possible, but Eugene Wigner was also was a Hungarian. Robert didn't like him and he certainly didn't like Szilard. They were too much alike. Then he had his trouble with Edward here during the war, but I don't want to get into it.

That one year that I was in A Building with Robert was the most meaningful from the point of view of my personal contact.

George Kistiakowski came here from Houston to head up the explosive work. He was the nation's most qualified person to direct the scientific approach to high-precision casting and machining of explosives, which was what was required. Deak Parsons got mostly interested in the delivery problem for the gun device, the one that was used on Hiroshima. The implosion work really fell into Kistiakowski's hands, and I was transferred from Deak's division into Bacher's. Robert Bacher had been head of the Physics and Research Division, and Robert chose him to head up what they called the Gadget, or G, Division.

A component of the gun device was a little capsule that contained beryllium, which makes neutrons, and polonium, which makes alpha particles, so that when the impact came, those two could come together (they were separated by a nickel layer) to create the neutrons and that would time the bomb to go off at the right time. My main interest at that time was this thing, called the initiator, so they transferred me to Bacher's division.

But the theorists said, "You don't need an initiator." Robert was very good at putting people he didn't know what to do with into jobs. They were hard jobs but didn't bother anybody else. And so that's where I was—with the initiator. But then it turned out in the winter or early spring of 1945 that the only way to do an implosion in time to get into this present war was to just implode a solid—almost solid—sphere, and that needed an initiator. So all of a sudden, the work we were doing was not only important, it was essential.

At that time, we didn't have the electronics to prove that the neutrons came out on time. We knew that lots of them came out, but that was after we found them in the field and brought them into the lab and measured them. In the bomb, they had to come out in one microsecond, or you're dead. Robert got very worried that we weren't going to be able to do an implosion device because the initiator might not work. There wasn't anything I could do except to say, "Look, it works in the lab. That's all I can say."

So he appointed a committee of Niels Bohr, Enrico Fermi, Hans Bethe, Cyril Smith, and Ken Bainbridge, I think, to meet with me every week to assure them that the initiator was going to work. But that's all they could do. It would be unbearable if it didn't work. So they got Bohr and Isador Rabi to tell Robert to quit worrying. He'd lost I don't know how many pounds.

In the beginning of the project, Robert seemed to be completely indifferent to whether the thing was going to work or not. It was just a scientific inquiry and we wanted to find out. If it didn't work for us, it wouldn't work for Hitler, you see. But now he was worried.

That leads to another thing that involves the *Gita*. Remember that famous saying that he made when the bomb finally went off: "I have become death, the shatterer of worlds." It's always said that it's a quotation from the *Gita*, but of course it isn't because it's in English. So I looked through these three volumes of *Gitas* for that line and it's there. But it's very different from the way Robert says it. I have written that down to quote it. This is a translation by Ann Sanders, a Stanford poet who made a first translation of the *Gita*. Chapter 11 is called *The Book of the Manifesting of the One and Manifold*. In it, this soldier finally persuaded God (he was his charioteer) to reveal to him what God was like, to see. Then he had a terrible dream; it was terrible, full of frightening things, which, incidentally, are narrated in the poem by a third party who was in the other army. (I don't know how that works.). In Verse 12 of that chapter, it says, "If a thousand suns should at once blaze up in the sky, the light of that mighty soul would be all their brightness"—the "mighty soul" being God, of course. In Verse 31 of that chapter, the soldier Arjuna says, "Tell me, you awful form, who are you?" Krishna says, "I am time, destroyer of worlds." Then in one of these translations by Eliot Deutsch, a professor of philosophy in Hawaii, he points out that the word "time" here is the Sanskrit word "karma", which is used in a sense that means "Father Time" and, therefore, can be associated with death and with the Supreme Deity. So what I suspect is that either Robert had another translation or he made up his own because he read Sanskrit. I wouldn't put it past him to have rehearsed this saying so that he'd be prepared to be dramatic, because he liked to be dramatic.

There are a number of other things—I couldn't understand the Greenglass case; I didn't understand why he was against going on with the H-bomb; or why he wanted people to leave here after the war. But I'll stop here and give time for you to talk.

Question: This is thrilling to hear you talk about this now, and I wonder if you were thrilled at the time, or did you just think you were doing a job that was rather odd at best? Can you remember what your initial impression was during the '40s?

Critchfield: Well, we were kept informed that the Germans were ahead of us, which they weren't. We had to do the best we could as fast as we could. The main bottleneck was really not Los Alamos. The big problem was to get the actual material. I can't speak for everybody because some people did have misgivings about their positions here. I always felt a scientist has to do what he can to support the society that supports him when nobody else can do it.

Question: Did you feel really important? Did you realize what kind of a position you were in?

Critchfield: Well, I did. That April when the people met in San Francisco to form the United Nations, I went to my boss, Bob Bacher, and said, "Look, it doesn't make any sense to form a United Nations without their knowing about what we're doing." He said, "Shut up. They're obviously not going to put up anything like that." So I didn't have a bad conscience. I just knew you couldn't do it. Then after Bob went off to Socorro County for the test, I went to Robert, who, incidentally, had lost his voice and talked in a whisper for about two weeks. I said, "Robert, this is not an ordinary bomb. It's wrong to drop it without some kind of consultation with nations. Like George Washington said in his farewell address: 'Good faith and justice should be used in dealing with other nations.'" I didn't have any idea what to do except that, but now I know that was wrong because you certainly couldn't have trusted Stalin with the head start he had with Klaus Fuchs and his own mentality. It would have been wrong to take him into confidence.

Robert was so emotionally upset that all he would tell me was, "George is an angel." What he meant was that George Marshall would convince them that they had the bomb. Now I've read quite a bit about what really went on. James Burns was quite aware of the danger of telling Stalin anything. George Marshall and Jack McCoy and others all thought seriously about doing something else, but they just didn't see how to do it. I think if they'd had theoretical physicists in there, then they'd have run, but they had diplomats, so they didn't do it. So I never felt any compunctions. Some people did. Seth Neddermeyer, the guy who invented the implosion, would have nothing to do with it afterwards. He wouldn't even come to the Trinity Shot to watch it. He went up on Highway 4 with Don Kerst and watched it from their automobile, 180 airline miles away.

Question: What was Robert's emotional makeup? I read in Richard Rhodes' book that he was sometimes a very depressed person. Did he go with what was happening at the Laboratory at the time? Was he full of vim and vigor or depressed? Did he work 80 hours a day?

Critchfield: Yes, as you know, he was an extremely brilliant man, and it was easy to get him to get an idea, work on it, and to switch his thinking. When the project started, he was quite indifferent, very well composed, but also a very compassionate man. But when it came down to whether the test shot would work, he changed. He became very worried and lost a lot of weight, but I didn't think he was depressed. I didn't have much of a chance to talk to him directly in those days until after the shot. Then I didn't get in touch with him, but I didn't see any great instability except that one period of worry, which was very unlike him. If you are going to be a good Hindu, you can't take life's ups and downs seriously. You've got to wait for the great bliss. Of course, I don't believe he was a Hindu; don't get me wrong about that.

Question: Isn't Sanskrit something of an odd skill for a physicist, even a brilliant one?

Critchfield: He did it for fun. It has an alphabet of 50 letters, 14 vowels. So does ours, but we don't admit it. We still stick with 26.

You notice, in my talk, I have referred to "Robert" a lot. Early in 1944 Kistiakowski came here and everybody called him Kisty. And, of course, everybody called me Critch. Captain Parsons' secretary had a boy friend in Syracuse, New York, who said he could send her a case of Scotch if she'd send him $50. Hazel thought that was quite a risk, so she asked me, "How would you like half a case of Scotch for $25?" I said I'd take a chance. Of course, it would be $250 now. She sent the money and her friend sent her a cardboard box marked "Gold Ink"—it was 12 bottles of Hudson's Bay Scotch. This was particularly nice because we were expecting another child and we knew we'd need some Scotch for the doctor.

On one occasion we took a bottle of Scotch to Kistiakowski's house, which was the Red Cross building on The Hill. He was a bachelor then. He and Kitty and Robert Oppenheimer and Jean and I worked on that bottle. About half-way through it, Kisty was feeling pretty good. He said, "Everybody calls me Kisty and I don't like to be called Kisty. I wish people would call me George."

Robert said, "I understand. Everybody calls me Oppie and I don't like Oppie because it sounds to much like the Dutch word for ape—which is aap, a-a-p."

I wasn't about to be left out of this. I don't mind being called Critch, but to get into such fine company, I said, "Well, everybody calls me Critch and I don't like to be called Critch. I want to be called Charles."

After that, we always called each other by those names. It was always Robert and Charles and George. I have seen in print that George called Robert "Oppie" after the shot, but I doubt it. All his friends called him Oppie, and I don't mean to say they're wrong. I'm just telling you a real-life story of how we changed our habits, and I'm still in the same habit.

*Charles L. Critchfield came to Los Alamos in 1943 with his family after being urged by Robert Oppenheimer and Edward Teller to participate in the wartime project. Critchfield's work with the Gadget Division produced the initiator that was crucial to the successful detonation of the first atomic bomb. After post-war years in Washington D.C., Minnesota, and California, Critchfield returned to the Laboratory in 1961 and remained until his retirement in 1977. He died February 12, 1994, at the age of 83. In an informal talk at the Unitarian Church in Los Alamos in 1992, Critchfield recalled his close association with Robert Oppenheimer during his wartime stint on the project. The talk was transcribed for this publication. Critchfield was introduced by Kay Manley, another of the earliest Los Alamos pioneers.

BEHIND TALL FENCES

Karan McKibben*

During the latter half of the 1940s while wary scientists and their administrators pondered over the future of Los Alamos now that its original *raison d'etre* had dissipated along with the two mushroom clouds over Japan, the first children born in this hilltop community embarked with scarcely a thought at all on a comprehensive discovery of the town the United States government had fenced off from the rest of northern New Mexico. As the Hill's war babies, to put it demographically, roamed through the hastily constructed town, down into the dark canyons, and over the lonely mesa fingers, they found growing up here much the same as anywhere. Still there was something persistently suspicious about a town enclosed entirely by wire mesh fence topped by strands of barbed wire and guarded assiduously at all three gated exits by men in dark, police-like uniforms. None of the other towns in northern New Mexico were encased in such fences and thus we kids knew something was peculiar about our home town.

The real purpose of these fences and gates always eluded my more immediate perspective of those years. Whether they were to keep people in, or to keep people out seemed equally probable explanations since exit as well as entrance was permitted only once the capped faces at the gates nodded their approval of the passes required of all over a certain age. This age limit was extended progressively through the years from five to twelve. Excluding people, however, was the more likely since those residing inside had only to flash their permanent passes to get out while those residing outside had to be vouched for by those inside. Whenever my family wanted to leave, it was necessary only to stop at the gate long enough for the security guard to glance at our passes. But whenever Grandma and Grandpa came rolling into Lamy on the El Cap, it was necessary for us to dash to the AEC pass office to obtain visitors' passes. Before we picked them up it was necessary to engage in a lengthy discussion on whether their stated intention of staying two weeks was firm. The resolution was always a signed decision to renew the two week pass if they should change their minds.

One beneficial by-product of the pass system was that no out-of-town friends and/or relatives could drop in unexpectedly and catch one in the embarrassment of having house and family in complete disarray. There was always ample time while someone obtained the proper piece of paper and rescued the perplexed visitors at the gate for a whole house and family to be put in their proper order.

Once inside the fence surrounding the town, visitors and residents alike encountered other wire mesh fences and more men in dark blue who kept Los Alamos divided into working and living areas. Since these additional fences controlled access to the various technical areas, they opened only to the holders of the special badges issued to those who worked in the areas, and closed resolutely to meandering children and their mothers. The number of fences behind which our fathers disappeared every work day added an aura of intrigue to their already mysterious work in sundry, odd shaped buildings. Until the advent of Family Days when the secrets were tucked away for a weekend and fathers escorted their families through portions of the tech area, the working areas were never within our purview.

The living areas, however, were very much within our purview. As the town changed rapidly from its army camp atmosphere to the tentative permanency of a government owned town, we became intimately acquainted with the houses and buildings that sprung up before our small eyes. The original, small residential area around Ashley Pond Pond (one Pond is a man's name and the other Pond is a geographic feature) was vastly expanded when Western Area was built with houses and duplexes made monotonously similar but ornamented brightly in beige, white, pink, or pale green stucco along with grass and shrubbery. It was a delightful contrast to the previous single offering of camouflage green and mud with the "temporary" Sundt apartments. The original, camouflage green school was also brightened and joined in the new area by a new elementary school and a high school built with such luxuries as an indoor swimming pool and a civic auditorium. Yet despite the expanded territory, the whole living area was readily accessible by an inexpensive bus service used primarily by maids and kids. We could ride on the red and white bus from the western-most houses to the brand-new Community Center that had replaced the few army-built shacks and boys-school cabins with more of the usual small town businesses, not the least of which were two movie theaters featuring Francis the talking mule and other wonderful stars.

Beyond the new houses and buildings but still within the fence were large areas untouched by the busy bulldozers. To the east were the pinon and juniper dotted mesa tips upon which the main gate had been thrust like a wedding ring on one of the fingers pointing to the distant Sangre de Cristo Mountains. To the west were the dark wooded areas filled with tall ponderosa pines and low scrub oak that grew on the foothills of the nearby Jemez Mountains. This latter world became more mysterious and awesome than the James Bond world of the tech areas because it was more accessible to our imaginations. In the cold months the woods became the haven of all manner of frightening creatures. In the warm months the woods became a lively, James Fenimore Cooper world with Indians and cavalry forts holding out against the destructive forces of the wild, i.e., other kids from other canyons. There were daring scouting feats where rough barked trees and the slick water storage tanks were scaled for an inclusive survey of the town. Even more daring were the excursions into the depths of the woods that brought back incredulous reports of holes in the fence big enough for one to crawl through to the foreign lands beyond.

Exit to the foreign lands was, of course, more easily accomplished via the three gates. In fact, exiting to foreign lands became a frequent and habitual activity for Hill people since not many could endure the constant enclosure for long. My own family drove nearly every Saturday to Santa Fe expressly to pick up frozen meat at a locker plant there, but actually to savor the colorful variety of the shops, people, and architecture. The strangeness and variety of this centuries old city contrasted sharply to the familiarity and homogeneity of our town constructed entirely within a decade. Thus when our new Chevy sedan returned home in the crisp night along the moonlit ribbon that curled over the hills near San Ildefonso Pueblo, bridged the Rio Grande at Otowi, and switched back and forth up the steep incline to the blinding lights of the main gate, I carefully hoarded all the impressions I'd gathered along the Plaza or in the restaurant on Cerrillos Road where we'd sampled like green tourists mild, native food amid a warm decor created by giant Mexican hats tacked everywhere and flickering candles dripping brightly colored wax. As the flashlight eyes of the security guard at the gate swept across our faces, I felt mischievously guilty, as if I were smuggling pieces of Santa Fe in the packages stuffed in the trunk, or perhaps a foreign spy instead of the piles of frozen meat stacked under a blanket at my feet. The guards never really looked in the trunk or down behind the front seat. It was so easy to go in and out and to bring back anything you wanted from those alien lands just beyond the gates.

Still the fences remained so that I was convinced they were there because God and the federal government, commonly known as AEC, had set aside a piece of northern New Mexico for our exclusive use. After all, the fences had signs screaming in red; "Government Property. No Trespassing." Even lost pilots who happened to stray into this forbidden territory were rudely escorted out of our sky by jet fighters. Los Alamos was clearly reserved for those who lived and worked behind the fences. Although life inside was about as normal as anywhere, interaction with the rest of New Mexico was strained by the aura of exclusivity fostered by the security system. As long as home was behind wire mesh fences, our New Mexico neighbors remained mistrusted and exotic foreigners, particularly in the eyes of the Hill's war babies who knew no other way of life.

Today, in 1973, the fences around the townsite have been down for almost two decades and Los Alamos has found itself a home, albeit at times uneasily, in northern New Mexico. The pondering scientists and administrators have found a permanent future in multifaceted scientific research. The town also has found a sense of permanency with its homogeneity diffusing as the population acquires a more normal distribution of age and interest groups and the housing acquires the growing variety normal with private ownership. All that remain of the gates are an abandoned shack on the West Jemez Road, a shack at a target shooting range on the East Jemez Road, and at the war time gate site only a few peach trees that sprung up from the seeds the security guards had thrown away. The later, main gate with more lanes than were ever necessary, has been transformed ironically into a restaurant serving hot, native food in a warm decor of giant Mexican hats and brightly colored, dripping candles. Above all, there are now a Chamber of Commerce, a Science Museum, and any number of helpful citizens willing to aid strangers who might wander by in discovering Los Alamos as fully as possible, if not as fully as those who grew up behind its fences had discovered it.

*Karan McKibben was born March 12, 1944, in the Post Hospital at Los Alamos. In September 1952, she contracted polio leaving her severely paralyzed; she used a respirator to sleep and an electric wheelchair to get around. She attended Los Alamos grade and high school using a speaker phone system and graduated valedictorian of her class of 1962. For her college education she attended night classes in Los Alamos and day classes at the College of Santa Fe and at the University of New Mexico at Albuquerque. She received her degree from UNM at Albuquerque as top senior, Phi Beta Kappa and Phi Kappa Phi. After moving to Riverside, California, in 1975 she did graduate studies at the University of California Riverside, receiving her MA and Ph.D in English Literature and Composition in 1984. She taught a short time at the English Department of this University. In 1988 she developed breast cancer. She came through her treatment at Loma Linda Hospital and went on to some tutoring, editing, and writing at home. Then the cancer spread to her liver and she died on April 24, 1992, after a brief illness.

OUR NONLINEAR WORLD
Serguei Kapitsa*

It is a singular honor to speak here, at this great Laboratory. The Laboratory was founded 50 years ago for a very special purpose by a very remarkable man, whose memory is now celebrated by these lectures. I never met Oppenheimer, although I suppose my father did. Perhaps he came to my father's house in Cambridge 60 years ago. It so happened with Weisskopf, and a few years ago at his birthday party at Boston I could recall meeting Vicky in 1933 and asking my father why he is called Weiskopf when his hair is black? Since then much has changed. Weisskopf was among those many scientists who came here to build the bomb at the height of World War II—probably never was such a collection of the best brains of the world assembled together to produce the most powerful weapon ever known.

Now that is part of history, and it is for the next generation to handle the legacy of those great pioneers. Among them was Bohr. He was the senior of that remarkable group, a teacher of many of them, mentor of that generation of scientists. It was Bohr who then attempted to look beyond the immediate horizon of events then taking place by the efforts of his former students and collaborators. He tried to look beyond the immediate issues and he came to the conclusion that with the appearance of the bomb the world had irrevocably changed. He explored these new departures and came to the paradoxical conclusion that war, that is nuclear war, was no longer a possible way of resolving conflicts of the future and that the security can only be guaranteed by openness. This result was shocking for the secrecy of the nuclear establishment: for politicians like Stalin or even Churchill, it was new thinking well beyond its time. Bohr did not manage to make himself heard; his letter on an Open World, written in 1950 to the United Nations, was not heeded and was lost in the emotions generated by the Korean War.

Now, more than 40 years later, it makes interesting and instructive reading in the new openness of the world after the collapse of the closed society of the Soviet Union. It is in this world that a new sense of mutual understanding and security is to be generated. Bohr summed it up as follows:

> Although, it would appear that, by making the demand for openness a paramount issue, quite new possibilities would be created, which, if purposefully followed up, might bring humanity a long way forward towards the realization of the cooperation on the progress of civilization which is more urgent and, notwithstanding present obstacles, may still be within nearer reach than ever before. The consideration in this memorandum may appear utopian, and the difficulties of surveying complications of non-conventional procedures

may explain the hesitations of governments in demonstrating adherence to the course of full mutual openness. Nevertheless, such a course should be in the deepest interests of all nations, irrespective of differences in social and economic organization, and the hopes and aspirations for which it was attempted to give expression in the memorandum are no doubt shared by people all over the world.

While the present account may perhaps add to the general recognition of the difficulties with which every nation was confronted by the coincidence of a great upheaval in world affairs with a veritable revolution as regard technical resources, it is in no way meant to imply that the situation does not still offer unique opportunities. On the contrary, the aim is to point to the necessity of reconsidering, from every side, the ways and means of cooperation for avoiding mortal menaces to civilization and for turning the progress of science to lasting benefit of all humanity.

These words, written in a rather dense and difficult style reflecting the complexity of Bohr's thinking, sound very modern and relevant to what is happening nowadays. In the strange setting of history a nuclear component in the emergence of social changes and *glasnost* was considerable. For it was Chernobyl that finally demonstrated to the people of the Soviet Union, to its government and ruling elite, the political impossibility of running things as in the past. The country then passed a decisive threshold, however painful and tragic that experience may be. Some even say that it was a played down version of a nuclear war, like an inoculation when a mild virus is introduced to generate immunity against the real thing.

In mentioning these historic events we see how slowly does the world react to the discoveries of science and developments in technology. It took five years to develop the bomb and now, 50 years later, we are reappraising its meaning and assessing its impact on our security and power. This disparity is not the only one that strikes an observer of world affairs, but here in Los Alamos it is probably the best, as it was here that these scientific ideas were conceived and then brilliantly carried out.

I have brought up these issues not only for their own sake, but as examples of the complexity of the world. This complexity comes out especially when we think in terms of the time scale of events.

Most of our thinking is linear. We always extrapolate in terms of continuation of the present at rates that we now observe. There is nothing wrong in such an approach. In fact, in human society the strength of tradition, of continuity, of a correlation between the past, present and future, was always with us. It is this spirit that gives guidance to our everyday behavior, to the recursive patterns of our life. It is a powerful stabilizing force and most necessary part of our existence, of our life and development, as we strive for a linear world, stable and cozy, predictable and secure.

As the title of my talk indicates, our world is to a great extent nonlinear. Today invoking nonlinearity has become quite fashionable, to the extent that it has become an intellectual fad, even an addiction. Chaos and thresholds, order and fractals have rapidly moved from the realm of nonlinear mechanics, where they rightly belong, to the titles of books and articles, to the headlines and news items. I am not sure that this is really what matters, for when after some hesitancy I chose the subject and, heading for my lecture, I was not trying to join this modern nonlinear bandwagon. What is really true is that we are now going through a very special stage of our human history. Without understanding its peculiar and singular character it is difficult, if at all possible, to try to comprehend what is happening.

I am sure that this fundamental difference of our time from any other is essential in understanding many of the problems that face us in one way or the other. In a sense we are living in nonadiabatic conditions, in a shock wave—things change in our lifetime so fast that many individuals have a difficulty in adapting to these changes. The human society is even in greater disarray. Social institutions, law and order, take time to develop, to set up the business of organizing social behavior. Most of these processes are evolutionary; by trial and error society works out how to handle its problems. In this century we have seen how vulnerable and unstable these social institutions are—how easily the society as a system can collapse and generate chaos, and how slow and difficult is the return to order and systemic behavior.

At one time, with the emergence of modern science in the 17th century, the discoveries of the regularities in the solar system and development of classical mechanics, a rational, linear deterministic model of the world emerged and for 200 years dominated our thinking. From the realm of the sciences that with some arrogance called themselves exact, these concepts of law, order, and determinism penetrated into the social sciences. They still are much in the grip of social determinism and linear thinking, and only slowly does the understanding come that the world is much more complex than it seems. Not totally random, not deterministic, but somewhere in between, chaotic as it is now called.

This is a very important concept, and we know how fruitful it is in extending our understanding into randomness of complex systems operated by microscopic laws, those that we sometimes can explain at a deeper level. In social systems this is far from achieved, and the collapse of the whole ideology of Marxism is a good example. Marxism was the logical development of this mechanistic, deterministic, rational and in a sense linear thinking. The collapse of this ideology has a broader meaning than the demise of a political system that took at least lip service from these ideas, especially in its last stages of decay, when it could not even evolve, so as to adapt to change.

Two years ago here in Los Alamos I attended a conference on climate change and energy policy. I had the privilege of making an opening statement and there I drew attention to the issues of population. In the course of the conference a paper was presented on a model that does describe world population growth. This complex problem has since been my main occupation, and I hope in these days at LANL [Los Alamos National Laboratory] and at Santa Fe to speak on the details of that model. Here and now I will only say that the model is essentially nonlinear, and the concept of scaling is its important component.

Why nonlinear? Let's have a look at simple linear models. Today the world population increases with 90 million people arriving each year, 2 million per week, 3 persons per second. As today's world population is 5.5 billion, then in a linear world 60 years ago, I could have seen the beginning of humankind. But as far as I remember I was taught at school that the world then had 2 billion people.

Next consider that the world population multiplies at a constant compound rate, doubling as it is nowadays every 40 years. As 5×10^9 is approximately 2^{32} then 32 generations or $32 \times 40 = 1280$ years ago we all began with Adam and Eve in the 8th century, not leaving any time for ancient Rome. Even assuming a Malthusian 400-year doubling time, then the origin of humankind is removed to the 11 millennia B.C. This is enough for history, but not for anthropology. That means that both linear and exponential growth cannot describe our development on any extended time scale. In other words linear modelling is useless in treating this problem, if we are to find a general law describing global population growth.

What works surprisingly well is the simplest nonlinear model assuming that the growth rate is proportional to the second power of the number of people, the next in terms of powers of N after exponential and linear models. Essentially it describes human growth and development as cooperative phenomena.

It is well known that such growth rates—faster than exponents—lead to divergences. To cope with them a cut-off has to be introduced, a time constant of 40 years, that regularizes the infinities and leads to a 14-billion limit in world population. I am not going further into the details, or I will have nothing to talk about later.

What is important is this time constant of 40 years as a characteristic time of the human lifespan, an estimate all will find fitting. You can start a family at 20 and the present life expectancy is now 70 years, so 40 is a good guess. As I mentioned this growth rate proportional to N^2 leads to infinite growth in a finite time and this time is desperately close—2007, less than 15 years away, much shorter than the 40 years I mentioned. In other words we are now living in the middle of a global population singularity!

This is a singularity both in the technical mathematical meaning—a pole in the growth rate and in terms of history. This singular period with a width of some 80 years is like a resonance on a scale of human development some 4 million years long—a very special time indeed. Up to this very peculiar period the world, as measured by human population growth, followed regular growth. This can be traced right from our origins 4 million years ago or 100,000 generations back. Over all this time our development pursued a certain pattern—not linear, but hyperbolic, only to hit this discontinuity, a break in laws established ages ago. I do not know the real origin of this law, one can surmise that it is the result of a superposition of many different processes happening in our history and seen as the result of the recursive nature of human affairs.

Probably here it would be best to illustrate the origin of a power law of scaling by reminding you of the change of radioactivity observed after fission. It was worked out by Wigner working in the early years of the Manhattan Project. The result is that from 0.1 second to 100 years—over ten orders of magnitude—the activity changes as $t^{-1.2}$. When you want to gauge the activity after the closure of a reactor or nuclear explosion, this is the practical law of radioactive decay. But we all know that each and every one of all the processes of radioactive decay are exponents. When we add them all up assuming a certain randomness in the fission fragments we arrive at a power law, get scaling into the picture. The same is true with the complexities of human development—here again all different processes studied by social sciences, demography and economics lead to scaling, a power law operating over a vast time scale. This is how to picture the world we are living in, and moreover have the luck or misfortune to experience its most critical period.

As with the example taken from radioactive decay, human population growth is described by a power law operating over five orders of magnitude of time and population growth and is limited at both ends in the immediate future and distant past. This is done by introducing into this phenomenological theory a time constant equal to 40 years as the microscopic (in terms of this model) scale of the human life span that can be taken from current demographic data. This leads to an estimate of the origin of the genus Homo some 4.5 million years ago, and the beginning of nonlinear systemic development associated with the appearance of Homo Habilis 2.2 million years ago in continuous development up to the present. At the other end it describes the current demographic transition.

In the framework of this model one can introduce the local time of growth—the time it will take the population to double or to be mathematically minded, increase by e = 2.73 times. The answer is very simple—it is equal to the time into the past reckoned from the singularity. As we are practically there it means that 100 years ago population grew e times in 100 years, 1000 years ago in 1000 years, and a million years ago in a million years. Only when we come close to the singularity, this simple law breaks down with the scaling that determined our development on all previous epochs. This expanding time scale gives you an explanation of why the Paleolithic was so long and slow, why the Roman Empire took 1500 years to decline and fall and why today empires go in decades rather than millennia on a contracting time scale with an accelerating growth rate.

In developing this model two points are important. One is that the global population is seen as an interactive system. The other is that the global human system is unlimited in terms of resources and growth, although locally environmental constraints do appear. The real limit to growth is its inherent systemic rate. Today's world, coupled by travel and trade, communication and migration, certainly is an entity, a dynamic evolving system. It can be described by a universal law averaging out statistically all things happening locally and following different laws, describing various stages of development. The concept of self-similarity of this development is a powerful concept of the overall constancy of the principal forces determining growth. This leads to scaling, a power law, in describing growth of the population imperative.

Of all problems of today the issue of population growth looms on our common horizon, but much has been and more is said about the environment. Certainly the environment is most important for our development and well-being. But imagine a world where only, say, 10 million people live being just as intelligent and developed as we are today. In such a world with a thousand times less people there would be no problems of the environment as long as everyone would not crowd into one city like Moscow or New York! You must recall that in ancient Rome two million people of the 200 million of the world population lived in those days. You can only imagine the environmental problems they faced!

The environmental problems to a great extent are the result not only of the total number of people inhabiting our planet but also of their spatial distribution. If we want to understand what is to happen with the environment and the impact it will have on our well-being, we should first have to gain greater insight into global population issues. Here again only if we treat this problem as nonlinear are we to expect a sensible result.

The remarkable thing is that now, after two million years of development, we are at a threshold: a fundamental change in the pattern of our growth is taking place. The world population is now passing through the time of a demographic transition, a critical period in all our history. Without introducing nonlinear thinking we would lack an understanding of the magnitude and significance of this very singular event, similar in a way to a phase transition, as the paradigm of our growth is changing.

This transition is a key to understanding of what is now happening worldwide. It should be seen as the most important of all global phenomena now encountered by the world community. The transition will lead to a stabilization of the world population at a level of 14–15 billion people in the foreseeable future. The global transition began at approximately 1965 when the global population was 3.35 billion and will culminate at 2007 at $N=7$ billion and will reach 90% of the limit in 2150. The transition is rapid and we are now right in its very middle, when the relative growth rate is at its highest—on the average 1.7% annually.

The lack of ideas as to how to describe and govern our world is a great challenge. Probably the way the world may negotiate the difficult passage through the population transition is the key problem of our time. It is a global issue, when we really have to think in a new way, recognizing the new priorities of the world.

The demographic transition has already occurred for the developed world as it started in the beginning of the 19th century. Now for the remaining 80% this is to happen on a very short time scale, even more rapidly than in the case of the developed world. The very rate of this transition when the exponential instantaneous time constant is 56 years, or a doubling time of 40 years, will lead to great social strains in world society.

This demographic transition through which we are now passing ultimately will lead to a stabilized world with a radically new age structure. Probably of all changes this is the most significant in its long-term social consequences. The percentage of people older than 65 years will reach 25% as compared to 6% in 1992 and the number of young people will accordingly drop. The median age from 24 years in 1993 will grow to 43 years according to UN projections for world population. It has already happened in the developed countries that have passed through the demographic transition and are now limited in their population growth. This is already leading to major changes in the care of the old, with a growing burden on public health. On the other hand, if we look at the military potential of the population, these developed countries have difficulties in manning large armies. At present in Russia this has become a major problem for our military, which has to change from numbers to quality. In the southern republics of the former Soviet Union the opposite is true. The experience of Afghanistan and especially the Gulf War demonstrated the same demographic mismatch of the warring parties in a striking manner. These are some of the consequences of the demographic transition. They are happening now with a short time scale and in military planning we should take these factors into account.

This transition to zero or very low growth rates will have many other consequences that I can only mention now. As the kinematic time constant will rapidly grow after the transition, does it mean that the rate of progress will decrease? Are we heading for millennia of stagnation and decay or will we find another dimension for growth, rather than sheer numbers? This is a very fundamental question. If we cannot grow quantitatively, then the only dimension is quality. The issue of quality in its broad sense is really the priority of intelligence and culture, of science and education, in an emerging scale of values. Probably that is what is going to happen and we already see this trend in the development of societies that have passed through the demographic transition.

There is yet another point that I will mention, an issue brought up in a recent conversation with the last British Labour Prime Minister, Lord Callahan. Of all problems of the developed countries he singled out complacency as the one that matters most. Many things can be read into that remark by a conscientious observer of modern society of the extreme self-satisfaction so widespread in the West.

The environmental issues that are so high on the public agenda, as demonstrated by the conference in Rio, have yet an indirect effect on population. It seems from the kinematics of world population growth that there is no overall limit to population that would be set by global environmental effects. However powerful, locally, are the effects of the environment, especially in large towns, in overpopulated countries of the developing world, there is yet no overall global limit. If we look into the past then, throughout human history seen on a large scale, we survived many ice ages; the level of the ocean changed by more than 100 meters. In spite of all these drastic changes, that had a time scale of thousands of years and hundreds of generations, the human race not only survived but multiplied and spread throughout the globe. These major changes in climate are seen by anthropologists as a stimulating factor in human development and demonstrate both the power of survival and the constancy of systemic growth relentlessly pursued by humankind in an unlimited world.

In considering the environmental factors of today much attention has been given to global changes in climate due to human activities. We certainly are observing a marked increase in the CO_2 content in the atmosphere. I must say that in some countries like Russia and Canada this warming is not perceived as an immediate menace to our well-being, and we would like to have a better understanding of the consequences of the expected global warming. Moreover, the time constant of these changes is certainly long, because these changes are damped by the thermal inertia of the oceans. It has been indicated that a loss of stability and a rapid switchover to a new metastable state can happen. Unfortunately we know very little about such changes, although recent research on ice cores has provided us with remarkable records of the past climates.

To illustrate the complexity of these issues I will mention the case of the Caspian Sea. Some ten years ago its level was falling and our technocratically minded civil engineers were so scared that great plans of turning the northbound rivers southward were made and even started to be carried out. By the way, nuclear explosives were considered for this huge project. A large gulf in the southern part of the Caspian was dammed off, so as to cut the loss of water by evaporation. But now the sea has started to grow so rapidly that the rising level is a new menace for the surrounding population. No reasonable explanation is offered, although an enormous amount of data has been accumulated and many papers written. All I have been told is that such oscillatory behavior of landlocked seas is an inherent property of these systems, not suggesting a more detailed explanation.

In these cases of complex systemic behavior it is indeed very difficult by the very nature of nonlinearity to explain these patterns in terms of cause and effect. Probably conceptually this is a great stumbling block for all who are educated in a reductionist and analytical mindset. In no field is it so obvious as in computer modelling. The early attempts of "The Limits to Growth" approach pioneered by the Meadows show this best. If their first book was an important event in making us aware of the issues discussed, their last publication, 20 years later, has not produced a vision of our future that seems to be both right and encouraging.

This difference between analytic reductionist thinking and a more synthetic, I would even say holistic, approach is intimately connected to the difference between linear, rational, and deterministic behavior and the conduct of systems where complexity, chaos, and unpredictability have to be taken into account. Today in our modern world the first attitude is largely associated with the West, with the European intellectual tradition. The second approach is to a great extent Eastbound. The Russian tradition in a certain way is caught in between these two extremes. I do think that the contributions of Russian scientists to nonlinear science is no accident and follows from this deeply entrenched attitude, the roots of which one can trace to the schism between the Eastern and Western Christian churches and see in the social history, arts, and values governing these two different ways of looking at the real world. Today, when Russian culture and science are meeting the West, this should be kept in mind and seen as our asset in international collaboration.

The difference is also seen in the attitude toward education. I do think that the Russian system, following the continental European tradition, is basically better than the American pragmatic approach, a point worth discussing. Recently this was demonstrated by Russian high-school students who won the International Physics Olympiad held in Virginia, where 40 countries participated.

Matters of education should also be seen in the light of the demographic transition. As the time constant of change in population has become shorter than the life span and the changes in science and industry are so rapid, we see how our training in specialized fields very quickly gets antiquated. As a student I learned vacuum-tube electronics, long surpassed by transistors, and now we have integrated digital circuitry. These changes are widespread and the issue of retraining is becoming more and more part of our life. On the other hand, what sort of basic education should then be provided at our universities—an education good for life or a training for a specific job? This balance is what education policy is all about.

Concerning the factors that limit population growth, the Population Principle of Malthus has dominated much of our thinking since the beginning of the 19th century. This again is an attempt of a reductionist moral philosopher to explain the factors in limiting population by the direct effects of poverty and wealth. Malthus was certainly influenced by the rational philosophy of the 18th century, and it is surprising that this approach is still pursued much as it was done by a remarkable pathfinder in economic and demographic studies.

Today there should be not only a modern revision of these ideas in terms of nonlinear systemic thinking. We have to construct a new way of thinking about social phenomena where the recent intellectual instruments developed in nonlinear studies have to be transposed into the studies of society. This is no easy task. In the first place the social scientists have a profound humanistic tradition of their own. Next they think in terms of history, usually dismissing the intellectual training of the hard scientist. It would be very arrogant to suppose that this great heritage can be disregarded. What I think is necessary is to gradually educate both the hard scientists in social issues and to introduce to the social sciences the methods, concepts, and ideas by which we have been brought up. It is no accident that Malthus had such an impact on economics and social thinking: when educated in Cambridge, he was the Ninth Wrangler in the Mathematical Tripos in 1788! I would be happy if modern historians, economists, and social scientists would have a similar educational background to that an aspiring young clergyman got at Christ College 200 years ago!

In all cases of analyzing wealth, space, and numbers of people we have to look not at the average dealt with by politicians, not at the extremes that capture the eye of the media, but at the statistical distributions describing incomes in terms of Pareto's law, scaling of cities and the self-similar pattern of population growth. It so happens that in all these cases we have to deal with stable hyperbolic power law distributions. The origin of these power laws should be seen in the recursive nature of human affairs, in setting up the spatial or temporal correlations determining these distributions in an evolving system. In terms of nonlinear kinetics we are dealing with the result of stochastic processes of self-organization. Before going into a detailed elementary analysis of the numerous social factors, it is most important to establish and describe in general terms these statistically valid entities. Only then can we expect at a later stage to understand not only on a phenomenological, but a more fundamental basis, these processes.

In considering population growth over the last decades it should be kept in mind that world population since 1950 has doubled in 40 years, but energy production has increased seven times. This trend, when the growth rate for energy, the key to all industry, is at least twice the growth rate of populations, is a decisive factor for global development. In spite of local famines, of undernourishment of many people in the world, food production has reached a level when it can satisfy the basic requirements of humankind, for in a modern society 3 to 4% can feed the whole country. World authorities on food production have stated that the planet can sustain a population of 15 to 25 billion. In other words the world has enough resources in terms of energy and food to support the expected world population. Can it be stably managed is the problem. What matters here most is the stability and sustainability of such a future state. Stability and security today should be seen not only in military terms but as economic, environmental, and, most decisively, demographic security.

I am sure that at present it is most necessary in a systematic way to explore this new world with a stationary population. First we should be concerned in the transition period with short-term stability. The present events in Russia can be taken as a crude model of what we could expect to happen on a larger scale, as the Soviet Union accounted for one-sixth of the world population. The population disparities are probably the most important factor contributing to the wars on the southern borders of the country. In these conflicts the ethnic factor is dominant as the expression of strains and stresses set up by the demographic processes.

The world demographically is in a nonequilibrium state, and that is why stability may be lost. I can remind you that the demographic disparities of the developed countries contributed to the instability that culminated in World Wars I and II, as has been noted by such an eminent observer of global matters as Keynes. Today Paul Kennedy has indicated that the demographic disparities are essential in understanding regional conflicts that could lead to a global loss of stability as an indication of events that could happen.

In a certain way before 1985 the world, balancing in a metastable state of deterrence, was drifting toward a global nuclear conflict. Although all responsible statesmen considered a nuclear war to be inadmissible, we were relentlessly arming for it and nowhere more than here, as you know best. The situation was similar to that in 1914. In Europe of the Belle Epoque, the world never had it so good. Trade and industry were flourishing, science and art set the pattern of development for the decades to come, and we still live on the technical and cultural legacy of that remarkable time. At the same time with the very rapid build up of population, the armies of the great powers were set for a war that no one wanted and whose outcome was well beyond the wildest fantasies of those who started it. It was an instability triggered by a seemingly trivial event—the assassination of an archduke in Sarajevo, of all places. I do hope that today, with the new situation, the world as a whole has the power to retain its stability, in spite of all the local conflicts now questioning our common security. This is the challenge for world governance on an international scale. It is of the greatest importance.

The causes of these numerous conflicts are not energy or resources, not even space. It is mainly the ethnic factors and demographic pressures that drive these bloody encounters, where the sudden appearance of a young, unsettled, often rootless generation is a prerequisite for war. One can even conjecture that due to the rapid rate of change we see the collapse of the restraints of culture and civilization when in these conflicts the participants rapidly degenerate into a primitive, if not primordial tribal behavior.

In a sense today, in those marginal wars happening all over the world, we see again how stability is lost and the extent to which population imbalance fuels these conflicts. It seems that these wars are inevitable, but what should be controlled at all cost is a military conflagration, a flare-up of these local conflicts into a regional or worldwide war. This humankind cannot afford, especially if it becomes nuclear. In this sense the next 50 to 60 years are crucial. In discussing the chances of such events it is difficult, in fact impossible, to make predictions. What one can and should do is to indicate the factors that may matter, draw analogies, draw up meaningful similarities and then leave the final conclusions to readers, or history, for that matter.

This again is a lesson we can learn from chaos, from modern nonlinear thinking. It is no accident that history has difficulty in understanding the past, in interpreting events and defining the decisive factors in bygone days, but even more difficult it is to look into the future! For a Russian the attitude expressed by Tolstoy is very relevant in *War and Peace*. With remarkable intuition and insight he described the chaotic, in the more technical sense of the word, outcome of battles, war and history itself. On the other side we have Clausevitz, to whom we owe the systemic approach to war as the ultimate instrument of politics. It was his dictum that war is a continuation of politics by other means that was revoked by the statement that a nuclear war should never be fought and cannot be won. This deterministic and mechanistic approach still has remarkable influence on military thinking. For World Wars I and II it is a key to understanding the disastrous consequences of those events. Unfortunately, this spirit is still well and alive in the minds of military planners the world around. In the case of Tolstoy, as it often happens, the powerful imagination of a great writer gives greater insight into the real world than that of political and military theorists. We should remember that Clausevitz in writing "On War" introduced the concept of friction as a factor in the study of conflict, accepting some element of chaos.

The long-term sustainability will have to deal with energy, food, water, space, and the environment. Here again we have to treat these issues as they interact in the synergisms of nonlinear coupling. For this world to which we are relentlessly heading, the new global factors that will be the result of these interactions have to be of our concern. It is no accident that in treating the global population by a simple nonlinear theory one cannot, just because this model is nonlinear, consider this model as a superposition or addition of all its partial components. Right from the beginning we have to consider the world population as an entity, as a system, the whole behavior of which we try to describe. In this way the population model follows the ideas of nonlinearity right from its inception, not treating nonlinearity as a perturbation of a linear system. This is what global thinking is all about.

I have in this talk used both the metaphor of nonlinear systems and the technical discussion of their properties to discuss some major issues facing us all in an interconnected world. I can only hope that the originators and practitioners of nonlinear thinking, many of whom worked at Los Alamos and were brought here and inspired by Oppenheimer, will have the intellectual courage, the imagination and even audacity to go beyond the obvious, pass the threshold of conventional wisdom, and contribute to an understanding of the world to come.

This world will operate where collective modes are most significant. We already see that in global communication networks, in the dealings of transnational corporations, international trade, transport and finance. For all of us, modern science is a truly global intellectual enterprise, one that we are happy to be associated with. This emerging world will certainly generate new collective states in its being as it is to happen in a complex nonlinear system. Perhaps that is why today the forces of isolationism, separatism and parochial sovereignty generate such strong opposition.

This laboratory was founded to demonstrate the collective mode of behavior of an assembly of metastable nuclei. I can only hope that the collective modes of our emerging world will not be explosive, but regular and well-behaved, like a reactor, not a bomb.

I tried to demonstrate the imminent transition in considering the cut-off in the explosive development of global population growth. Strangely enough, I cannot offer you an explanation of this stabilizing effect in the patterns of our behavior to which we all personally experience and contribute. Modern demography can only say that this is happening with a resolution and persistence that goes beyond our control and even, as you see, understanding. Probably this illustrates how poorly we comprehend human behavior in its most fundamental function of multiplying its numbers.

I also hope that those who have contributed so much to the hardware of our new world will also share their experience and expand their thinking to the social issues emerging in this new world. On many occasions we see that a mechanical, "technically sweet" solution does not lead to the expected results. No wonder it is not the outcome of poorly conceived decisions in handling the political gadgetry of our world. I am sure that what is lacking is the software—conceptual, operational, even legal.

As you know today, the effort to produce software for computers is an order of magnitude greater than in making the hardware. Our own human growth and development shows the same, for it takes a couple of decades to educate a person as compared to the time in producing the hardware, if you allow me to use this analogy. In these 20 years of making a man, to use the old expression, we again encounter the fundamental time constant of human development. This is the microscopic time constant that determines the pattern not only of our personal development, but of humankind at large. It is this time of change and growth that sets the real pace for our development. Today we are forced to recognize this threshold, this limit, and the purpose of my talk is to bring it to your attention.

Fifty years ago this great laboratory was founded. Now, two generations later, the world has changed and the laboratory has to have a new agenda, find a new mission. I do hope that the software, the ideas and concepts will appear in time for these pressing changes.

*Serguei Kapitza is Vice-President of the Academy of Natural Sciences of Russia and of the European Physical Society. He holds the Chair of Physics at the Moscow Institute for Physics and Technology and has served in many advisory capacities for his Nation and has been a leader in technical and societal issues, including education, global security, disarmament and peace. His paper, delivered at the Twenty-Third J. Robert Oppenheimer Lecture in August 1993, is presented here as an epilogue to those early war and postwar events helping to end fear of nuclear annihilation, reminding us that continued resolve, commitment, and cooperation by all nations is essential for meeting future potential catastrophes.

A DIFFERENT COUNTRY
Richard Rhodes*

Fifty years. What extraordinary changes in warfare and in world politics. You really started something, didn't you?

After I published *The Making of the Atomic Bomb*, a metallurgist wrote me, asking me to correct the next edition. He said he wanted to complain. Those damned *physicists* didn't make the atomic bomb, he said; he and a couple of his buddies made the atomic bomb, literally—reduced the ^{235}U to metal, cast the bullet and the target rings. He's right. I should have looked into that and said something about it, but the passage of time works like sunlight, fading away the details.

You have your reminiscences, more numerous and far richer than the scant collection of stories that I and other historians of the Manhattan Project have managed to assemble in our books. So I won't repeat your stories back to you tonight—you tell them much better than I could. I'd like to do something more speculative. I'd like to try to assess, to a first approximation, fifty years along, what happened as a result of the work you did here, and what it meant. It's a cliché at reunions to remind people that the world has changed. I'd like to remind you of something altogether more remarkable: that you changed the world. You changed the world irrevocably, and short of the destruction of human memory there will be no changing it back. That's certainly what Robert Oppenheimer meant, in 1946, when he said that "...the atomic bomb was the turn of the screw. It has made the prospect of future war unendurable. It has led us up those last few steps to the mountain pass; and beyond there is a different country."[1] That different country is our country now, our world. How did we get here? What accommodations have we made, and what accommodations remain to be negotiated?

My discussion will carry us into what Victor Weisskopf once called "the most cruel part of reality"—necessarily, since the work you did here was accomplished in a time of terrible war. That might be painful. I hope you will bear with me, because I believe with you that the intention of your work was honorable and the outcome humane. I believe indeed with Robert Oppenheimer that the development of the atomic bomb made the prospect of at least total war unendurable, and thereby charted a millennial improvement in the conduct of human affairs.

With the discovery of the electron in 1897, less than one hundred years ago, J.J. Thomson first demonstrated the physical reality of the atom itself. The discovery of radiation the previous year had already revealed that the atom was a storehouse of energy, continuously releasing penetrating radiation and making elements like radium warm to the touch for hundreds of years. When James Chadwick discovered the neutron in 1932, a potent mechanism for perturbing the atomic nucleus came to hand.

The discovery of nuclear fission by Otto Hahn and Fritz Strassmann in Germany on December 21, 1938, was nevertheless a great surprise. Niels Bohr, when he heard of it, slapped his head and exclaimed, "Oh what idiots we have all been!"[2] In all previously identified nuclear reactions, energy in had been comparable to energy out. Nuclear fission, by contrast, was fiercely exothermic, ten millions times as much energy released as the neutron that initiated the reaction carried in. When experiments in the United States, in France, and in the Soviet Union early in 1939, determined that more neutrons as well as more energy came out of the reaction, physicists everywhere understood that here at last was a process that might be exploited to release the vast energy latent in matter. Leo Szilard wrote Lewis Strauss on January 25, 1939, that nuclear energy might be a means of producing power, and mentioned "atomic bombs."[3] Philip Morrison remembered later that "when fission was discovered, within perhaps a week there was on the blackboard in Robert Oppenheimer's office [at Berkeley] a drawing—a very bad, and execrable drawing—of a bomb."[4] "These possibilities," Bob Serber remarks, "were immediately obvious to any good physicist."[5] Otto Hahn brooded on the probable military applications of his discovery and seriously considered suicide. Within months of the German news, Enrico Fermi would stand at his panoramic office window high in the physics tower at Columbia University, look across the gray winter length of Manhattan Island alive with vendors and taxis and crowds, cup his hands as if he were holding a ball and say simply, "A little bomb like that, and it would all disappear."[6]

If the discovery of fission was surprising, it was also, to use Philip Morrison's word, "overripe." Everyone who heard of it kicked himself for missing it and ran to his laboratory to demonstrate it with off-the-shelf equipment. If Hahn and Strassmann had not discovered nuclear fission in Germany, others would have discovered it in some other laboratory somewhere else soon after. Here was no Faustian bargain, as movie directors and other naifs still find it intellectually challenging to imagine. Here was no evil machinery that saintly scientists might have hidden from the politicians and the generals. To the contrary, here was a new insight into how the world worked, an energetic reaction older than the earth that science had finally devised the instruments and arrangements to coax forth into the light of day. "Make it seem inevitable," Louis Pasteur used to advise his students when they prepared to write up their discoveries.[7] But it was. To wish that it might have been ignored or suppressed is barbarous. "Knowledge," Niels Bohr comments, "is itself the basis for civilization."[8] You cannot have the one without the other; the one depends on the other. Nor can you have only benevolent knowledge; the scientific method doesn't filter for benevolence. Knowledge has consequences, not always intended, not always comfortable, not always welcome. "It is a profound and necessary truth," Robert Oppenheimer once remarked, "that the deep things in science are not found because they are useful; they are found because it was possible to find them." And once they are found, wishing will not make them go away.

The first application that the discovery of nuclear fission suggested to those who understood the reaction's prodigal energetics was a devastating new weapon of war. Since Germans discovered fission, the emigré physicists who alerted the British and American governments feared from the outset that Germany might already be at work on such a weapon. But it's inaccurate to say that the Allies therefore committed their resources to build the atomic bomb so that they might use it on Germany. Rather, we began work on the atomic bomb because we understood that possession of such a weapon ourselves would be the only defense against an enemy similarly armed.

Deterrence had already been debated publicly and at length during the 1930s in the context of aerial bombardment. It found its first documented expression in the context of nuclear weapons in a secret report prepared early in 1940 as a warning to the British government by the emigré physicists Otto Frisch and Rudolf Peierls, a report that also first laid out on paper the basic mechanism of an atomic bomb. "If one works on the assumption," the two physicists wrote, "that Germany is, or will be, in the possession of this weapon, it must be realized that no shelters are available that would be effective and could be used on a large scale. The most effective reply would be a counter-threat with a similar bomb. Therefore it seems to us important to start production as soon and as rapidly as possible, even if it is not intended to use the bomb as a means of attack."[9]

In the course of the Second World War, every major industrial nation at least initiated a program to build atomic bombs: the Germans, the British, the French before their surrender, the Soviets, the Americans, even the Japanese. But the atomic bomb required a massive commitment of government funds that would have to be diverted from the conventional prosecution of war. If atomic bombs could be built they would be decisive, in which case no belligerent could afford not to pursue them. Negotiating such a commitment nevertheless depended critically on how much scientists trusted their government and how much government trusted their scientists.

Trust would not be a defining issue later, after the secret, the one and only secret—that the weapon worked—became known. This first time around, however, it was crucial, as the Russian physicist Victor Adamsky, who worked on the Soviet bomb, recently pointed out:

> The tension [between the scientists and their governments], stemmed from the fact that there existed no *a priori* certainty

of the possibility of creating an atomic bomb, and merely for clarification of the matter it was necessary to get through an interim stage: to create a device (the nuclear reactor) in order to perform a controlled chain reaction instead of the explosive kind. But the implementation of this stage requires tremendous expenses, incomparable to any of those previously spared for the benefit of scientific research. And it was necessary to tell this straight to your government, making it clear that the expenses may turn out to be in vain—an atomic bomb may not come out.... The American nuclear scientists...addressed the President...directly and described that complicated situation to him.... After a number of procrastinations, which are inevitable even in a democratic society, a decision was taken in the USA to make the research as comprehensive as required by logic, disregarding the [un]certainty of the final result.

...There was [no such confidence and mutual understanding] in Germany.10

In the United States the trust was there, and Franklin Roosevelt duly authorized a full-scale atomic-bomb program on October 9, 1941. In Germany the trust was not there on either side and the German program fragmented and stalled. After 1942 Werner Heisenberg, Otto Hahn, and Richard von Weizsäcker turned their attention to building a nuclear reactor and the bomb went by the board. Nor did the German scientists believe the Allies could do what they themselves had not judged feasible.11

The French program was stillborn. The Soviets, whose agents passed them the minutes of British government meetings concerning the atomic bomb as early as October 1941 but who were suspicious that the reports might be deliberate disinformation, and who in any case were fighting for their lives against a relentless German invasion, put their early work on hold, and only revived it in 1943 after the Red Army had pushed back the Wehrmacht outside Moscow and after further and confirming espionage in England and the United States. The Japanese saw that a bomb program was beyond their resources, estimated incorrectly that it was also beyond American resources, and restricted their efforts to laboratory studies of uranium separation and geological exploration for uranium and thorium ores in northern Korea.

At the time we knew very little of these developments. Until 1944, the Manhattan Project raced against an imaginary German clock, calculating that from the discovery of fission forward, the Germans might have at least a two-year lead. Then another and more terrible clock ticked off the project's hours: the clock of the war itself, of the young men dying on the battlefields of Europe and the bloody Pacific beaches.

The arduous road to the bomb would turn out to be industrial production on an enormous scale—more than two billion dollars worth by the end of the war in 1945 dollars, about the same as it cost, twenty years later, to go to the moon. What began as a benchtop experiment in Germany in 1938 became, in the United States, an industry comparable in scale to the U.S. automobile industry of the day.[12] Niels Bohr had returned to Denmark from an American visit in 1939 secure in the conviction that no nation could afford to build such an industry in time of war. The United States not only did so, it did so redundantly, pursuing three different and expensive paths to accumulating the necessary quantities of fissionable materials. The Manhattan Project commanded a higher priority for materials and staff than any other program of the war—not because anyone thought the atomic bomb would win the war, but because its sole possession by an enemy might turn Allied victory abruptly into defeat.

But we did use the bomb, use that remains publicly controversial even now, almost fifty years after the fact, and that use needs to be addressed. Historically, it's the first manifestation of the larger ambiguity that complicates understanding the consequences of the discovery of how to release nuclear energy—the fact that nuclear weapons are weapons of mass destruction—an ambiguity that each of you has undoubtedly evaluated many times over the years.

"In Los Alamos," Victor Weisskopf told a reporter several years ago, "we were working on something which is perhaps the most questionable, the most problematic thing a scientist can be faced with. At that time physics, our beloved science, was pushed into the most cruel part of reality and we had to live it through. We were, most of us at least, young and somewhat inexperienced in human affairs, I would say. But suddenly in the midst of it, Bohr appeared in Los Alamos.

"It was the first time we became aware of the sense in all these terrible things," Weisskopf went on, "because Bohr right away participated not only in the work, but in our discussions. Every great and deep difficulty bears in itself its own solution.... This we learned from him."[13]

What the sense in all these terrible things might be, I will come to. Clearly the use of the first atomic bombs on Japan at the end of the Second World War was different from their prolonged and remarkable *non-use* afterward.

At the Potsdam Conference in July 1945 Harry Truman was waiting eagerly for word of a successful test. News of the Trinity shot bucked him up. The Soviet Union was still officially neutral in the Pacific War; Stalin had promised to begin fighting the Japanese on August 15, and until the word came from Trinity, Truman's major concern had been to shore up Stalin's commitment. The test changed the stakes; now Truman could hope to end the war *before* the Russians joined it. "Believe Japs will fold up before Russia comes in," Truman confided to his diary. "I am sure they will when Manhattan appears over their homeland."14 General George Marshall, the Army's chief of staff, whose judgment everyone respected, remembered later why there was not more discussion in those final days of summer about demonstrating or withholding the bomb:

> We regarded the matter of dropping the [atomic] bomb as exceedingly important. We had just gone through a bitter experience at Okinawa [the last major island campaign, when the United States had lost more than 12,500 men killed and missing and Japan more than 100,000 killed in eighty-two days of fighting]. This had been preceded by a number of similar experiences in other Pacific islands, north of Australia. The Japanese had demonstrated in each case [that] they would not surrender and would fight to the death.... It was expected that resistance in Japan, with their home ties, would be even more severe. We had the one hundred thousand people killed in Tokyo in one night of [conventional] bombs, and it had seemingly no effect whatsoever. It destroyed the Japanese cities, yes, but their morale was not affected as far as we could tell, not at all. So it seemed quite necessary, if we could, to shock them into action.... We had to end the war, we had to save American lives.15

And in truth the first atomic bombs would not represent even a quantitative extension of the destruction that strategic bombing had already wreaked on the cities of Japan; since March 10, Curtis LeMay's B-29s had been systematically firebombing Japanese cities one by one to utter destruction, killing hundreds of thousands of civilians in the process; by August 1, the B-29s were burning down cities of less than 50,000 population, almost the only cities left in Japan to attack. Hiroshima and Nagasaki survived to be atomic-bombed only because they had been deliberately reserved.

The devastation of Hiroshima on August 6 was complete. Flying home from the Hiroshima mission, Luis Alvarez wrote his son Walter a letter. "At this moment," Luis wrote from ten miles off the Japanese coast, "only the crew of our three B-29s and the unfortunate residents of the Hiroshima district in Japan are aware of what has happened to aerial warfare. Last week the 20th Air Force, stationed in the Marianas Islands, put over the biggest bombing raid in history, with 6,000 tons of bombs (about 3,000 tons of high explosive). Today, the lead plane of our little formation dropped a single bomb which probably exploded with the force of 15,000 tons of high explosive.... A single plane disguised as a friendly transport can now wipe out a city."[16] Of 76,000 buildings in Hiroshima, 70,000 were damaged or destroyed, 48,000 totally. Ninety percent of all Hiroshima medical personnel were killed or disabled. Up to September 1 at least 70,000 people died. More died later of the effects of radiation.

George Marshall remembered that he was surprised and shocked that the Japanese didn't immediately sue for peace. "What we did not take into account," he said, "...was that the destruction would be so complete that it would be an appreciable time before the actual facts of the case would get to Tokyo.... There was no communication for at least a day, I think, and maybe longer."[17] The Air Force distributed millions of leaflets over Japanese cities in the next several days suggesting that skeptics "make inquiry as to what happened to Hiroshima" and asking the Japanese people to "petition the Emperor to end the war."[18] The firebombing continued relentlessly.

But there was now a struggle for power in the Japanese government, no surrender emerged, and on August 9 Fat Man exploded over Nagasaki with a 22-kiloton yield, killing many thousands more Japanese civilians and combatants and devastating another Japanese city. Finally, breaking tradition, Emperor Hirohito demanded that the government communicate its surrender, and reluctantly it did. In his historic broadcast to his people on August 15, Hirohito specifically cited "a new and most cruel bomb, the power of which to do damage is indeed incalculable," as "the reason why We have ordered the acceptance of the provisions of the Joint declaration of the Powers...."[19]

The atomic bombs exploded over Hiroshima and Nagasaki didn't *win* the Pacific war, but without question they *ended* the war. What might have followed had the war continued, no one can say with certainty, except that Hiroshima and Nagasaki would certainly have been firebombed, probably to equivalent loss of life—the Air Force launched the largest bombing raid of the Pacific War on August 14. The Japanese might have surrendered. Or the Allies might have had to invade the Japanese home islands, as we were vigorously preparing to do. The Soviets would have joined in that invasion, and having done so would certainly have insisted on a larger share of the spoils than the Kurile Islands. Japan might have been partitioned as Korea and Germany were partitioned.

Those first atomic bombs, made by hand here on this mesa, fell on a stunned pre-nuclear world. Afterward, when the Soviets exploded a copy of

Fat Man built from plans supplied by Klaus Fuchs and then went on to develop a comprehensive arsenal of their own, matching ours; when the hydrogen bomb increased the already devastating destructiveness of nuclear weapons by several orders of magnitude; when the British, the French, the Chinese, the Israelis and other nations acquired nuclear capabilities, the strange new nuclear world matured. Then the "sense" that Bohr saw "in all these terrible things" revealed itself.

Bohr proposed once that the goal of science is not universal truth. Rather, Bohr thought, the modest but relentless goal of science is "the gradual removal of prejudices."[20] The discovery that the earth revolves around the sun has gradually removed the prejudice that the earth is the center of the universe. The discovery of microbes is gradually removing the prejudice that disease is a punishment from God. The discovery of evolution is gradually removing the prejudice that *homo sapiens* is a separate and special creation.

The closing days of the Second World War marked a similar turning point in human history, the point of entry into a new era when humankind for the first time acquired the means of its own destruction. The discovery of how to release nuclear energy, and its application to build weapons of mass destruction, has gradually removed the prejudice on which total war is based: the insupportable conviction that there is a limited amount of energy available in the world to concentrate into explosives, that it is possible to accumulate more of such energy than one's enemies and thereby militarily to prevail. So cheap, so portable, so holocaustal did nuclear weapons eventually become that even nation-states as belligerent as the Soviet Union and the United States preferred to sacrifice a portion of their national sovereignty—preferred to forego the power to make total war—rather than to be destroyed in their fury. Lesser wars continue, and will continue until the world community is sufficiently impressed with their destructive futility to forge new instruments of protection and new forms of citizenship. But world war at least has been revealed to be historical, not universal, a manifestation of destructive technologies of limited scale. In the long history of human slaughter that is no small achievement.

I live on four acres of land in Connecticut, land completely surrounded by a forested wildlife preserve. We have abundant wildlife: deer, squirrels, raccoons, a woodchuck, turkeys, songbirds, a Cooper's hawk, even a pair of coyotes. Except for the hawk, every one of these animals constantly and fearfully watches over its shoulder lest it be caught, torn, and eaten alive. From the animal's point of view, my Eden-like four acres are a more lethal environment than you and I would find in the South Bronx or Sarajevo. Only very rarely does an animal living under natural conditions in the wild die of old age.

Until recently, the human world was not much different. Since we are predators, at the top of the food chain, our worst natural enemies historically were microbes. Natural violence, in the form of epidemic disease, took a large and continuous toll of human life, such that very few human beings lived out their natural lifespans. By contrast, manmade death—that is, death by war and war's attendant privations—persisted at a low and relatively constant level throughout human history, hardly distinguishable in the noise of the natural toll.

The invention of public health in the 19th century and the application of technology to war in the 20th century inverted that pattern in the industrialized world. Natural violence—epidemic disease—retreated before the preventive methodologies of public health to low and controlled levels. At the same time, manmade death began rapidly and pathologically to increase, reaching horrendous peaks in the two world wars that scarred our century. Manmade death has certainly accounted for not fewer that 150 million human lives in this most violent of all centuries in human history, a number that one writer vividly characterizes as a "nation of the dead."[21]

The epidemic of manmade death collapsed abruptly after the Second World War. Losses dropped precipitously to levels characteristic of earlier interwar years. Since then, the epidemic of chartered violence has smoldered along, flaring in guerrilla conflicts and conventional wars on the nuclear periphery, accounting for an average of a million lives a year.

Manmade death became epidemic in the 20th century because increasingly efficient killing technologies made the extreme exercise of national sovereignty pathological. And it was evidently the discovery of how to release nuclear energy and its application as nuclear deterrence that reduced the virulence of the pathogen. In a profound and even a quantifiable sense, the weapons that enforced nuclear deterrence these past fifty years served as containers in which to sequester the deaths they held potential, like a vaccine made from the attenuated pathogen itself. It required three tons of Allied bombs to kill a German citizen during the Second World War; by that quantitative measure, the strategic arsenals of the United States and the Soviet Union at the height of the Cold War held latent some three billion deaths, a number that corresponds closely to a 1984 World Health Organization estimate, arrived at by other means, of potential deaths from a full-scale nuclear war.[22]

Packaging death in the form of nuclear weapons made it visible. The sobering arsenals became *memento mori*, blunt reminders of our collective mortality. In the confusion of the battlefield, in the air and on the high seas, it had been possible before to deny or ignore the terrible cost in lives that the pursuit of absolutist ideologies entails. Nuclear weapons, the ultimate containers of manmade death, made the consequences of sovereign violence starkly obvious for the first time in human history. Since there was no sure defense against such weapons, they also made the consequences certain. A new caste of arms strategists tried to discover ways to use them, but every strategy foundered on the terrible possibility of escalation. Every great and deep difficulty bears within itself it own solution. Nuclear weapons, encapsulating potential human violence at its most extreme, paradoxically demonstrate the *reductio ad absurdum* of manmade death. These fifty years have been a dangerous but probably inevitable learning experience. As the latest revelations about the course of the Cuban missile crises make clear, we almost lost our way.

Robert Oppenheimer examined many of these issues forty-eight years ago in a speech to the Association of Los Alamos Scientists here on the Hill on November 2, 1945. Some of you were there. It was harder then to hear what Oppy had to say than it is now, in the aftermath of the long Cold War, when the nuclear arsenals are standing down. Let me repeat some of his words:

> There are things which we hold very dear, and I think rightly hold very dear; I would say that the word democracy perhaps stood for some of them as well as any other word. There are many parts of the world in which there is no democracy. There are other things which we hold dear, and which we rightly should. And when I speak of a new spirit in international affairs I mean that even in these deepest of things which we cherish, and for which Americans have been willing to die—and certainly most of us would be willing to die—even in these deepest things, we realize that there is something more profound than that; namely, the common bond with other men everywhere.[23]

With the discovery of how to release nuclear energy, and the long, progressive demonstration of its inevitable consequences, science became the first institution powerful enough to challenge the system of nation-states that had aggrandized itself with technology to the point of pathological destructiveness. Oppy also spoke of that phenomenon, and explained how it happened that an unarmed, peaceful, international institution such as science had quietly but decisively become a dominant political influence in the world:

> But when you come right down to it, the reason that we did this job is because it was an organic necessity. If you are a scientist you cannot stop such a thing. If you are a scientist you believe that it is good to find out how the world works; that it is good to find out what the realities are; that it is good to turn over to mankind at large the

greatest possible power to control the world and to deal with it according to its lights and its values.... It is not possible to be a scientist unless you believe that the knowledge of the world, and the power which this gives, is a thing which is of intrinsic value to humanity, and that you are using it to help in the spread of knowledge, and are willing to take the consequences.[24]

So now, fifty years later, fifty years after this city on a hill opened its doors, when we know what the consequences are, I believe the world owes you, and those of your colleagues who are gone now and no longer among us, an immense debt of gratitude. The work you did was analogous to the work that the first public health reformers undertook two hundred years ago. With courage, with vision, and with intelligence, braving the most cruel part of reality, you started us down the road toward removing a terrible scourge from the earth. Knowledge is itself the basis of civilization, and you helped civilize us.

NOTES

1. J. Robert Oppenheimer, The Atom Bomb and College Education. *The General Magazine and Historical Chronicle*. University of Pennsylvania General Alumni Society. 1946, p. 265.

2. Quoted in Stefan Rozental, ed., *Niels Bohr*. North-Holland, 1967, p. 145.

3. Spencer Weart and Gertrude Weiss Szilard, eds., *Leo Szilard: His Vision of the Facts*. MIT Press, 1978, p. 62.

4. Quoted in Charles Weiner, ed., *Exploring the History of Nuclear Physics*. AIP Conference Proceedings No. 7. American Institute of Physics, 1972, p. 90.

5. Robert Serber, *The Los Alamos Primer*. University of California Press, 1992, p. xxvii.

6. Quoted in Daniel J. Kevles, *The Physicists*. Vintage, 1979, p. 324.

7. Quoted in Gerald Holton, *Science and Anti-Science*. Harvard University Press, 1993, p. 75.

8. "Open Letter to the United Nations," in Stefan Rozental, ed., *Niels Bohr*. North-Holland, 1967, p. 350.

9. Serber, ibid., Appendix I: The Frisch-Peierls Memorandum, p. 82.

10. V.B. Adamsky, "Becoming a Citizen," in B.L. Altschuler et al., eds, *Andrei Sakharov: Facets of a Life*. Editions Frontieres, 1991, p. 26. Translation edited.

11. Evidence to this point is abundant in the newly released Farm Hall tapes.

12. Bertrand Goldschmidt, *Atomic Adventure*. Pergamon, 1964, p. 35.

13. Quoted in Ruth Moore, *Niels Bohr*. Knopf, 1966, p. 330.

14. Quoted in Robert H. Ferrell, ed., "Truman at Potsdam." *American Heritage*, June-July 1980, p. 42.

15. Quoted in Leonard Mosley, *Marshall*. Hearst, 1982, p. 337ff.

16. Luis Alvarez, "Dear Walter," 6 August 1945. Personal communication.

17. Quoted in Mosley, ibid., p. 340.

18. J.F. Moynahan to L.R. Groves, May 23, 1946, MED 317.7, History. National Archives.

19. Quoted in Herbert Feis, *The Atomic Bomb and the End of World War II*. Princeton University Press, 1966, p. 248.

20. Niels Bohr, *Atomic Physics and Human Knowledge*. John Wiley, 1958, p. 31.

21. Gil Elliot, *Twentieth Century Book of the Dead*. Charles Scribner's Sons, 1972, p. 187 and *passim*. Cf. also Richard Rhodes, Manmade Death: A Neglected Mortality. *JAMA* 260:5 (5 Aug 88).

22. International Committee of Experts in Medical Sciences and Public Health to Implement Resolution WHA34.38: *Effects of Nuclear War on Health and Health Services*. Geneva, World Health Organization, 1984.

23. Quoted in Alice Kimball Smith and Charles Weiner, eds., *Robert Oppenheimer: Letters and Recollections*. Harvard University Press, 1980, p. 320.

24. Smith and Weiner, ibid., p. 317.

---

*On the evening of June 10, 1993, Richard Rhodes, the Pulitzer Prize-winning author of *The Making of the Atomic Bomb*, spoke to a full house at the Los Alamos Civic Auditorium. His address, reprinted here with his permission, was the closing event of the Fiftieth Anniversary Reunion of Los Alamos Pioneers. He brings to this collection of stories an overview and credence that none close to it could possibly achieve. Paula Schreiber Dransfield, who came to Los Alamos with her parents in 1943, introduced Richard Rhodes.

GLOSSARY

accelerator—A device for producing particles of high speed and energy. In this volume, the Van de Graaff accelerator, invented by the physicist Robert J. Van de Graaff (1901–1967), plays a large part. This accelerator conveys charge to a high-potential head by the motion of an insulating belt. In the 1940s it was the accelerator that could produce the highest voltages, hence the highest particle energies.

alpha particle—The helium nucleus. See helium.

atomic mass—The number of protons and neutrons contained in an atomic nucleus.

atomic number—The number of protons contained in an atomic nucleus. The chemical behavior of a nucleus is determined by its atomic number, or nuclear charge. The nucleus contains roughly the same number of neutrons as protons at low atomic numbers, with the preponderance of neutrons increasing at high atomic numbers. A variation in the number of neutrons produces an *isotope*, a variety of an element with nearly identical chemical behavior to that of its sister isotopes, but a different atomic mass.

electron—Sir Joseph John Thomson (1856–1940) is recognized as the British scientist who discovered and identified the electron. It is a fundamental particle that occurs in two charge states, positive and negative. The positive variety is called the positron; it is a state of antimatter.

fission, nuclear—The splitting of an atomic nucleus into two or more parts. The total mass of the fragments is less than that of the original nucleus; hence the process of fission releases energy. Fission is the source of energy in fission weapons and nuclear reactors.

helium—The second lightest element, with atomic number two. Naturally occurring helium has two protons and one or two neutrons, resulting in He^3 or He^4. Helium is the first of the "noble gases," so called because they are chemically inert. Its nucleus usually has two protons and two neutrons and is called the alpha particle, named by Pierre and Marie Curie. George Gamow named the nucleus of He^3 the "tralpha."

hydrogen—The first and lightest element. It occurs in three isotopes: hydrogen, deuterium, and tritium, with 0, 1, and 2 neutrons in the nucleus. There is 1 electron in the atom, the same as the atomic number.

lithium—The element of atomic number three. In nature its nucleus may have 3 or 4 neutrons. It is the most abundant naturally occurring element.

neptunium (see plutonium)

neutron—The English physicist James Chadwick (1891–1974) discovered the neutron in 1932 and won the Nobel prize in physics for this discovery. With nearly the same mass as that of the proton, the neutron was needed to explain certain observations of nuclear physics. Absorption of a neutron may cause fission of certain heavy elements, notably thorium, uranium, and plutonium.

pile, graphite—First used at the University at Chicago, the graphite pile enables scientists to measure the neutron multiplication of fissioning elements, uranium for example. Neutron multiplication means the number of neutrons released in fission per neutron absorbed. If the multiplication is greater than one, the possibility of a chain reaction is raised; chain reactions operate in nuclear reactors and weapons.

plutonium—Plutonium and neptunium are the first two manmade elements ever produced in large quantities. Uranium of atomic mass 238 becomes ^{239}U upon absorption of a neutron. This isotope decays to ^{239}Np by emission of an electron, or beta particle, thence to ^{239}Pu by a second beta decay.

primacord—A cord of explosive material that detonates at a high rate with a shock wave with sufficient shock pressure to initiate an explosion in another explosive. Primacord can be used to produce nearly simultaneous explosions of two or more pieces of high explosive.

proton (see hydrogen)

reactor, nuclear—A nuclear reactor consists of an array or other system of fissionable material, usually immersed in a medium such as graphite or water, that can slow the neutrons that result from fission to low speed and energy. Nuclear reactors were first used for production of plutonium, later for generation of electric power and propulsion of submarines and ships with the energy released in fission.

uranium—The heaviest naturally occurring element, atomic number 92. Uranium occurs naturally in two isotopes, ^{235}U and ^{238}U.